T0305194

Clipped Coins, Abused Words, and Civil Government

Also available:

Civilizing Money:
Hume, His Monetary Project, and the Scottish Enlightenment
George Caffentzis

"Caffentzis is a practical philosopher and a pure teacher. His reasoning even at its most abstract always tends to the political. The street is his classroom. This is truly vulgar Marxism, that is, it is a critique by, with, and for the vulgus, or common people (you and I)."
—Peter Linebaugh, author of *The Magna Carta Manifesto*

Clipped Coins, Abused Words, and Civil Government

John Locke's Philosophy of Money

NEW EDITION

George Caffentzis

Edited and with an introduction by Paul Rekret
Foreword by Harry Cleaver

First published by Autonomedia, 1989

New edition first published 2021 by Pluto Press
345 Archway Road, London N6 5AA

www.plutobooks.com

Copyright © Constantine George Caffentzis 2021

Every effort has been made to trace copyright holders and to obtain their
permission for the use of copyright material in this book. The publisher apologizes
for any errors or omissions in this respect and would be grateful if notified of any
corrections that should be incorporated in future reprints or editions.

The right of Constantine George Caffentzis to be identified as the author of this
work has been asserted in accordance with the Copyright, Designs and Patents Act
1988.

British Library Cataloguing in Publication Data
A catalogue record for this book is available from the British Library

ISBN   978 0 7453 4205 4 Hardback
ISBN   978 0 7453 4207 8 Paperback
ISBN   978 1 78680 768 7 PDF
ISBN   978 1 78680 769 4 EPUB
ISBN   978 1 78680 770 0 Kindle

Typeset by Stanford DTP Services, Northampton, England
Printed and bound by CPI Group (UK) Ltd, Croydon, CR0 4YY

Contents

Acknowledgments

It is a good tradition for the author of a book to thank the people and institutions who inspired it and helped in its production. Continuing this tradition, I want to thank several scholars of Locke who have been central to my writing of *Clipped Coins, Abused Words, and Civil Government: John Locke's Philosophy of Money*.

First among them Carl Wennerlind, for our early discussions concerning Locke's and Hume's monetary thought.

Thanks also to:

Margaret Schabas who, by publishing my early work, introduced me to the academic research on the social roots of eighteenth-century philosophy and science.

To the Bristol Radical History Group that has opened up a radical methodology to uncover the class struggle in Britain.

To Peter Linebaugh for his decades-long support of my project on the philosophy of money and for his unmatched contribution to the history of England's enclosures and thanatocratic rule.

To Harry Cleaver whose invaluable political reading of Marx set a model also for my reading of the history of monetary theory.

And to the members of the Midnight Notes Collective, who have continuously urged me to make my philosophy of money relevant to the contemporary struggle for social justice.

Thanks also to Jim Fleming, of Autonomedia, who published the first edition of *Clipped Coins, Abused Words, and Civil Government: John Locke's Philosophy of Money*.

To the late Gaspare De Caro, of the Istituto della Enciclopedia Italiana, who gave an early hearing and translated for my class analysis of Locke's philosophy in Italy. And thanks to Silvia Federici who admirably translated *Clipped Coins* into Italian.

To Arlen Austin, who with his passion, humor and multifarious technical and humanist skills has assisted my work for the new publication of *Clipped Coins* and made an irreplaceable contribution to its completion.

Acknowledgments

Above all, I thank the staff of Pluto Press who in the midst of a pandemic are devoting a major effort to publishing two books on the philosophy of money, back to back, one on John Locke's and another David Hume's philosophy of money. In particular, I want to thank Thérèse Wassily Saba.

Not last, heartfelt thanks to my companion Silvia Federici, whose reconstruction of the history of capitalist development has greatly influenced my understanding of the patriarchal dimension of monetary theory, and with her love and solidarity has been an essential part and supporter of all my intellectual and political projects.

Note on the New Edition

This new edition of George Caffentzis' study of John Locke includes the text of *Clipped Coins, Civil Government and Abused Words: John Locke's Philosophy of Money*, a monograph originally published by Autonomedia in 1989 and very slightly revised here. In particular, some references have been updated to newer, more readily available editions. The original manuscript of *Clipped Coins* is included here with a new Foreword, Editor's Introduction, and a new Postface that was originally published as a pamphlet in 2008 by the Bristol Radical History Group (*John Locke: The Philosopher of Primitive Accumulation*). This new edition of *Clipped Coins* appears in conjunction with Caffentzis' new study of David Hume titled *Civilizing Money: Hume, His Monetary Project and the Scottish Enlightenment*, also published with Pluto Press. Readers are advised to consult the "Autobiographical Preface" in that volume for an account of the context in which these two books (along with a third volume in the series, Caffentzis' study of George Berkeley, *Exciting the Industry of Mankind: George Berkeley's Philosophy of Money* (London: Kluwer, 2000) were written.

Paul Rekret

Foreword

Harry Cleaver

The recent preoccupation with "financialization"—of economists, government regulators, and their critics—makes the republication of George Caffentzis' study of John Locke's philosophy of money especially timely. Never has the importance of money among the weapons that capitalists use to maintain their regime of domination, exploitation, and alienation been greater. This has been especially clear since the financial crisis of 2007–08 revealed how contradictions in the deployment of that weapon could have sudden, unexpected, and disastrous consequences for millions of workers who, losing jobs, housing, and prospects, were suddenly thrown into poverty and homelessness—while those directly responsible for the crisis through their fraud and reckless speculation (bankers and other money capitalists) were bailed out and none wound up in jail. Since then, over a decade of "recovery," slowed by the onset of the Covid-19 pandemic, has done little to reverse those consequences. Even the disbursements of the Biden administration's American Recovery Act of 2021 have proved weak palliatives. City streets and highway overpasses are still filled with makeshift campgrounds of the homeless, unemployment remains high and suffering is widespread. Largely uncurbed by effective regulations, speculation and fraud are once more on the rise.

Within this context, George's study stands out as an illumination of long past practices that throws light on current problems. While Locke was certainly a philosopher, one of those providing early rationales for the structures of capitalism, and George took his degree in Philosophy from Princeton University and taught in Departments of Philosophy for many years, neither man can be pigeonholed as only a philosopher. As George highlights, Locke was actively involved in the capitalist management of money to support the capitalism of his day, both at home in Britain and abroad in the Empire's colonies and expanding world of trade. He brings this aspect of Locke back to the foreground as one moment of his own activism in struggles against the capitalist use of its money weapons in recent decades, both at home during the New York City financial crisis of the mid-1970s and then abroad in struggles against the use of money to impose austerity on workers in Nigeria and elsewhere through the International Monetary Fund's programs of "structural adjustment," rampant in the 1980s and 1990s. Not surprisingly, therefore, George reads and amplifies both Locke's philosophy and his favored monetary policies through political perspectives gained in contemporary struggles. One result, this book is not just an addition to library shelves holding books on philosophy or to the much narrower field of Locke Studies by academics – analyzed by Paul Rekret in his Introduction to this new edition. Another result, unlike many an academic tome whose specialized jargon impedes understanding by the uninitiated, *Clipped Coins* is written in a way that makes its contemporary relevance to anti-capitalist militants quite clear.

I make this claim because when I first decided to read this book—upon its original publication in 1989—I did so with a certain trepidation. My own study of Locke's writings had only included his justification for a "labor" theory of value/property, his theory of the effects on price of variations in the quantity of money, and his thoughts on the kinds of education appropriate to different classes. Of his "general theory of semantics and language"—essential to George's argument—I had no clue. Although I had known George since our undergraduate years and conspired with him in the political activities of the Zerowork collective in the mid-1970s, I had never dared to dive deeply into his previous writing on philosophy, such as his 1978 PhD dissertation "Does Quantum Mechanics Necessitate a Theoretical Revolution in Logic?". Philosophy was his field of study; mine was economics and its critique.

I should have known better, not only from our collaboration on Zerowork, but because I had long been familiar with drafts of George's critical dissection of Paul Samuelson's *Economics* textbook, carried out with his classmates at Princeton Mark Linder and Julius Sensat and later published in two volumes as *Anti-Samuelson* (1977). However obscure his dissertation may be (I still haven't gotten beyond his Preface), his studies of economics and his political activism against capitalist strategies and tactics during crises should have given me confidence that those things would inform and shape his more recent studies of philosophers, especially of their writings on money. Indeed, brief moments of such influence were already apparent in his 1980 essay on the "Work/Energy Crisis and the Apocolyse" in which he analyzed the connections between the evolution of scientific thought on energy and thermodynamics and the evolving character of the class struggles of capitalism. And sure enough, once taken up, I found *Clipped Coins* not only revelatory about Locke's thinking and practices but in ways that sharpened my own thinking about the capitalist use of money against workers in the class war of our times and about the theories they use to both organize and justify their actions. For while providing a new analysis that shows the interconnections among diverse aspects of Locke's thoughts and actions, George does so in a way that provides a methodology applicable to other thinkers and other times, including those we are having to deal with today. While John Locke and his times—the late seventeenth century—may be unfamiliar to some readers, even uninteresting to them, they will be happy to discover how George links Locke's ideas to phenomena with which we are still coping, including the never-ending enclosures of what Marx called "primitive accumulation" and the neoliberalism of capitalist policies that have besieged us for the past 40 years. Those linkages should prove inspirational, pushing the hitherto uninterested to recognize the importance of this seemingly distant past and its thinkers to contemporary struggles. Given the appalling degree to which the American educational system produces historical ignorance among those it processes for the workforce, any work, like this one, that demonstrates the truth of Nietzsche's argument that studying history is useful because it can help us improve our lives today should be welcome.

For those anti-capitalists weary of top-down histories, focused on the "great men" of the very class they despise and anxious to include the role of bottom-up forces at work shaping the history of class struggle, they too will be pleased to discover how George's reinterpretation of Locke's thinking reveals how the latter's acute awareness of those "others" influenced his ideas. Not only coin clippers and counterfeiters of coin and language but the "quarrelsome and contentious", the lazy idlers who might work to live but who refused to live to work, all of whose actions threatened and undermined capitalist management of money for its own purposes, shaped his proposals for policies both at home and abroad. Whether we are reinterpreting the past or deciphering the present, we must, as George writes of ideology (and hence also in policy) in footnote 21 to Chapter 1, "not only see the interests of the dominant class expressed in it, but also the fears that are not expressed." Fears, of course, of those "others"—those of us whose struggles undermine and go beyond the plans of that dominant class.

Therefore, I want to recommend this book (along with the other two of George's trilogy) to anti-capitalist activists. Those struggling to understand the class politics of money, to figure out how to best oppose the capitalist use of money and to find ways beyond both capitalism and money, should find it well worth their time and energy.

That last objective—escaping money—has only recently returned to the agenda of revolutionaries. After a brief period of consideration by communists after the revolution in Russia, and in the wake of the debates over planning vs. markets of the 1930s, it largely disappeared. In the "East" the experience of planning in Soviet-style economies revealed both the limits of central planning and the existence of a "black economy" of widespread markets for both commodities and money. In the "West," where various mixes of planning and markets reigned, social democratic parties and their theorists came to embrace markets and money—to be tweaked, of course, in the direction of fairer, "socialist" forms. But a combination of factors, including the recent central role of money in the class struggle, the development of modern computers and their capacity for handling the information necessary for redistributing use-values from those exercising their abilities to those in need and the ever multiplying examples of what economists euphemistically call the "negative externalities" associated with markets—from the persistence of poverty to the mass extinctions threatened by the money-hungry, market-driven rape of the planet—have made growing numbers of those looking beyond capitalism conclude that the decommodification of life and escape from money are essential to the conceptualization and building of new, non-capitalist worlds.

This perspective is a far cry from either the "sanctification" of metallic money by Locke and his contemporaries that George analyzes or the continued imposition and acceptance of the much less sanctified money prices on anything and everything that we live with every day. It is not a call for all of us to "drop out of the club of money users" into some isolated, demonetized commune, it is one to free society from a money (or even labor) measure of the value of all things and to celebrate the diversity and richness both of "needs/desires" and of our abilities to satisfy them—creating a multiplicity of values in place of an imposed and impoverished singular one.

Austin
May 2021

Introduction to the New Edition

Paul Rekret

"...from the abstractions of philosophy to who'd put the kettle in the workhouse."

Peter Linebaugh, The London Hanged (2006)

MONEY ON THE MIND

The question of the relationship between thought and money is an especially awkward one for philosophy.[1] The ideal of the love of wisdom upon which it is founded implies that philosophical activity be pursued as an end in itself, having no bearing on the philosopher's personal interest or quest for survival. But such a heroic notion of the pursuit of knowledge, inherited from ancient Greece, has disposed philosophy to neglect its own material conditions; from slavery in Athens to modern divisions of labor, or the ongoing marketization of higher education today. Of course, one could insist that such concerns regarding the wider context of philosophy fall outside its own proper terrain and are, instead, more appropriate pursuits for intellectual historians or sociologists of knowledge. But not only would such a claim entail a rather truncated and idealized conception of philosophy, for where one can discern the effects of social institutions at the level of the concept itself (this is, after all, one way of thinking ideology), the question of social conditions recoils back upon theoretical inquiry anyway.

The claim for a formal correspondence between thought and its social context—an emergent capitalist society in seventeenth- and eighteenth-century Britain, in particular—is at the center of George Caffentzis' three-volume study of the philosophy of money, of which the first volume is republished here. Caffentzis is certainly not the first thinker to have delineated an intersection between money and philosophy, but the significance of his work rests in part with the intricacy with which he characterizes the relationship between them—one defined ultimately by the exigencies of class struggle. While the best known iterations of the genre have tended either toward positing the identity of philosophy with money or, in contrast, their complete autonomy from one another, Caffentzis has sought instead to trace out in detail instances in the work of particular philosophers where money and conceptual thought intersect and the terms upon which they do so.

By way of comparison, take the German sociologist and philosopher Georg Simmel's monumental 1907 book *The Philosophy of Money* (Simmel 1990). Simmel characterizes his work as an investigation of the metaphysical preconditions necessary for the categories of value that create a monetary world. This then forms the foundation for his analysis of the effects that money has on inner life and culture. Simmel claims to have erected "a new storey beneath historical materialism," one that rests with his account of the psychic essentials of the economic (Simmel 1990: 56). But to seek the formal conditions of money in this way, as Caffentzis notes, is to assume the stability of its meaning across history. In addition, it implies a category separation of philosophy and economy insofar as the former is used to articulate the conditions for the latter (Simmel 1990; Caffentzis 2021: 6). For Caffentzis, such an account "dichotomizes" philosophy and money. That is, in pursuing the conditions of money as such, Simmel poses philosophy as independent of the economic and, in turn, fails to consider how the meaning and nature of money might have changed over time and the role philosophical interventions might have had in these transformations.

We also find a restricted historical view if we look to a very different, perhaps even inverse, approach to the philosophy of money from Simmel's: that proposed by the Frankfurt School fellow-traveller, Alfred Sohn-Rethel in his 1978 book *Intellectual and Manual Labour*. Here, a formal identity is posed between philosophy and money, one where the latter is afforded temporal priority since, on Sohn-Rethel's reasoning, the abstraction that occurs in acts of exchange between commodities precedes and conditions abstractions in the human mind. It is in this sense that *Intellectual and Manual Labour* relates the emergence of philosophy to the development of coinage in classical Greece as that society's primary means of exchange, that is, the Greek conception of 'being' as something that is unchanging and timeless is premised, the book argues, on the use of money as timeless and immutable substance (Sohn-Rethel 1978: 64 and 59). Along these lines,

Sohn-Rethel traces the development of knowledge from antiquity, through the medieval period to the rise of merchant capital and the development of industrial capital. In each instance, he advances an abiding causal relation between money and philosophy, one running from the Greeks to Kant, whereby the expansion and intensification of the circulation of commodities constitutes a growing abstraction and alienation of cognition from sensual experience. This might amount to a reversal of Simmel's argument insofar as money here provides philosophy with its formal and historical conditions rather than the obverse, but it nonetheless entails a history as monotonous as Simmel's. Whether philosophy is presented as wholly dependent upon money for its existence (as in Sohn-Rethel) or wholly independent of it (as in Simmel), an anachronistic understanding of money prevails.

Caffentzis evades this Scylla or Charybdis of identity and dichotomy between philosophy and money by opting not to pursue *the* philosophy of money altogether. Instead, he restricts the scope of his enterprise to the study of specific philosophers—the trio of so-called British empiricists John Locke, George Berkeley and David Hume to be exact—whose work, in engaging in questions of policy, constitutes what Caffentzis calls a "monetary act" (Caffentzis 2021: 7). Doing so allows him to attend to the more restricted, historically refined terrain of how particular epistemological, ontological and political formulations inform monetary ones. Equally, his work is characterized by a depth of research that undergirds deliberation upon the ways historical events, and monetary debates more narrowly, have shaped philosophy. This is what Caffentzis has in mind in referring to his method as "ampliative," one which finds conceptual architectures first averred in a work of philosophy, to later be refracted in policy proposals, or vice versa.

One of the more intriguing aspects to Caffentzis' understanding of the philosophy of money is the way in which he calls attention to modern thought itself as a capitalist class project. At the core of such a framing lies the recognition that, as the mediator between people and their means of subsistence in a capitalist society, money is a form of command (on this point, see Cleaver 1996). Homing in on what Caffentzis calls the "money face" of the wage relation—the reflection of labor as money—permits us to examine how labor-power comes to be fixed as an abstract measure; it also helps us to consider that the institution of the wage is neither frictionless nor absolute but rather, entails a long history of struggle. It is with these issues in mind that we can understand the motivation behind Caffentzis' delineation of his three-volume study of the history of the philosophy of money to the oeuvres of Locke, Berkeley and Hume, poised as they are at crucial junctures of capital's development in the seventeenth and eighteenth centuries; each faced with urgent questions and crises around the generalization of exchange relations and the compulsion to wage labor: the state's role in money's creation and management; the social employment of money in the imposition of a universal form of value; overcoming resistance to capital's generalization; and money's civilizing function as a spur to industriousness and entrepreneurial behavior.

But attending to the *reciprocity* of philosophy and money, as I have suggested Caffentzis does, further entails examining how these problematics are shaped by and come to shape theoretical inquiry. In *Clipped Coins*, Caffentzis reveals Locke's liberalism to be mobilized by the problem of the universalization of money in the late seventeenth century, the criminalization of pre-capitalist forms of survival, and the legitimation of enclosure and indefinite capital accumulation underpinned by a metaphysical notion of personhood and a conception of knowledge as a mode of labor.

If Locke can thus be said to be "the philosopher of primitive accumulation," then Berkeley is the theorist of "import substitution" and economic diversification (Caffentzis 2000: 118). For while Locke's fundamental concern was the generalization of a mode of property that would subject the whole of the world to the impersonal power of the market, Berkeley's conundrum, framed by his experience as Bishop of Cloyne, is centered upon compelling his recalcitrant Irish flock into wage labor while inciting the Anglo-Irish gentry's investment of its wealth in Ireland. It is through this problematic of needing to "excite" or stimulate productive activity that Caffentzis reads Berkeley's defense of a paper currency. Given his setting in an underdeveloped economy, for Berkeley, the function of money does not rest merely with its capacity to store value but with its potential to stimulate and regulate economic behavior. In other words, it is a wider monetization of life itself that Berkeley seeks. And it is in these terms that Caffentzis interprets the development of the conception of "notion" in the Irish philosopher's later work: here is a referent to volitional impulse inseparable from the view of money as a reflection of the "spirits" that guide it.

Focused upon Ireland and the rebellious Scottish Highlands respectively, Berkeley's and Hume's monetary programs emerge from a common problem. The process of expropriation associated with Locke, it turns out,

4

is insufficient as a compulsion to wage labor. Yet while Berkeley calls for a temporary withdrawal of Ireland from the world market as a means of transforming social relations along capitalist lines, Hume proposes complete integration into the national and world market as a means of "civilizing" Scotland's Highland cultures (Caffentzis 2021). Hume's defense of a metallic money standard is, therefore, not a sign of regressive essentialism as is often assumed but, as Caffentzis shows, a response to the promiscuous issuing of promissory notes widespread in eighteenth-century Scotland, along with the ensuing balance of payments crisis that followed. Read through the frame of Hume's functionalist ontology, his defense of a metallic standard for money is centered upon a moral argument against paper money's ability to sever the "barbaric" Scottish Highlanders from a gift economy in order to compel them to the capitalist discipline of frugality, work and investment (Caffentzis 2021).

Together then, these three studies (the study of Hume is published for the first time as a companion to this new edition of *Clipped Coins*) offer an expansive examination of the intersections of biography, philosophy and monetary policy. In doing so, they illustrate not only how the function of money as an equalizer between different objects and activities is crucial to the imposition of capitalist power but broader still, they show philosophical concepts to be inextricable from their class content.

Caffentzis is best known for his work in radical political economy, especially through the collectives Zerowork and Midnight Notes which he co-founded, and his incisive attempts to understand the changing dimensions of labor and the production of value over recent decades continue to influence and inform scholars and activists.[2] Yet, despite the clarity and edifying style of his work, Caffentzis is all too often overlooked where study of the history of philosophy is concerned. Even if we restrict our gaze to the more widely referenced book on Locke, it is apparent that undue neglect of the theoretical terrain it has opened has entailed the unnecessary persistence of confusions in the English philosopher's contemporary reception. Caffentzis' work, it is held here, merits further examination.

Admittedly, situating Locke's philosophy in the context of an emergent global capital in late seventeenth-century Britain, as Caffentzis does, is not in itself a unique proposition. At least since C.B. Macpherson's formative 1962 study of *The Political Theory of Possessive Individualism*, left readings of Locke have been premised upon his place in the rise of market society and the theoretical priority given to the individuals who inhabit it (Macpherson 2011). It is worth stressing, then, that the significance of *Clipped Coins* is not exhausted by its account of an inherent relationship between Locke's philosophy and capitalism, but rests, rather, with the more nuanced claim that a peculiarly capitalist ontology of money, at a decisive moment for modern value relations, acts as the hinge around which both Locke's political theory and his epistemology revolve. Such a claim, as we will see, not only resolves a host of tensions in the reception of Locke, it also offers important insights into the history of modern thought more broadly. Looking to Caffentzis' study of Locke in what remains then, this introduction seeks to show the importance of that project for both the study of Locke and of liberalism, more broadly. In doing so, it hopes to persuade the reader of the significance of Caffentzis' philosophical project for understanding both the origins of capitalism and the conceptual architecture through which we understand it.

BETWEEN NATURE AND CONVENTION

Money is poised equivocally between being a natural substance and a social convention. This ontological axiom is, as far as Caffentzis sees it, key to unlocking the manifold tensions and uncertainties pervading Locke's work. Caffentzis first discerns this idea in what ends up as Locke's winning case in a polemic that has come to be known as the "recoinage debate," and it bears a bit of unpacking here. Having become severely undervalued relative to the price of silver on the world market by the 1690s, it had become highly profitable to trade English silver coins on world bullion markets for their silver content alone. This not only produced a severe shortage of coins—exacerbated by rampant counterfeiting and the clipping of coins for bullion—but, in turn, led to chronic price inflation.[3] While broad agreement existed for the minting of new clip-proof coins, dispute revolved around whether to set the current market price for silver at London Mint parity (the denomination set for a given amount of silver) or to instead keep the official Mint parity unchanged. Tasked with drafting a recommendation, Secretary of the Treasury William Lowndes proposed devaluing English coinage by re-minting coins with lower silver content while maintaining their nominal value. Opposed to this deflationary strategy, Locke instead proposed re-minting coins with their formal silver content while simultaneously bringing all-out discipline and justice upon counterfeiters and clippers (see Locke 1991).

While the conventional reading has long taken Locke's opposition to Lowndes as a reflection of his "metallist" money fetishism, Caffentzis instead works against the grain of this established view. On his reading, Locke's proposal for re-minting silver coins reflects a broader need for a stable measure of value to underpin contracts and transactions upon a burgeoning world market. This interpretation has the merit of understanding the motivations behind Locke's fervent opposition to Lowndes' inflationary proposal. For it's given that it effectively deflated the value of money from its metal content, that Lowndes' program would be viewed by Locke as a threat to trust in both money and in the state. For one thing, Lowndes' plan to devalue English currency would endanger world trade by failing to impose a spatial and temporal identity upon financial contracts. For another, it would enrich hoarders and manipulators of bullion while also effectively transforming the state itself into a coin clipper. Certainly, on Locke's re-minting plan deflation would occur, but this would only be the case when viewed from the relative myopia of a British idea of value and not from the perspective of a global market dealing in the objective value of silver coins determined by their weight (on this point, see also McNally 2014). As we will see later, the question implied here of the relation of value to substance brings monetary policy immediately into the ambit of epistemic questions regarding the universality of knowledge; for, if experience is essential to knowledge, as Locke holds, then where the relation between money's metal content and its value is severed, ideas of money lose coherence (see page 36).

Here then lies the key to Locke's "mercantilist prejudice." While money is subject to convention, it is only assured a level of objectivity beyond subjective intention through its substantial qualities (Caffentzis 2000: 186). This is a claim to which we shall return, but suffice it to say that holding the universality of money as of a higher order than the nation-state, as Locke does, extends beyond local questions of inflationary policy to underlie the issue of the emergent dominance of capital on a world scale along with Britain's rise to global power in the eighteenth century (see also McNally 2014: 20).

MONEY AND NATURE

The priority attending the universality of money in Locke's position in the recoinage debate is also reflected in the role that money is assigned in the account of the origins of political society presented in the *Second Treatise on*

Government (see Locke 1823g). This is insofar as in both arguments we can detect the effects of Locke's conception of money as lying somewhere between subjective convention and its objective qualities. In fact, as Caffentzis shows, not only does the introduction of money function as "efficient cause" of the social contract but moreover, its ambiguous ontological status between convention and nature forms the basis for Locke's program of political reform. Before examining the consequences of this claim for understanding the wider implications of Locke's political philosophy, let us see in more detail how this is the case.

As is well known, in the *Second Treatise* Locke establishes "life, liberty, and estate" as rights that are temporally and logically prior to civil government. Where Robert Filmer and other seventeenth-century defenders of absolutism had held property in biblical terms as a royal inheritance from Adam, to whom the Earth was given, Locke's argument sets off from the claim that everyone is a "proprietor in his own person" and in the products of his labor (Locke 1823g: II, 27 and 44). "I labour on X, therefore X is part of me," as Caffentzis puts it. While the notion of self-ownership allows man to inscribe property in the natural commons, Locke further insists on a natural law to "preserve God's creation," implying moral limits to appropriation (Locke 1823g: II, 6). A so-called "spoilage limitation" limits property to what can be used before it spoils, while a "sufficiency limitation" means that one is duty-bound to "leave enough and as good" for others (Locke 1823g: II, 31 and 34). Only with the invention of money and men's mutual consent to put a value upon it are both limitations overcome so that man may "fairly possess more land than he himself could use the product of" (Locke 1823g: II, 50). In other words, money's capacity to store value frees the subject from moral limits to appropriation of that with which he mixes his labor or, implicitly, free to sell his labor for a wage. From this moment, property ceases to encroach on anyone's natural rights since the universal consent conferred upon the value of money amounts to a universal consent to the "disproportionate and unequal Possession of the Earth" it engenders (Locke 1823g: II, 50). So far this is a relatively orthodox account of Locke's theory of property, but the perspicacity of Caffentzis' reading comes into view where we see how it overcomes tensions and aporia that have plagued reception of the *Second Treatise*.

The dominant strain of Locke scholarship in recent decades has been characterized by a "religious turn" that emerged in response to Macpherson's influential framing of Locke as *the* philosopher of market society. Against the view of Locke as a theorist of "possessive individualism," John Dunn (1969), Quentin Skinner (1998), Peter Laslett (1963), James Tully (1980) and others, have centered Locke's Protestant faith rather than his mercantile activity as the key to understanding his political philosophy. At its core, their argument rests upon a sequential understanding of the role of money in Locke's political theory: money marks a step *out of* man's natural state and thus, occurs as a fall from grace. By therefore insisting upon the conventional rather than natural character of money in the *Second Treatise*, these scholars seek to rescue Locke from those interpretations—Macpherson's in particular—which view him as having naturalized a capitalist economy. Moreover, in foregrounding the moral limitations that the natural law places upon acquisition, such a "religious" reading also seeks to preserve an egalitarian spirit in Locke's work. However, as Onar Ulas Ince has shown in a shrewd analysis informed by Caffentzis' work, it remains unclear why, if Locke understands money as wholly conventional rather than originary to the state of nature, he does not simply call for its eradication instead of invoking the necessity of the state to manage its effects (Ince 2011: 38)? But equally, as Ince argues, to view Locke as naturalizing capitalist social relations, as Macpherson has it, only works by awkwardly discarding the moral limits Locke ascribes to accumulation. That is, the conventional left reading hinges upon the rather tenuous assumption that, contra Dunn, Skinner, et al., Locke is not deeply invested in the moral foundations he ascribes to property. But if this were truly the case, Ince continues, then he would have no reason to insist upon the moral right to property even where "disproportionate and unequal Possession of the Earth" occurs, since this would be *prima facie* self-evident anyway (Locke 1823g: II, 50; Ince 2011). It seems that logical consistency eludes accounts of the *Second Treatise* that take money as either wholly natural or as wholly conventional.

Here, Caffentzis' reading guides us to the conclusion that the tension between these two interpretive frames cannot be overcome since, for Locke, the very being of money oscillates between them. Given Locke is explicit that the use of money is based on consent, readings such as Macpherson's that hold him up as naturalizing a market society simply do not work. Still, it is only insofar as the consent to recognize the value of money is understood by Locke to be a universal yet pre-political event, one that precedes the constitution of the commonwealth, that he can make accumulation of property as a moral right without at the same time making the grossly dubious claim that inequality is a religious commandment (Ince 2011). Money, it turns out, is neither wholly natural, nor wholly conventional, and moreover, it is only on the equivocation between these two states that money can become universal.

Likewise, if we remain with that moment in the "state of nature" where men consent to the use of money, *Clipped Coins* outlines a further moral economy central to Locke's political theory. On the one hand, man's chief moral obligation is said to be "the preservation of God's creation" such that the central purpose of labor and the appropriation it engenders is to "improve [the Earth] for the benefit of life" (Locke 1823g: II, 32). On the other hand, "land that is left wholly to nature, with no improvement through cultivation ... is rightly called 'waste'" (Locke 1823g: II, 42). Only given its enclosure through social relations founded upon money as a mechanism for preserving things that would otherwise perish and be wasted, is land improved.[4] Not only therefore, does property trump common possession, it is determined in opposition to indigenous relations to non-human nature or webs of local use-rights specific as these are transformed into discrete units of abstract value (see Neocleous 2011; Goldstein 2013).

In centering the role of money in the justification of processes of enclosure, Caffentzis also anticipates those interpreters who, in growing numbers in recent years, emphasize the Atlantic colonial context as the focus of Locke's theory of property (see especially Tully 1993; and Arneil 1996). Broadening the focus onto the colonial dimension certainly allows for a shift beyond the parochialism of English debates around absolutism to Locke's role in providing moral foundations for the settler colonial project. But it's only by foregrounding the logic of money and the compulsions of capital accumulation more broadly, as all too many scholars fail to do, that we can understand the global forces that induce both enclosure and prole-tarianization in England along with the project of Indian "removal" in the Americas (an exception here is Ince 2018). Whether the native in America or the English peasant, Locke's theory of property amounts to a sanction against both those not working for a wage and against land not being worked by wage labor; "idleness" becomes viewed as a criminal disposition that fails to engage in "improvement."[5]

Introduction to the New Edition

MONEY AND CRIMINALITY

This brings us to the close relation discerned in *Clipped Coins* between money and criminality in Locke's political philosophy. As Koshka Duff argues, Locke's dual moral economy of improvement and waste was "instrumental in delegitimating those uses of nature he finds undesirable, and criminalising the people engaged in them" (Duff 2017: 36). Locke's notion of criminality implied a policy of enclosing the English commons since, it was widely held, if left unimproved the commons would generate an idle and disorderly mass while profits would be lost (Neocleous 2011: 510–512; Wood 2002: 276; Goldstein 2013). It further entailed support for the colonial enterprise since indigenous American failure to use money meant land was allowed to lie in waste. Along with attacks upon customary entitlements to workplace materials, expropriation of land and trade made independent survival all but impossible insofar as they eradicated access to grazing, hunting and gathering. In fact, so extensive was the criminalization of subsistence beyond the wage in Locke's time that Silvia Federici has described life lived outside the capital relation as "always one step away from the whip and the noose" (Federici 2004: 85). In a similar vein, in a reference to the widespread use of capital punishment, Peter Linebaugh refers to the epoch as a "thanatocracy" (2006). For, as Locke argues in the "Second Treatise," while the end of government is the protection of "life, liberty, and estate," those who transgress against them might "deserve [...] death" (Locke 1823g: II, 182).[6]

On one level, the relation between money and criminality is quite patently self-evident. If the imposition of money wages and prices was necessary to compel labor to be sold to capital, this in turn required the state to both control the creation of money and to impose it as a universal measure. But Caffentzis' argument extends further, not merely to underline money as the theoretical mechanism by which the whole of the Earth is viewed as a source of potential profit, but also as the device by which, to borrow a turn of phrase from Duff once more, subsistence beyond the wage is excluded from the body politic (Duff 2017: 16).

At this point, the intimate relationship between Locke's ontology of money and his conception of criminality ought to be apparent. Ultimately, for Caffentzis, it hinges upon the peculiar temporality of money. For while money's relative permanence, as we have seen, overcomes the

11

moral limitations to appropriation in the state of nature, it only does so, as Caffentzis maintains, by introducing a hiatus between the acts of appropriation and consumption. Accordingly, if money preserves property and makes unlimited accumulation possible, it also bears the corollary of an insecure temporal space characterized by "fears and continual dangers" and populated by criminals (Locke 1823g: II, 123) (see pages 63–65). To begin with, the point here merely revisits money's ambiguous state of being between nature and convention. Metal content exerts a certain "power of objectivity," yet unlike any other substance direct knowledge of the real essence of money is unattainable through its material content alone. Accordingly, though it affords a certain permanence to property, money nonetheless generates a new temporal site of "dangers" and uncertainty that, in turn, demands leaving the state of nature to form a civil compact.

In this context, Caffentzis presents us with a further thesis that bears examination. As we have seen, the state's function is in part to preserve money from criminality or, to use Locke's expression: the "corruption and viciousness of degenerate men" (Locke 1823g: II, 128). While the sources of such degeneracy are only ever fleetingly referenced in the *Second Treatise*, by referring us to Book II of the *Essay on Human Understanding*, Caffentzis gleans an account of crime that coheres quite seamlessly with Locke's ontology of money. For in that text we discover that it is a temporally bounded rationality, which leads the subject to fail to defer the satisfaction of his pleasure and thus, leads him to transgress against natural law. As Locke puts it,

> [f]or though he will be always determined by that which is judged good by his understanding, yet it excuses him not; because a too hasty judgement of his own making, he has imposed on himself wrong measures of good and evil.
>
> (Locke 1823a: II, xxi, 56)

Money, it would appear from this reading, stimulates the "evil" of easy gratification by inducing the subject to act in "haste." For if in the pre-monetary state of nature the satisfaction of pleasures is immediate, once a money economy generates a moral law of endless improvement then crime amounts to a failure to live according to the temporal discipline of capital's logic of accumulation.

This brings us back to the question of the state. For on this account, it is only upon the mutual consent to money, along with the scarcity and deferral of pleasure it entails, that it becomes necessary to exit the insecurity of the state of nature to form a civil compact. It is ultimately in this sense that the account of the state presupposes criminality, as Locke's widely cited formulation implies: "[t]he great chief end therefore, of men's uniting into commonwealths, and putting themselves under governments, is the *preservation of their property*" (Locke 1823g: 124, emphasis added).

Returning to the debate with Lowndes, Locke's defense of a metallic money standard, along with his desire to tackle counterfeiters and clippers, rests with the premise that money generates the social contract in the first place (see page 65). In this light, we can understand the *Second Treatise* as a foundational instance of the liberal theory of the state, anchored upon property, money and the obfuscation of legally constituted violence.

Moreover, such a line of thought also gestures toward the way the liberal state is an abstraction in theory as well as in practice. For where a regime of property and money exists, the society can have no common interest except, as Lucio Colletti once put it, "by dissociation from all contending interests" (Colletti 1975: 35). That is, the indirect, impersonal authority of the state appears as a power that belongs to no one and stands for everyone where class rule is mediated by the rule of law and so, to quote Colletti again, "the eternal category is substituted for the historical concrete" (Colletti 1975: 27).

SUBJECTIVITY AND PROPERTY

The peculiar temporality ascribed by Locke to the money-form does more than condition criminal subjectivity on Caffentzis' account. In perhaps his book's most dazzling argument, the abstract conception of property that appears in the *Second Treatise* is shown to presuppose the metaphysical notion of personhood and identity. That is insofar as the indefinite circulation of commodities presupposes continuity in the identity of their owners: in order for what is mine today to be mine tomorrow "I" must continue to be the same person; I must be the "proprietor of one's own person," as Locke puts it (see page 53). This insinuates a formal affinity between the notion of self-ownership reflected in Locke's notion of "property in the person" that we have seen is central to his political theory and the account of memory in Book II of *An Essay Concerning Human Understanding*. The latter text presents memory as an act of appropriation of past action by present consciousness. Identity, it would seem, consists in the continuity of a claim to ownership of one's self or, at least, this appears to be what Locke has in mind:

> consciousness always accompanies thinking and it is that which makes everyone to be what he calls self [...] and as far as this consciousness can be extended backwards to any past action or thought, so far reaches the identity of that person.
>
> (Locke 1823a: II, xxvii, 9, quoted on page 53)

Caffentzis sees the intersection of subjectivity and property further refracted through Locke's theory of language. Locke ascribes words the function of transporting ideas from a private self so they may be "re-privatized" by an interlocutor or preserved for a future self against oblivion (see page 84). The conclusion that Caffentzis draws in this light rests with the notion that Locke in fact transforms the Cartesian deduction of the self into a deduction for the creation of property in the self along with private property more broadly: "cogito ergo habo," as Caffentzis puts it (see page 52).

This is a bold claim, for it entails a reformulation of the conventional history of modern philosophy: the Cartesian philosophy of consciousness is recast by Locke's notion of self-appropriation into a conception of identity persisting across time. Caffentzis is not entirely isolated in conveying such an argument. Indeed, he anticipates Étienne Balibar's own study of the English philosopher, *Identity and Difference*, a decade later (Balibar 2013). Not unlike the assertions in *Clipped Coins*, Balibar discerns the constitution of identity in Locke's philosophy as an act of self-appropriation. On his reading, this is mobilized through a linguistic contradiction whereby the self divides its unity in the process of its self-naming. "I speak about myself," Balibar says, "therefore about my 'self'" (Balibar 2006: 322). Like Caffentzis then, Balibar also detects an unstable equivocation underlying the Lockean account of subjectivity; one that lies between the categories of identity and property. There exists an "anthropological doublet" between consciousness and language grounded upon an unstable relation between "being" and "having," between the "self" and the own" (see Balibar 2006; 2013: 23 and 32).

As we have already seen, to underscore the intersection of personhood and possession in Locke's philosophy is not in itself a wholly novel proposition, dating back at least to Macpherson's designation of Thomas Hobbes and Locke as philosophers of "possessive individualism" (Macpherson 1962). For Macpherson, Locke's political thought is built upon a relation of ownership to oneself and one's capacities as the ground for freedom. As the proprietor of one's own person, one owes the society nothing and liberty comes to be conceived as independence from the wills of others. Yet, as Balibar has suggested, Macpherson inaugurates a tendency among historians of political theory to view property as an external condition of freedom (Balibar 2013: 72). This is, to quote Balibar, "to subordinate anthropology to positive law," for it fails to understand the way in which identity itself is conceived as a form of property in the *Essay* (Balibar 2013: 72; Sanford 2013: xi–xlvi). Such a contention of continuity across the philosophy of subjectivity and of the polity aligns Balibar closely with Caffentzis' interpretation. For where the labor theory of property "projects the privateness of the person into the ontological transformation of the earth," as Caffentzis puts it, property and freedom are of the same ontological order (see page 52). Just as he understands property as external to subjectivity, so too does Macpherson assess its function too narrowly. In understanding Locke's central theoretical gesture as the naturalization of a society grounded upon market relations between individuals, Macpherson understands property as a limit upon the state rather than the very condition of its power. This belies a restricted view where capitalism is concerned, since it is a vision anchored upon an individual propensity to the pursuit of wealth instead of the compulsion to accumulate capital on a global scale in the context of which Locke was already operating. In other words, rather than the "petit bourgeois shopkeeper" that characterizes the notion of "possessive individualism," Caffentzis holds that it's more apt to speak of Locke's philosophy in terms of a "possessive universalism," to denote the generalization of the commodity form and wage relation that it implies (see page 95).

This argument for what I have called a formal affinity between subjectivity and property not only relates the political theory of the *Second Treatise* to the epistemology of the *Essay* in convincing fashion, it can further be made to stand in as a tangible philosophical manifestation for a broader argument for the historical co-emergence of abstract conceptions of property and of abstract will. Here, we might follow a line of argument put down by the philosopher of law, Evgeny Pashukanis. His path-breaking account of capitalist legal systems shows that while common law systems tend to apprehend contractual relations as occurring between concrete persons, this acts as a barrier to systems of exchange, so that the indefinite circulation of commodities becomes possible only where an abstract "free" will—a "purely social function" in Pashukanis' words—is established through the continual transfer of rights in the market (Pashukanis 1978: 115, 112 and 127).[7] It is through this process that the bearers of these rights come to appear as independent and substitutable: they become abstracted from any concrete bond. In capitalism, therefore, as Marx avers, "private property has become the subject of will," the will survives only as "the predicate of property" (Marx 1992: 168).[8] Nowhere is the articulation of these historical transformations clearer than in Locke's theory of property.

If the subject is constituted through property in the self, what of that occurrence where the self becomes the property of another? All too often Locke's readers brush aside the apparent contradiction between his principle of universal right and his investments in slave trading operations and plantations, or his role in drafting of the *Fundamental Constitutions of Carolina*; an especially regressive set of laws that, among other things, granted the British colonist "power and authority over his negro slaves" (see pages 154–156, n.9; see also 1823b). But to overlook Locke's enthusiasm for chattel slavery, whether implicit or explicit, to view it as a mere historical anachronism independent of the core principles of liberal thought, entails an altogether flimsy rhetorical gesture. Caffentzis rejects this sort of easy resolution of the tensions between biography and philosophy by probing for a *theoretical* reconciliation between them.

As Caffentzis points out, there is at least one explicit justification of slavery in Locke's work: the *Second Treatise* rationalizes a forfeiture of freedom to despotic power for the criminal who transgresses the natural law. As Locke writes, the criminal "having forfeited his life by some act that deserves death, he to whom he has forfeited it may […] delay to take it and make use of him to his own service" (Locke 1823g: II, 23). Here we thus find a rationalization of slavery as a sort of suspended death sentence for the transgressor of the natural law and accordingly, of the slave as existing in a sort of zombie state of living death. And yet, this merely begs the question since, on Locke's terms, this monstrous logic might apply to English criminals shipped to the colonies, but how could it possibly warrant the capture of slaves by traders or the confinement of children born into slavery? For these are people who have committed no transgression against the natural law and, as such, would not seem subject to the punishment Locke's liberalism metes out to its offenders. The condition for a logical consistency in Locke's support for the institution of chattel slavery would thus need to lie elsewhere and it is here that Caffentzis' reading of Locke's 'anthropological' study of Africa in *The Whole History of Navigation from its Original to this Time* stands as a crucial reference. For it is in that text that Caffentzis uncovers an account of racial and cultural inferiority by which, one can surmise, Locke had vindicated the terror with which he was so closely embroiled, through his moral philosophy. Given that Africa is described by Locke as "scarce civilized," barbarous and where slavery is commonplace, Caffentzis infers that Locke had held Africa itself and Africans as a whole as fallen from natural law (quoted in Locke 1823d: 414). Such an interpretation, where the view of blackness itself as criminal is ascribed to Locke, has the merit of squaring the circle of his view of slavery as a deferred death sentence for the transgressor of the laws of nature. It also brings Caffentzis into dialogue with those accounts, Cedric Robinson's, Fred Moten's and Stefano Harney's above all, of black social life as disruptive of social order so that its criminal character is inherent to its resistive nature (see Robinson 2000; Moten 2018; Harney and Moten 2013). In any case, Caffentzis ultimately concludes that Locke's omission of any explicit examination of the enslavement of Africans or the consistency of his own political commitments in itself signals a profound moral indifference. However, we might here advance the further claim that Locke's silence is inherent to his politics, that is, that the withdrawal of self-ownership and the "forfeiture" of all rights upon which the Atlantic slave trade was premised, is, as Sybille Fischer shows, as much a structural necessity for liberal thought as much as it is logical contradiction (I draw here on Fischer 2015). How else might liberal empire have been founded and continue to persist, except by supplementing the ideal of universal liberty with the despotic right to enslave and to kill?

COMMODITY AND CONCEPT

All of this insinuates a continuity in the social function of private property from Locke's epoch to our own. In turn, it brings Caffentzis' study into dialogue with other assessments of Locke as a fervently bourgeois ideologist. Ellen Wood is significant in this regard insofar as, in a number of books, she has contested dominant currents of thought in political theory that postulate the relative autonomy of Locke's discursive context from the categories of capitalism. Partly under the sway of hermeneutic methods imported from continental philosophy, Anglo-American scholarship—under the guise of the "Cambridge School" especially—has sought to isolate Locke's work from the forces of the commodity form by situating his oeuvre within the historical horizons of the Grotian tradition of natural law (see Wood 2008: 1–27).[9] While Ellen Wood has undermined such claims and the deeply atomized view of history they entail by situating Locke and other modern philosophers in their wider socio-economic contexts, Neal Wood, in reading the bourgeois concepts plainly perceptible in the *Second Treatise* back into the *Essay on Human Understanding*, complements the assessment offered in *Clipped Coins* and so, deserve further scrutiny.

Seeking to situate Locke's political theory as an articulation of the institutional architecture necessary for the cultural renewal proposed by his epistemology, Wood locates the peculiarly bourgeois character of Locke's philosophy of knowledge across four distinct themes: a Baconian natural history of the psyche that implies a commitment to social reform; a celebration of independent reason against conformity; a self-directed industrious subject; and empiricism as a meritocratic form of philosophy, where intellectual or moral inequality is a result of circumstance (Wood 1983: 180–181). In discerning the work of bourgeois ideology at the level of Locke's concepts themselves, Wood's theoretical enterprise is not at odds with Caffentzis'. But while Wood perhaps risks the determinism that accompanies a mostly linear causative relation between politics and philosophy, the "deep coherence" between philosophy and money discerned in *Clipped Coins* and elsewhere is less reducible to such a potentially reductive logic.[10]

In this regard, it is instructive to examine more closely the intersections identified by Caffentzis between Locke's famous doctrine of primary and secondary qualities and his ontology of money. As is well known, in the *Essay* Locke gives ontological primacy to what he takes to be the objectivity of the "primary" qualities of substances (such as solidity, extension, motion) over "secondary" qualities (such as color, taste or heat) since the latter promise to be explained on the basis of the former. That is, while absolute knowledge of the essence of natural substances is unattainable, observation is possible and we can still acquire knowledge on the basis of experience (see page 90). Even if human organs do not directly observe bodily motion or structure, sensory ideas are still generated by a determinate corpuscular world. In short, even if human knowledge is by definition incomplete, nature provides it with objective limits. From here, it is possible to assert, along with Neal Wood, that to free knowledge from innate ideas by grounding it in sensory experience is to liberate it from the fetters of superstition (Wood 1983; Faulkner 2011). One might further speculate, as Wood does, that the social force of the distinction between primary and secondary qualities reflects a modern capitalist experience of nature as an abstract object of production, whereby labor and land are increasingly reduced to the qualities of number, weight and measure in order to be exploited and exchanged. In *Clipped Coins*, the argument goes further to locate a *formal affinity* between the philosophy of primary and secondary qualities and capital at the level of the form of value itself. It is here that the intimate relation between concept and commodity becomes especially apparent, for if the value of money is to be universally established as Locke wants, it cannot be wholly embodied in the sensuous qualities of the commodity nor in the primary qualities of precious metals. That is, as a measure of value money is conventional, its existence hinges upon consent and yet, as we have seen, the preservation of value across time and space demands its stability. Accordingly, what Caffentzis refers to as the "bond between convention and nature" represented by metallic money amounts to a unique synthesis of primary and secondary qualities (see page 94).

The point becomes even clearer when we see how this view of money further coheres with Locke's taxonomy of ideas. Where ideas of substances are concerned, words are said to merely "tag" an already coalesced idea and so are not subject to whim. Since substances are discovered and not invented, for Locke their names are "passive and external" (see page 71). Conversely, insofar as they lack a natural external standard, abstractions are not confronted by reality and, thus, are said to bear an inherent indeterminacy. There is a continuity discernible here between Locke's ontology of money and a "mercantilist" conception of language where words give stability to ideas so they may be smoothly exchanged (Caffentzis 2000: 193). As Caffentzis suggests, while for Locke a coin signifies both the particular idea that is produced upon its appearance *and* the abstract quality of gold or silver it represents; it is only the corpuscular metallic nature of the coin that assures its bearer that the abstract idea of value will have a continuous objectivity in the world, and therefore, preserve property through money's "power of objectivity" (see pages 92–93; Caffentzis 2000: 187; and 2021: 6).

Conceived as marking a particular intersection of the commodity and the concept, Caffentzis' study is thus not restricted to detecting the bourgeois desire motivating his philosophy as other historical materialist accounts have sought to demonstrate, but rather to show how "the abstractions to which capital submits social life," to employ Alberto Toscano's formulation, are uncovered at the level of the history of ideas (Toscano 2008). This insinuates the potential for the arguments discussed above to offer a wider contribution to debates regarding the material sources of mental abstraction as such. Alfred Sohn-Rethel's influential theoretical enterprise centers upon an attempt, not entirely unlike Caffentzis', to locate the conditions of cognition in the exchange of commodities and therefore merits a brief detour, so as to further appreciate the significance of Caffentzis' argument.

MONEY AND ABSTRACTION

Sohn-Rethel's philosophical project begins with the premise that, in posing an equivalence between two different objects, money necessarily involves abstracting from their physical qualities. This entails what he calls a "real abstraction," for while the subject of exchange thinks of the qualitative properties of the object, the practice of exchange takes place in terms of the form of the exchange value of the object. Abstraction in the mind is preceded by abstraction in practice (Sohn-Rethel 1978: 28–29). Drawing on this basic premise, Sohn-Rethel seeks to trace the development of conceptual knowledge from antiquity through the medieval period to the rise of merchant capital and finally, to the development of industrial capital. Of course, the crucial juncture in this narrative occurs with the emergence of capitalism, since here the separation of manual from mental labor becomes stark. Sohn-Rethel's contention is that the epistemic project of modern science and philosophy is inseparable from capital's need to posit a mental labor autonomous from manual labor since it permits the imposition of abstract knowledge over labor and so, control by automation over artisanry (Sohn-Rethel 1978: 113, 122, 141 and 179–180). In this reading, the dualism of mind and world inaugurated by Descartes and later presented as a transcendental necessity by Kant reflects a dualism inherent in a society wherein social control is grounded upon a knowledge of nature that is based on intuition and sources that are non-sensuous (Sohn-Rethel 1978: 77–78 and passim).[11]

Sohn-Rethel is widely regarded as contributing to a truly historical materialist account of conceptual abstraction insofar as he locates the sources of the latter in the practices of class societies. Yet in taking the consumer's relation to the product as the source of abstraction, it has been argued that he obscures what Marx views as the specific basis of abstraction in capitalism, namely, the commodity form of abstract labor. *Pace* Anselm Jappe and Moishe Postone, Sohn-Rethel seems to presume capitalism to be defined only by the sphere of exchange, circulation and distribution of commodities, while labor in production is seen as a neutral activity not alienated by its commodification (Jappe 2013; Postone 2006: 177–178, 156, n. 90). Moreover, given the priority he accords to abstraction in exchange rather than in labor, Sohn-Rethel's historical narrative centers upon the gradual expansion of exchange from Ancient Greece to modern capitalism, culminating with Galileo's concept of inertial motion as the founding gesture of a truly capitalist form of knowledge no longer derived from nature but deduced from abstractions that are themselves derived from the "pattern of motion contained in the real abstraction of commodity exchange" (Sohn-Rethel 1978: 128). This is an account that provides little distinction between a situation of widespread commodity production and a capitalist society where social reproduction is dependent upon the market.

Abjuring the sort of monotonous historical narrative espoused by Sohn-Rethel, the scope of Caffentzis' study of Locke does not extend to setting out the sources of mental abstraction as such. At stake is not merely a question of analytic scope but also a methodological proposition. Or, at least, this seems to be the case where a more detailed historical perspective suggests a crucial transformation in early modernity in the philosophical understanding of thought from a form of activity to a form of labor (Caffentzis 2013: 165), that is, where Sohn-Rethel sees a continuous division of mental and manual labor running from Ancient Greece to eighteenth-century Europe culminating in industrial capital's taking direct control of the labor process through industrialization, Caffentzis insists that only with Locke is the idea conceived as property or chattel and, thus, on the ontological order of the products of labor (Caffentzis 2013: 192). Where for Plato, for instance, thought consists in contemplation of and participation in ideal forms, its products could not be alienated. Similarly, if for Aristotle thought is distinct from labor, this is to the extent that labor has a telos, while thought is an end in itself (Caffentzis 2013: 168). In either case, an unequivocal gulf in the being of master and slave classes, between thought and labor, excluded any discourse between absolutely distinct ontological orders. While he ascribes to Sohn-Rethel's (and indeed, Federici's) view of Descartes as inaugurating a separation of mind and world as a reflection of capital's view of the world as a mechanism to be mastered, Caffentzis indexes the modern rupture with the Platonic separation of knowledge and property to Locke, since it is only with the latter that the equation of subjectivity with property extends to the level of thought itself (Sohn-Rethel, 1978: 123; Federici 2004: 138–155; Caffentzis 2013: 167).

This much becomes patently apparent if we take Locke's philosophical enterprise as centered upon a critique of the notion of innate abstract ideas, for it appears particularly clearly from this perspective as a project, as Caffentzis suggests, grounded upon a conception of knowledge as effort and of ideas as the objects of labor. As a matter of fact, Locke views the exercise of mental labor as a moral compulsion; in the *Essay* he asserts that, "God having fitted men with faculties and means to discover, receive and retain truths, according as they are employed" (Locke 1823a: I, iv, 22). The activity of thought, it would seem, coheres perfectly with the labor theory of property (Caffentzis 2000: 199). While Locke holds the mind as passive in the reception of simple ideas, he nevertheless obliges it to act upon them not unlike the requirement to labor upon the commons in order to transform it into private property. What Locke calls the "workmanship of the understanding," therefore, seems to amount to a sort of "improvement" in the realm of ideas (Locke 1823a: III, xiii, 13). Thought thus becomes a form of appropriation and its products come to be potential commodities. *Cogito ergo habo* indeed.

I have suggested, however, that given the constraints Caffentzis places upon the scope of a given history of thought, this accounting of Locke's philosophy of money is not the last word, nor does it account once and for all for philosophy's relation to the commodity. In this light, Locke's philosophy is read as a particular attempt to assert the priority of capital over the state and the imposition of a universal form of value upon labor. Locke's project thus differs from Berkeley's attempt to monetize the everyday life of a resistive peasantry or Hume's desire to break Highlanders' gift economy.

We might discern these projects as foreshadowing Keynesian versus neo-liberal monetary policies, or whatever else might supersede these, but all in all, the point is that, if we understand money as a form of command, this implies that where the philosophy of money is involved so too are the coordinates of struggle. George Caffentzis has left us with a method for mapping their conceptual history and reverberations in the present. We are lucky to see this important work back in print (appended here with a 2008 pamphlet on primitive accumulation) along with the previously unpublished book on Hume.

Preface

thirty spokes share the wheel's hub;
it is the center hole that makes it useful.
shape clay into a vessel;
it is the space within that makes it useful.
cut doors and windows for a room;
it is the holes which make it useful.
therefore profit comes from what is there;
usefulness from what is not.

—Lao Tsu

This essay is part of a longer work on Locke's, Berkeley's and Hume's philosophies of money. Its structure is ampliative, beginning with what might be considered a relatively minor interpretational problem in Locke's economic writings and ending with a reconstruction of Locke's ontology and genealogy of money.

The method I employ with Locke (as with Berkeley and Hume) is also ampliative. For my purpose is to demonstrate that Locke's writings on money cannot be adequately understood without placing them in the context of: (1) his general theory of semantics and language; and (2) the socio-historical fears, possibilities and challenges that confronted Locke and his circle. Within this more encompassing manifold, we can better understand some of the reasons for and causes of Locke's theoretical choices and creations, and not "merely" remain at the level of philosophical narrative.

I suppose one could call this a study in ideology, but only if by "ideology" is meant neither an illusion nor a *Weltanschauung*. That is, Locke's theory of money was not "invented" to "justify" a pre-determined policy on the basis of false premises and/or fallacious inferences. True, it is easy to make a fool of anyone, as the Sophists showed long ago; but economic policies in capitalist societies necessitate thought and knowledge. It would be foolish to say otherwise, considering that the accumulation of an enormous cognitive patrimony has been an essential element of the general accumulation process over the last 500 years. However, we must be precise as to the kind of thought and knowledge theories like Locke's present. For they are only as illusory as the process they have been part of.

Furthermore, I do not have a Leibnizian or Hegelian notion of ideologies as either co-present or serially ordered conceptual totalities reflecting or progressing toward a larger totality. Perhaps God, the dead and Brecht's happy souls "who shall emerge from the flood in which we are sinking" can now see "around the corners" of their concepts, but the theories of *this* period are *not* totalities. There is inevitably much "reality" showing through that cannot be said, too much of the obvious that is concealed. Our investigation of Locke's writings shows more consistency and coherence than expected, but it will *also* show the recognition of an intractable "*other*" in the world, limiting and threatening any "totality." That, if anything, is Locke's "greatness."

In the context of Lockean studies, I see this book as part of a trend typified by some recent works of Peter Alexander (1980; 1981) and Michael R. Ayers (1981), which try to "make sense of Locke." This trend arises after a period in the 1960s and early 1970s, which reached its zenith (or nadir) in Jonathan Bennett's *Locke, Berkeley, Hume: Central Themes* (1971), when interpreters reveled in revealing the lack of clarity, the incoherence and the plain contradictions of the very same philosopher who, in the 1930s, was considered the founder of the "analytic tradition." Such are the ways of time, interpretation, and perhaps, the changing needs of socio-philosophical memory. Certainly, our times have forced me to go beyond the easy criticism of the past.

However, anyone familiar with the work of Drs. Peter Linebaugh and Silvia Federici will recognize little that is new in the following pages. At best this effort, as well as the titles on Berkeley and Hume, can be seen as attempted confirmations of their theoretical conclusions and an application of their historical method. For I have been enormously helped by their work. I refer specifically to Linebaugh's *The London Hanged* (in press) and Federici's contributions to *The Great Caliban* (published in Italian as *Il Grande Calibano* in Milan, 1984).

Many friends have helped in this work, but I would like to single out three: first of all, Mike and Pat Athay, who for nearly two decades now have kept me philosophically coherent with their concern, criticism, conversation and love. And I am especially grateful to Dr. Mariarosa Dalla Costa, of the Institute of Social and Political Science at the University of Padova, Italy, for the contribution her theoretical work has made to the development of my thought.

As for institutions, I would like to mention two. First, the students and staff of the Department of Philosophy at Millersville State College in Pennsylvania, who encouraged me to present my initial course in the philosophy of money (in the spring of 1980), and who received the result with patience and good grace. Second, the students and staff of the Department of Religious Studies and Philosophy at the University of Calabar, who gave me "shelter from the storm" and a beautiful environment in which to write, think, and speak.

July, 1984 Calabar, Nigeria

Introduction

I know nothing of Edmund Metcalfe convicted at Derby Assizes of counterfeiting the coin ... but ... it's better to let him suffer ... for these people seldom leave off. And it's difficult to detect them.

—Sir Isaac Newton (1724)

Many commentators on Locke's economic writings have noted a contradiction or paradox in his views on money. On the one side, Locke is considered one of the earliest and clearest exponents of the "quantity theory of money"; on the other, he sponsored monetary legislation that any quantity theorist could see would create catastrophic consequences for an England in the midst of stabilizing a "Glorious Revolution" and fighting a world war with Louis XIV.[1] I claim that this paradox is only apparent, but its resolution will require a new and better understanding of the relations obtaining among Locke's economic, semantic and metaphysical views.

Locke was quite aware of the tension between the quantity theory and his parliamentary proposals; however, a higher theoretical imperative was called for by the monetary situation of late seventeenth-century England. This imperative, ultimately grounded in Locke's *ontology of money*, overrode any quantity theoretical considerations. By "ontology of money," I mean a specified set of social and natural conditions that are said to be presupposed by the existence of a monetary system. In interpreting Locke's practice at that time, I argue that he preferred short-term economic dislocation over total monetary collapse and, perhaps, the onset of what he would consider an "Inglorious Revolution." In making my case I will, of course, examine Locke's major "economic works": *Some Considerations of the Consequences of Lowering the Interest and Raising the Value of Money* (1823f) and *Further Considerations Concerning Raising the Value of Money* (1823c).

But I will also show how his more "philosophical" work is essential to his economic argument. Thus, my analysis will involve Locke's *Two Treatises of Government* as well as the *Essay Concerning Human Understanding.*[2] These two works were published and republished in the same period as his

27

monetary pamphlets (1690–1696) and were immediate "hits," although they were in preparation for a long period, including a decade of exile on the Continent.

A word about these books and their environment might be in order. Seventeenth-century England was a dangerous place for a writer. On the one side, during the Civil War and after, an immense pamphlet literature developed whereby the experience of an "instant replay" of ideas—political, economic and religious—could tempt the enthusiast and the unwary. On the other, it was a period riddled with politically motivated self-censorship, pseudonymity and the posthumous.[3] Locke was a skilled but cautious navigator in these cross-currents, but with his return to England in the Queen-to-be Mary's van, he organized a publishing campaign that brought him into a public identity with the new state. As a consequence we must assume, as Locke did, that his audience was familiar with the political and philosophical background of his monetary argument. That we cannot always make such an assumption for a philosopher writing on economics today should not blind us to the radically different situation philosophy experienced then.

1

Clipped Coins

"The shears supply the place of one witness, the filings of another, and the rough clipped money of another."

—Sir Isaac Newton (1724)

The monetary system of England and its empire at the end of the seventeenth century was largely metallic. Coin of the realm—but not necessarily of the English realm—still magnetized desire. When Henry Morgan, with some 400 buccaneers, seized Porto Bello in 1668—the port from which the Spanish silver fleets sailed to Europe—his men brought back to Port Royal a quarter of a million "pieces of eight," a world currency:[1]

> [It was] a silver coin worth 8 reals or 272 maravedis. It was also known as the hard or strong peso, and later as the piastre, which became the precursor of the dollar … these coins, produced in Mexico as well as in Spain (Madrid, Seville and Segovia) invaded the whole world (including Africa and Asia).
>
> (Vilar 1976: 138)[2]

True, there were "experiments" with non-metallic currencies: tobacco in Virginia and "traditional" cowrie shells in West Africa, while at the center of the empire the Bank of England, formed in 1694, started to issue "paper money."[3] But the hierarchy of metal still held sway in the English mind: tin, copper, silver and gold. However, since gold was largely a *"deus absconditus"* then, "the only true coin of the country was silver—crowns, half-crowns, shillings and sixpences" (Craig 1946: 5).[4] This explains why Locke could begin his *Further Considerations* so axiomatically:

> SILVER is the instrument and measure of commerce in all the civilized and trading parts of the world.
>
> (Locke 1823c: 139)[5]

But this civilized "instrument and measure" was in deep crisis in the 1690s. The cause of the crisis was a collective antagonist who had no unified face, force or plan. Unlike "the enemies of government" during the Civil War, who identified themselves and tried—through arms, land occupations and public demonstration—to "turn the world upside down,"[6] the new antagonists to order were, literally and figuratively, marginal, cryptic and fluid: coin-clippers, counterfeiters, bullion smugglers and the like.

Whereas the Quakers, Diggers and Ranters expressed themselves in the categories of revelation, the Holy Spirit and conscience—the language of the political theology of the time—the new subversives expressed themselves with tools: shears, dies and presses, kilns and sloops. But their persistent activity accumulated into a profound social disorder, according to Locke, who helped organize the theoretical and practical struggle against them. Moreover, they had "friends in high places." Just as the "lunatic fringe" had, at times, secret supporters in the official opposition, so too these subterranean figures (who could at best speak in "lies") had an echo in the legitimate debate concerning the monetary strategy of the state.

In all his writings of the 1690s, Locke saw himself as the chief spokesman against the public defenders of either the camp of religious enthusiasts or the den of monetary and semantic criminals. His efforts were not merely verbal; for example, he arranged for Newton to leave Cambridge and become Warden of the Mint. From this position Newton became the detector, interrogator and prosecution of the actual miscreants, helping fill Newgate and providing much employment for the hangman at Tyburn.[7]

What was wrong with the silver coin of England? It was clipped, for a start.

An experiment was made which showed that £57,200 sterling in silver coin, which should have contained 220,000 ounces of pure silver, contained only 141,000 ounces. It was calculated that at least 4,000,000 out of 5,600,000 sovereigns in circulation had deteriorated in this way.[8]

(Vilar 1946: 218)

This experiment involved *physical* measures; the *economic* measure could be found in the Dutch international money market, where silver bullion was going for 77 pennies an ounce, though its official and legal English price was 62 pennies. The ratio between the physical and the economic measures was important; although there was a 36 percent drop in silver content, there was only a 24 percent increase in the penny price of silver bullion. There was thus a 23 percent "margin of error" that may have been due to the information lags common during that period, that is, the totally informed "rational" trader should have been trading bullion for about 96 pennies an ounce.

By 1695, it was clear to Locke and to Lowndes—then Secretary of the Treasury—as well as to other informed figures that the coin was physically crippled and was not a standard. Moreover, the international market was noting this fact, though not to its full extent. (However, in the course of the upcoming Parliamentary debates on the matter, it would.) Further, the experiment mentioned did not deal with the quantity of counterfeit coin—a statistic that by nature is always suspect—nor did it reveal the extent of bullion melting and smuggling, though both were acknowledged to be large-scale undertakings at the time. One need not be an accomplished economist to conclude that the clipping of coin was the obvious manifestation of an *inflationary/deflationary mechanism* operating outside of the state's control, and indeed, by Locke's definition, *against* the state. When we add to the network of clippers, counterfeiters and smugglers, the pirates of the silver fleets in the Caribbean and the Indian Ocean,[9] we glimpse behind the pages of *Further Considerations* an international counter-system of monetary creation, flow and appropriation threatening Locke's notion of civil government. As we shall see, for Locke, civil government has its origin and end in the regulation of money.

But surely clipping, counterfeiting, smuggling and piracy were not new; they had always been the other side of all monetary systems. After all, Diogenes the Cynic was said to have come from Asia Minor to "debase the currency" of ancient Athens. Why then the alarm?

In part, the problem stemmed from the very opportunities the English rulers saw in the immediate political and economic conjuncture. After more than half a century of isolation (during the Civil War), quasi-vassalage (in Charles II's relation to Louis XIV), and apprenticeship (to Dutch capitalism), the time seemed ripe for a new world-power hierarchy, with England at the top. This, however, required an international solution to the "economic problem." How could England face and rule the world market with a tattered and snatched silver dress? To accept a domestic "fix" might technically work in the short run, but it would kill the very fruits of world power that so many—Locke among others—risked so much for, including exile and execution. Again, a domestic "fix" would underestimate the enemy, for the threat too was worldwide and, if it were not dealt with (indeed, if England did not deal with it), then the very government called for by world trade (a "world government" that was to be provided by the English imperium and navy) would be put into question. Failure to deal with the problem of coinage on a world scale would open a space to "anarchy" and "treason" perpetually lurking outside the limited domestic interests of each state (as the explosion of piracy showed). If England could not represent the interests of the world market, then it would not be able to claim the legitimacy of its rule, especially if it gave in to the clippers' shears.[10]

Such was the political context behind the coinage debate. But what were the practical alternatives in dealing with the "deteriorated" silver coins? Surely there had to be a recoinage; newly minted coins had to replace the old. But under what conditions of exchange? There were two diametrically opposed ways to accomplish this task:

(1) take in the old coin at its "face value" and return reminted coins with the same "face value" but with about one-quarter less silver in every crown and shilling; or
(2) take in the clipped coin at weight and return coin at the same weight, where crowns and shillings keep their old silver content.

The first was, roughly, Lowndes' method. The second method was Locke's. Clearly, with Lowndes' solution, there would be the same number of coins (crowns, shillings and pennies) in the newly reminted currency as in the old. But with Locke's solution, there would be fewer coins. Since neither method could create silver *ex nihilo*, it follows that Lowndes' method spread less silver per coin over more coins, and Locke's spread more silver per coin over fewer coins. In both cases new, shining coins would be issued—with milled edges, designed to stop future clippers.

While physically these proposals did not seem radically different, economically and philosophically they expressed completely opposite views of money.

It is in Locke's debate with Lowndes over recoinage that the contradiction or paradox, which is the focus of this chapter, appears. In reviewing the argument Lowndes advances for his proposal, Locke locates three main sub-arguments, which I dub the *Price* Argument, the *Balance of Trade* Argument and the *Quantity Theory* Argument.

The Price Argument
The value of the silver in the coin ought to be raised to the foot of six shillings three pence in every crown; because the price of standard silver in bullion is risen to 6 shillings 5-pence an ounce.

(Locke 1823c: 153)

The Balance of Trade Argument
The value of the silver in the coin ought to be raised, to encourage the bringing of the bullion to the mint.

(Locke, 1823c: 115)

The Quantity Theory Argument
By making it "more in tale, will make it more commensurate to the general need thereof" and thereby hinder the increase of hazardous paper credit, and the inconveniency of barter.

(Locke 1823c: 177)

These arguments were meant to bolster Lowndes' official proposal:

that all such silver money as are ... not at all diminished by clipping, rounding, filing, washing ... be raised by public authority to the foot of six shillings and 3 pence for the crown and proportionately for the other species.

(Lowndes 1933)[11]

Since 6 shillings 3 pence come out to be 75 pence (for there were 12 pennies to the shilling), Lowndes' proposal amounted to recognizing the price of silver bullion on the international money market and literally making it the legal price. That is—in modern terms—declaring a devaluation of the currency. This sounds like a perfectly reasonable suggestion to the modern ear, hardened as we are to the almost daily manipulation of money by state authorities. So why was Locke's response such adamant opposition? Why did he support a position that left England with fewer coins, hence a decreased money supply, and so (by simple quantity theory of money reasoning) prone to price deflation and economic depression?

Let us consider Locke's reply to Lowndes. His reply to the *Price* argument has three parts. The first is a technical one, based upon the "informational lag" of the international money market, as mentioned above. Start with the following two equations:

$$1 \text{ legal crown} = 1.25 \text{ oz. of silver;}$$
$$6s\ 5d \text{ "clipped coin"} = 1 \text{ oz. of silver.}$$

The first equation is a socio-physical fact, while the second is a current report from the money market in Holland. But now consider Lowndes' suggestion:

$$(L)\ 1 \text{ legal crown} = 6s\ 3d \text{ "clipped coin"}$$

However, anyone combining (1), (2) and (L) would be able to violate the basic conservation laws of the market and create money *ex nihilo*.[12] Consider the following diagram, Figure 1.1:

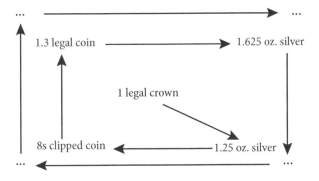

Figure 1.1

This presents a much-too-virtuous spiral for the trader. A clever and unscrupulous person could melt 1 legal crown down to 1.25 ounces of silver, then in Holland buy 8 shillings of the "clipped coin" on the money market, then transport the coin to England and trade it in to Lowndes' Treasury, where they would get 1.3 legal crowns which, of course, they could then melt down to 1.625 ounces of silver, etc. Such a circuit could theoretically be traversed until the Treasury was depleted. Surely the algebra could be corrected (e.g., by identifying the proper exchange for 1 legal crown as 8 shillings, or, equivalently, 96 pennies) to deal with the "informational lag," but where and when would such "corrections" end?

Whatever the technical problems Lowndes' proposal faced in bowing to the fluctuating prices of a far-from-"efficient" money market, Locke worried about a more abject capitulation:

> I cannot but wonder that Mr. Lowndes, a man so well skilled in the law, especially of the mint, the exchequer, and of our money, should all along in the argument speak of clipped money as if it were the lawful money of England; and should propose by that (which is in effect by the clipper's shears) to regulate a new sort of coin to be introduced into England.
>
> (Locke 1823c: 156)

The measured tone and irony of the passage barely hide the anger. To "regulate" is the essential power of the state, especially in defining the form and substance of money. Was the Secretary of the Treasury to become the lackey of the clippers? According to Locke, Lowndes' proposal was unacceptable especially because it validated the millions of criminal acts by the clippers themselves, as well as the many more millions of acts of negligence by the citizens and state officials that let the clipped coins "pass." Such a validation would quickly signal—to the clippers, the underworld, the money market and the average person—a deep deterioration of English civil government.

To measure is an exercise of power and objectivity; it requires a will and a standard. Locke questioned Lowndes' will, but he was not surprised by the lack of standards. The long decline of the English currency had led to an almost total disappearance of lawful money, that is, coins able to serve as an external standard of the substance of money. But if experience is essential to knowledge, then ideas about money inevitably break down and lose coherence and unity in the absence of ideas derived from sensation (Locke 1823a: II, xi, 15).[13] Thus:

> [I]t is no wonder, if the price and value of things be confounded and uncertain, when the measure itself is lost. For we have no lawful silver money current amongst us; and therefore cannot talk or judge right, by

our present, uncertain, clipped money, of the value and price of things, in reference to our lawful regular coin, adjusted and kept to the unvarying standard of the mint.

(Locke 1823c: 158)

The lack of an everyday standard immediately available to the exchanging community was, perhaps, the gravest consequence of the clippers' crime, and the reason why Locke saw clipping as much more damaging than theft. One might even call clipping a "philosophical" or an "epistemological" crime (Locke 1823a: III, x).[14] For theft is a one-time affair, but the clipper's work introduces a continuously deepening obscurity into our reality and into our ideas. It is an act that is repeated *ad infinitum*, making counterfeiters of us all.

For what is a coin's signification, according to Locke, but the association of the idea of silver with the ideas of specific weight and purity, plus the idea of universal exchange?[15] But we cannot hope to fix this complex of ideas and be sure of community-wide agreement concerning them without continuous testing with an external, substantial standard. Confusion, uncertainty and abuse slowly ooze from the clipped coin and seep into the mind of every person, so that universal equivalents turn into universal chaos. No wonder that in such situations officers of the state become servants of the underworld, the high descend below the low.

Locke's third main reply to the Price argument also appeals to the fundamental duties of civil government: guaranteeing the fulfillment of contracts. He points out that "all people, who are to receive money on contracts already made, will be defrauded of 20 per cent, of their due," if Lowndes' proposal were to be adopted (Locke 1923c: 164).[16] Lowndes' claim—that since silver had grown scarce, it had increased in price, and so being paid pence-for-pence in new money for old obligations would not be injustice—is brushed aside by Locke. In reply, he tells a tale of coconuts:

Suppose then you had lent me last year 300, or fifteenscore cocoa-nuts, to be repaid this year, would you be satisfied, and think yourself paid your due, if I should tell you, cocoa-nuts were scarce this year, and that forscore were of as much value this year as a hundred the last...

(Locke 1823c: 164–165)

36

One sees the immediate point, of course, but there is a deeper one: that money—gold and silver—is the positive *object of desire*; it is substantial, as well as relational; one can desire it as well as what it measures. Locke writes of silver:

> [It] is a measure quite different from all other. The yard or quart men measure by may rest indifferently in the buyer's or seller's or third person's hands; it matters not whose it is. But it is not so in silver; it is the thing bargained for as well as the measure of the bargain.
>
> (Locke 1823c: 141)

As a consequence, money contracts, like commodity contracts, have a physical presence and are not mere conventional objects. The duty of the state is to guarantee money contracts as assiduously as it would any other contract, and thus preserve the relation between past possession and future reappropriation. This is not an incidental aspect of the civil authorities, for just as personal identity is the foundation of judicial reward and punishment, so too is guarding the integrity of contract essential to the continued existence of the state (Locke 1823a: II, xxvii, 26).[17] Aside from defrauding countless individuals on fixed incomes, Lowndes' proposal would have made the state the very agent of a planned inequality of exchange, and thus undermine its own continuity.

Such were the pernicious implications of Lowndes' Price argument, according to Locke:

1. A scheme to make money market manipulators and hoarders rich;
2. A vindication of a capital crime;
3. A reneging on the civil authority's promise to impose a temporal identity and reciprocity in contracts.

Indeed, a swift reading of the last chapter of the *Two Treatises* might prompt one to conclude that the time for "the Dissolution of Government" was at hand! (Locke, *Treatises on Politics*, II, 211–243).[18]

Locke's reply to Lowndes' Balance of Trade argument is short but reveals his emphasis on the international character of English economy and polity. He holds that the world market is infinitely more powerful, more "analytic," "objective" and "just" than any single nation state's legal machinery or currency manipulation. Simply changing the denomination would not alter the balance of trade, which finally determines whether there is to be any silver left in the country to bring into the mint in the first place. That the Treasury calls an ounce of silver "one crown" or "6s 5d" means nothing to the foreign merchant, for he deals in silver *qua* silver and not in denominations.

Since England had no silver mines, silver could come into England only through trade or plunder. If silver is not in the country, there is no reason for anyone to bring it to the mint. However, if the country's balance of trade is favorable, then the active merchant will coin his money for internal purchases. But, in either case, the foreign creditor is not interested in the stamp on the coin but the substance and quantity "behind" it.

One can understand Locke's heat in rejecting Lowndes' Balance of Trade argument—a heat that is unusual in Locke, who is normally a cool and ironic controversialist—only in the light of the personal and social context of the question. The world-economy was a vital but delicate mechanism, for it combined violent nation-state rivalries with the most intense international trade and communication in history until then.[19] Most of this trade occurred outside of any one nation state's jurisdiction. "Who is to enforce my contract?" was always *the* question as you stood on the dock and watched your wares sail off to Asia. The personalities this type of situation fostered were undoubtedly cynical, shrewd and observant of human behavior. Locke had known them both in London (from his years on the Board of Trade and Plantations) and during his exile in Holland. They were already used to think not in terms of Nottingham, Newmarket and Westminster but of Cochin, Potosi and Calabar. These merchants judged people and nations on their words and deeds, and they judged them harshly. The little currency "game" that Lowndes was suggesting would never fool them, or convince them to keep and coin one more ounce of silver in London.

Let us turn to Lowndes' third and final main argument, the Quantity Theory argument. Locke's reply brings into focus the "contradiction" that commentators have found in his critique. For example, Vickers writes:

[Locke] failed to see that while money was current and widely accepted at its face value, even though it had been clipped and reduced to a lower intrinsic value, the effect of insisting that that money be recoined at the same standard of weight and fineness would be to engender a monetary deflation. He failed, that is, to recognize at this point the application of his own earlier propositions regarding the deleterious effects on activity of reducing the effective money supply in circulation.

(Vickers 1959: 70–71)

My purpose is to acquit Locke of such charges, but we may first ask: why do commentators think he "failed to recognize" a gross contradiction in his own thinking; indeed, a contradiction concerning matters of immense national importance on which he was bound to be attacked in the lively pamphlet literature surrounding the issue? The standard answer reverts to Locke's strict "metallism" or "bullionism" and argues that Locke's almost fetishistic devotion to the metallic body of money "blinded" him to the economic consequences of having too few coins for trade.

Joyce O. Appleby, in *Economic Thought and Ideology in Seventeenth-Century England*, amplifies this answer, and appears to take up the cudgel for the losing side of the recoinage debate, the late seventeenth-century "inflationists" (1978). She writes:

The basic assumption Locke built into his case was faulty: that men exchange goods for quantities of silver. In fact men exchanged goods for quantities of coin. The fact that coin was legal tender added value to the silver content as the acceptance of clipped shillings had demonstrated.

(Appleby 1978: 222)

Appleby assembles and quotes a series of excerpts from the pamphlet-writing opposition to Locke, which makes this point in many keys. For example, Sir Robert Temple:

The Money of every Country, and not the ounce of Silver, is the Instrument and Measure of Commerce There.

(Appleby 1978: 224)

James Hodges:

Silver, considered as money, hath, speaking properly, no real intrinsik Value at all [for] the whole Value that is put upon Money by Mankind, speaking generally, is extrinsik to the Money ... and hath its real Seat in those good things which it is capable ... to purchase.

(Appleby 1978: 222)

And Nicholas Barbon:

> Money is the Instrument of Commerce from the Authority of that Government where it is coined.[20]
>
> (Appleby 1978: 225)

Appleby clearly thinks that the "inflationists" (or equally, the "devaluationists") had a superior argument. Why, then, did they lose? "Ideology," in a word, according to Appleby. Her explanation of Lowndes' defeat is in the tradition of the most "mechanical" economic determinism. She identifies Lowndes with a group of thinkers oriented to domestic markets and domestic production, while Locke is identified with foreign market interests. The economic strategy of the domestically oriented group would necessarily have required increasing domestic mass consumption, "the expansion of the purchasing power of ordinary people," and so across-the-board wage increases—a nasty conclusion for most employers. However, Appleby writes,

> If markets are sought abroad, the dilemma is solved. Thus, while policies supportive of foreign trade did not equally benefit all groups in England, they did advance the social interest of the upper class in general.
>
> (Appleby 1978: 238)

Locke's ideological appeal to this class, which had the ultimate decisional power, presumably compensated for the lack of explanatory power and incisiveness of his theory of money.

So we have "ideology" versus "science" again, "reasonable" proto-Keynesians versus "ideological" proto-monetarists? Certainly Appleby is to be commended for her attempt to investigate the class determinants of Locke's theoretical speculation.[21] But there is no reason to give the scientific laurels to "old" Barbon & Co. One can equally say that Locke stripped the ideological veil off this consumerist, inflationist, domesticist and mediationist tendency. Locke points out, first, that the object of business is not to give others pleasure but to make "money, gelt, silver." Second, if people are willing to be defrauded they are simply fools—but for the state to "sanctify" the fraud is to call for a civil breakdown. Third, the world economy *is* the dynamic space of accumulation, which brooks no sentimentality about "Delight" but sets a clear standard and measure on exchange. Finally and most crucially, the "scientific" character of Locke's analysis lay in the recognition of the "Others"—the clippers, counterfeiters, smugglers—as a *dynamic* variable in the question of recoinage. (Indeed, in his analysis, Locke developed one of the first theories of "semantic crime.")

This is what Barbon and Lowndes refused to accept: that there were others who had been able to significantly erode the power of the state. According to Locke, their unwillingness to face the source of the deterioration blinded them to the *real* problem: for what was at stake was not simply an economic proposition, but social subversion, that is, not just theft but treason.[22] Lowndes' proposal set the nation up for an infinite cycle of devaluation–deterioration–devaluation–deterioration … It would not take many such phases to sap the very ontological roots of money.

I would conclude that the mantle of "science" be put back into the closet in examining Locke and Lowndes.

Let us return to Locke's supposedly contradictory attack on Lowndes' Quantity Theory argument: that devaluation would increase the supply of money, hence hinder the increasing use of paper credit and the inconvenience of barter. One might wonder why Locke would attack such a view, particularly when he himself had made reference to such a deflationist scenario in the 1691 *Further Considerations*:

> Supposing then, that we had now in England but half as much money as we had seven years ago, and yet had still as much yearly product of commodities, as many hands to work them, and as many brokers to disperse them as before; and that the rest of the world we trade with had as much money as they had before, (for it is likely they should have more by our moiety shared amongst them) it is certain, that either half our rents should not be paid, half our commodities not vented, and half our labourers not employed, and so half the trade be clearly lost; or else, that everyone of these must receive by half the money for their commodities and labour they did before, and but half so much as our neighbors do receive, for the same labour, and the same natural product at the same time. Such a state of poverty as this, though it will make no scarcity of our native commodities amongst us, yet it will have these ill consequences.
>
> (Locke 1823c: 49)

A clear enough expression of the "simple quantity theory of money" if ever there was one! Moreover, Locke was well aware of the "human capital" consequences of such a deflation for military policy and logistics; a "mercenary drain" would follow, as well as a "brain drain":

> [The halving of the money supply] endangers the drawing away of our people, both handicrafts, mariners, and soldiers, who are apt to go where their pay is best, which will always be where there is greatest plenty of money, and in time of war must needs bring great distress.
>
> (Locke 1823c: 50)[23]

This passage was written at the beginning of "King William's War," while the recoinage debates took place during a decisive point of that war—a war Sir George Clark described in the following way:

> It was the longest foreign war [England] had waged since Queen Elizabeth; it was the bloodiest and most costly. It was the first war of what may be called the modern type, the first of a series of wars lasting down to our own time, in which Britain had fought not only at sea but also on the frontiers of her colonies and as one member in a European coalition waging land war on the greatest scale.
>
> (Clark 1955: 159)

Add to this the fact that Locke firmly supported William and Mary's reign—indeed, held public office in the government—and we may conclude that Locke would be mightily concerned about a deflationary episode during wartime. His description of the military consequences of a deflation caused by a reduction of the money supply is stark. True, his "timorous temper"[24] reacted to the pervasiveness of clipped coins, but one would think that his concern for the continuation of William's rule would have far outweighed any worry over clipping. A government is much more likely to be destroyed by military defeat than by the presence or absence of a few grains of silver in its coinage, after all.

If Locke knew his proposal jeopardized the very government he risked so much for, why did he make it? Shouldn't the charge of "contradiction" be amplified to "irresponsibility" and even simple "stupidity"?

If we consider the situation from Locke's point of view, however, the facts appear quite different, either from a superficial modern appraisal or from Barbon & Co.'s angle. Let us compose a scenario that might capture the reality Locke saw.

Since the Civil War and the Restoration, the English monetary system had slowly driven itself into a sort of collective madness. Clippers, counterfeiters and other rogues had started it, but the Treasury and other state offices had begun to accept clipped currency in their accounts. This practice was emulated by the common traders, until the very formal distinction between clipped and unclipped coin disappeared. However, the simultaneous convergence of (1) a sharp increase in the domestic inflation rate, (2) an increasing gap between the official and actual price of silver bullion on the international market, and (3) an even sharper increase in the price of gold in shillings, stirred the population *out* of its abuse of monetary signs. Once the average trader knew that the silver content of most coins was short and, even more decisively, that the people he traded with knew this fact as well (and were becoming increasingly suspicious), there was no turning back; something had to be done before all confidence was lost in the monetary system itself.

Some decision had to be made, war or no war.[25] For to recognize the *fait accompli* of the clippers would have meant absorbing the unclipped coins into the spectrum of the clipped, and thus *de facto* allowing the clippers to control the value of the currency. But such a "solution" would not do. The custom of accepting clipped coins or, in Locke's psychological parlance, the association of clipped coins with exchange, was ending. People were asking questions of each other and of the state. To accept recoinage at full weight was to recognize that people would no longer accept the identity of clipped with unclipped coins in the exchange process. They would now look to their content, bring out the scales and weigh. Whatever the sounds that shilling, "pence," "crown," "pound" were to call up in men's breasts, according to Lowndes, the question "How much silver is in it?" had to be answered. For monetary signs signify the idea of a quantity of universally exchangeable substance, and it is the ideas we go by and not the sound. Surely the international market was already asking England the decisive question, and Locke continually and bitterly complains that Lowndes never says how many full-weighted shillings will buy an ounce of silver bullion! For to answer would have inevitably revealed the underlying fraud.

This is the scenario Locke viewed as the background of the social debate. But we come to the nub of our argument here. Did or did not Locke fail to "see" the consequences of his recoinage proposal? I claim he did not.

First, from Locke's viewpoint, the social and monetary history of England that had led up to the recoinage crisis was quite different from the hypothetical halving of England's money supply discussed in *Considerations*. Locke assumed in his theoretical example that *literally half* the silver and gold would leave the country and go to other states. By contrast, the actual amount of silver in England before and after full-weight, Lockean recoinage would *remain the same.*

Further, in his theoretical example, the deflation in value is *relative to an international standard*; that is, domestic prices are compared to what "our neighbors" receive for commodities and labor. But the "deflation" after the Lockean recoinage would be *relative to a mistaken collective English idea of value.* In other words, it would be relative to the English people's mistaken ideas about what an English coin had in it, their wrong association of a coin with a particular amount of wealth, and their continual abuse of monetary signs. They might feel poorer for a while after the recoinage, but they would not be, any more than they had been right in feeling richer before the recoinage.

Putting these contrasts together, *we* see that Locke's quantity theory of money enunciated in *Considerations* would not predict a deflation after a Lockean recoinage. Rather, *Locke* saw that his theory did not apply to the particular situation England faced in 1696. Or better, his quantity theory gave Locke assurance that *if* the transition from monetary madness was accomplished correctly, there would be no deflationary episode.

Second, Locke recognized that the transition from bad to good coinage could be traumatic and, if not handled gradually and carefully, could lead to a deflationary episode as devastating as the one described in *Further Considerations* (though it would arise for different reasons). His argument is not "unreasonable" on the basis of his contemporaries' categories. Consider the different ways to go about the transition:

If clipped money be called in all at once and stopped from passing by weight, I fear it will stop trade, put our affairs at a stand, and introduce confusion … If it be permitted to pass in tale, as if it were lawful, weighty money whilst it is recoining, and till all be recoined, that way also there will be an end of trade, or no end of clipped money.

(Locke 1823c: 147)

How does Locke propose solving this dilemma? His "ace in the hole" was the existence of a "Gresham hoard," a large amount of legal, unclipped coin that was not circulating. An estimate based on contemporary evidence suggests that this hoard could easily have included more than a million sovereigns. If that hoard could be brought into real circulation, the transition could be eased. For we must remember that by "money," in the early quantity theory, we mean actually circulating money (to such a point that there were proposals to enact laws against the hoarding of money during that period.) How was this Gresham hoard to be flushed out into the market? This was to be done by applying Locke's "metallism" full force, namely, taking out the scales *for a while* during the transition:

> If [clipped money] be made to pass for its weight till it all be recoined, both these evils [mentioned in the previous quote] are avoided and the weighty money, which we want, will be brought out to boot.
>
> (Locke 1823c: 220)

Mathematically, Locke was not far off the mark, assuming the correctness of the data, for the ratio of "legal" unclipped coins that were hoarded to the total stock of coins could easily have been 20 percent. If the bulk of that hoard was brought into circulation, then the 20 percent devaluation would have lost much of its cogency on even strict quantity theory grounds.

Joining these two arguments together:

(1) Full weight recoinage would not bring about a real deflation due to quantity theoretical causes; and
(2) A transition period of full-weight treatment of clipped coins would bring out hoarded "legal" unclipped coins into circulation;

we can conclude that Locke was by no means "blinded" to the problems inherent to his proposal, but he saw a good chance of escaping calamity with it. Whittaker is wrong in accusing Locke of not realizing the "distress" recoinage could cause (Whittaker 1940: 652). And it is equally wrong to assume that Locke did not account for the acceptance of clipped coin, as Appleby argues, or that his "strict metallism" caused him to fail to deduce deflationary consequences from his proposal, as Vickers claims. Rather, Locke saw a history of monetary confusion and public fraud, an imminent threat of civil collapse, and the possibility of social and economic disaster compounded by military defeat. The clippers *were* more serious enemies of the state, in Locke's view, than the French regiments at Namur.[26]

This picture dictated drastic action. For what were the alternatives? Lowndes' solution accepted defeat at the hands of the enemies of public order, refused to distinguish between intrinsic versus extrinsic changes in value—or, as we shall see later, *substantial* versus *mixed mode* aspects of money. In the short run, Lowndes proposed another cycle of the same; in the long run, he assured the end of the monetary system as a whole. Surely, taking a risk, even a big one, would be preferable to passively accepting calamity.

But our answer to the claim that Locke contradicted himself raises new questions. Locke's theory of money is based on an ontology whose most immediate consequences are the axioms of *Further Considerations*:

> SILVER is the instrument and measure of commerce in all the civilized and trading parts of the world.
>
> It is the instrument of commerce by its intrinsic value.
>
> The intrinsic value of silver, considered as money, is that estimate which common consent had placed on it, whereby it is made equivalent to all other things, and consequently is the universal barter, or exchange, which men give and receive for other things they would purchase or part with for a valuable consideration: and thus, as the wise man tells us, money answers all things.
>
> (Locke 1823c: 139)

How does Locke deduce and justify these axioms? Why, for example, is silver "the instrument of commerce by its intrinsic value," and why did "common consent" place this distinction on the moonlit metal? If "money answers all things," then what is the question that posed it? And, first and foremost, why does money—formerly the "root of all evil"—become an almost sanctified object for Locke and many of his contemporaries? An object for which the price of desecration is death?

These questions can only be answered by an investigation into Locke's ontology of money.

2
Civil Government

But as the king increas'd, they soon found Cause,
To limit forms of government by Laws:
Degenerate Nature soon seduc'd by Crime,
Quickly encroached upon the Power sublime:
And Reason found it needful to explain,
Laws to prescribe, and limits to restrain.

—Defoe (1701)

In Chapter 1, we solved the apparent paradox in Locke's political economy by demonstrating that the transition from a deteriorated coinage to one fully representing "value" (like the transition debated in 1694–1696) was not an example of *real* deflation in Locke's terms.[1] His quantity theory of money, which predicted a permanent depression following a permanent removal of a substantial quantity of the *material* money supply did not apply directly to the England of 1695 in Locke's perspective, any more than the physics of bodies can be applied literally to the motion of shadows. But this solution precipitates further questions concerning Locke's ontology of money.

In this chapter, we deal with one of the first paths of ontological knowledge, the path of the *Other*. After all, one of the best ways to understand a practice is to study its abuse; a structure, its limits; an entity, its antagonists. So too with money. Why does Locke consider the monetary crimes of clipping and counterfeiting (which were considered venal enough previously) serious enough to warrant capital punishment?

We have seen that Locke's post-Settlement texts certainly mark a deep change in the notion of the *social Other*[2] as violation of religious norms gave way to monetary crime as the fundamental disorder of the state. Locke, who is so tolerant of religious deviation, is almost religiously devoted to the quantitative and substantial "integrity" of silver and gold—so much so that the violators of the body of money become the real "robbers of the faith" in his demonology. Thus, according to his *Letter Concerning Toleration*, a pagan should be permitted to sacrifice a calf to his gods in the middle of London, and even "devil worship" and idolatry should be given free reign so long as the worshipers do not violate the laws of *civil* society;[3] but tampering with the coinage should be considered a capital crime of the most *detestable* nature:

> The use and end of the public stamp is only to be a guard and voucher of the quality of silver which men contract for; and the injury done to the public *faith*, in this point, is that which in clipping and false coining heightens the *robbery* into *treason*.
>
> (Locke 1823c: 144)

Such a view represents a momentous transformation in intellectual perspective and social policy. Clearly the locale of heresy had shifted from private religious conviction to public monetary faith—from the stake to the gallows.[4] A two-century long witch-hunt "officially" ended when such conceptual identities became common sense for the likes of Locke and his circle.

Simultaneously, a new "center of evil" and a new "thanatocracy" was founded,[5] for coin clipping and counterfeiting were now raised from the ranks of petty crime to the level of a semantic heresy against the state, one far more dangerous than reading the Bible backwards or conversing with one's cat.

The immediate cause for this change was perhaps the war-tension of the 1690s. For the semantic mendacity of the clippers and false coiners was most pernicious in times of emergency, and of socio-economic crisis, when the civil government was already weakened and threatened:

> Men in their bargains contract not for denominations or sounds, but for intrinsic value, which is the quantity of silver, by public authority, warranted to be in pieces of such denominations ... which, when they come to have need of their money, will prove but empty sounds, if they do not carry with them the real quantity of silver expected.
>
> (Locke 1823c: 14)

"Empty sounds" in the face of "need" is *the* prescription for state collapse (especially during a war when the troops *must* be paid!).[6] Hence, the drainers of the sounds' significations had to be extirpated. For once Silver, instead of the Bible, becomes the cornerstone of the state edifice, its violation becomes *the* capital crime.[7]

Locke however, did not limit his strictures to emergencies only, for they simply brought to the surface the mortal corruption in the state these crimes engender in "normal times." But what is the deeper source of the sanctity of money, and of the sudden elevation of clipping to the pinnacle of treason? Is this just a symptom of a long-term and growing "fetishism of commodities"?

To answer this question we must trace the notion of "semantic crime" back to its origin, that is, to Locke's discussion of the original use and abuse of money. Not surprisingly, it is in *An Essay Concerning the True Origin, Extent, and End, of Civil Government* that Locke tries to justify his "monetary axioms" and show the relation of crime to money and the state (particularly in that much-thumbed chapter, "On Property").

In the last generation of Lockean exegetes, especially since Macpherson's (1962) work, there has been an increasing recognition of the importance of money and monetary exchange in Locke's account of the social contract. Indeed, the place of money as the efficient cause of the contract is what differentiates his theory from those of Hobbes and Rousseau.[8] Moreover, due again to Macpherson's influence, there has been an increasing reluctance to accept analytic vocabulary at its face value. No more can we read the *Second Treatise* with the confidence that Locke's categories are synonymous with the pieties of contemporary democratic thought. (Although suspicion would have been in order in an era when the racism, sexism and classism of the "Western intellectual tradition" was being extensively uncovered.) Exemplary in this respect is the opening statement of *Two Treatises on Government*:

> Slavery is so vile and miserable an estate of man and so directly opposite to the generous temper and courage of our nation, that it is hardly to be conceived that an Englishman, much less a gentleman, should plead for it.
>
> (Locke 1823g I, 1)

It is generally acknowledged, however, that Locke was not against slavery *per se* in the practice of his time. He not only regulated the slave-trading activity of the Royal Africa Company through his various tenures on the Board of Trade and Plantations, he owned shares in the company himself, and, most explicitly, he sanctioned "negro" slavery in his drafting of the Constitution of Carolina for his "master," the then Lord Ashley.[9] Are we to "accuse" Locke of blatant "hypocrisy," or, rather, of attributing a different signification to the word *slavery*? Surely his notion, and abhorrence, of slavery did not extend to the African. But we are not interested here in beating a dead horse "Locke was a racist"—when there are plenty of living stallions about.[10]

Our aim is methodological: to question an easy "homophonic" interpretation of his political terminology. This hermeneutic principle is especially appropriate to the chapter titled "Of Property." The view of property found here has often been referred to as the "labor theory of property," because the *bulk* of the argument revolves around the relation between labor, personhood and appropriation. Only the last sections are devoted to money, and they appear almost as afterthoughts where the argument, in effect, ceases. But the ratio of attention does not match the ratio of importance. Though labor might have given the original title to property (and still did at the empire's margins, in the Americas), the ownership of property in Locke's England was not based on labor but on monetary exchange.

Locke presents a four-stage theory of the development of property:

(1) the divine creation and grant of the commonwealth of the earth to collective humanity;
(2) the private appropriation of the commonwealth through individual labor;
(3) the invention of money and the accumulation of wealth; and
(4) the recognition of the need for and agreement on the social contract.

Thus, though the introduction of money is an essential step in understanding the social contract, Locke does not apparently devote to it the lengthy examination he thought appropriate when analyzing the relation of labor and property.

Locke's unequal development of his theory of property and money can be partially explained in view of the political context that generated the publication of the *Two Treatises*.[11] Particularly relevant here is the Whig–Tory debate concerning the notion of political authority, which had an immediate bearing upon the legitimacy of William III's right to rule.[12] Locke was anxious to establish that property rights *precede*, both temporally and logically, the prerogative of civil government.

The political burden of "Of Property" is to explain the transformation from the God-given commonwealth of the world to the creation of "privateness" *outside of and before* the rise of government. What Locke presents is a self-conscious alternative to the "Tory theory" of Sir Robert Filmer "and his followers" that located the origin of property in the divine grant given to the original father (and king): Adam.[13] Filmer justified his claim on the basis of that most notorious of *Biblical* texts, Genesis, i: 28:

> And God blessed them, and God said unto them, Be fruitful and multiply, and replenish the earth and subdue it, and have dominion over the fish of the sea, and over the fowl of the air, and over every living thing that moveth upon the earth.
>
> (Genesis, i: 28)

According to Filmer, God founded the state and property simultaneously; thus, the title to all landed property is ultimately a royal prerogative deriving, via rightful inheritance, from the original monarch. The immediate political application of Filmer's theory was as a refutation of the Parliament's right to grant kingship to William.[14] For how could a representative body of property holders (whose property claims were granted and validated by the monarch) depose one monarch and recognize another?

Locke, anxious to find another basis for property, proposed the labor theory, which projects the *privateness* of the person into the ontological transformation of the earth. In the "labor theory of property," the metaphysical, political and economic strands of Locke's thought merge, for here we find one of the first attempts to derive the right to property from the categories and properties of the ego, whose outcome is in the form of *cogito ergo habo*.[15]

> [T]hough the things of nature are given in common, yet man, by being master of himself, and proprietor of his own person, and the actions and labour of it, had still in himself the great foundation of property; and that which made up the greater part of what he applied to the support of comfort of his being, when invention and arts had improved the conveniences of life, was perfectly his own, and did not belong in common to others.
>
> (Locke 1823g: II, 44)

With this deduction, immediately political and economic questions acquire a metaphysical character, for this theory presupposes the notion of the *person*, and the conditions of personal identity. Just because x at time t labors to *produce a*, it does not follow that x' at t' can consume or exchange a' unless it can be proven that $x=x'$. What is mine may need not be "mine" tomorrow unless I am the *same person*. It is not enough to be the same man or woman, one must be the master and "proprietor of one's person" to constitute the "foundation of property." But if the foundation of property be in the person, the foundation of the person is in consciousness:[16]

> For, since consciousness always accompanies thinking, and it is that which makes everyone to be what he calls self, and thereby distinguishes himself from all other thinking things, in this alone consists personal identity, i.e., the sameness of a rational being: and as far as this consciousness can be extended backwards to any past action or thought, so far reaches the identity of that person; it is the same self now it was then; and it is by the same self with this present one that now reflects on it, that that action was done.
>
> (Locke 1823a: II, xxvii, 11)

For the crucial question in Locke's theory and practice of property relations is not "Is the acorn I pick up and eat *now* my property?" but rather "Is this acorn, picked up yesterday and *not* eaten, my property?" Locke's answer points to the realm of consciousness and *memory*, whereby memory *too* becomes an act of appropriation of a past action by a present consciousness. The great enemy of property is oblivion, since the loss of conscious mastery over time and succession leads inevitably to the breakdown of property. Thus, the forces of oblivion are antagonistic to the self and property, while all the techniques of mnemonics are their essential allies.[17]

The relation of property to memory is the most important consequence of Locke's "labor theory of property"—which in fact might be more properly redefined as the "memory theory of property."[18] While its notorious problematic is not our immediate concern, we must point out a rather peculiar conclusion of this theory; property based on labor appropriation is ultimately *bounded* in two ways: the needs of the owner and the transitoriness of the object of acquisition. The stage in history Locke refers to here had obviously long since passed, however; the notion of property that was the basis of political struggle in Locke's day was quite different from the one typified by acorn gathering. As he pointed out, this older type of property was based upon and bounded by *use*; one owned not what one labored on *per se* but that much one labored on and could use. To labor on too much and have it rot or putrefy was to violate the natural law and be unreasonable to boot, as "one would literally be working for nothing." This was the state of affairs in the period before the accumulation of wealth was possible.

In the society Locke envisages at this stage (2) of property, there is a proportion of labor to consumption, a rough egalitarianism whereby there is no reason to argue about landed, or any other, property.

> Right and conveniency went together; for as a man had a right to all he could employ his labour upon, so he had no temptation to labour for more than he could make use of. This left no room for controversy about the title, nor for encroachment on the right of others; what portion a man carved to himself was easily seen; and useless it was, as well as dishonest, to carve himself too much, or take more than he needed.
>
> (Locke 1823a: II, 51)[19]

Idyllic indeed. One could almost mistake Locke for a closet anarchist.[20] Plenty of land, fish and fowl for all, as the good Lord promised; in fact, the very fruits of theft would only serve for immediate use and so the risk would not be worth the candle. Reasons for envy, that "uneasiness of the mind, caused by the consideration of a good we desire obtained by one we think should not have had it before us" (Locke 1823a: II, xx, 13), could not exist in front of the Heraclitean river which was the world:

> Nobody could think himself injured by the drinking of another man, though he took a good draught, who had a whole river of the same water left him to quench his thirst…
>
> (Locke 1823g: II, 33).[21]

Thus, Locke could insist that the origin of property could be derived independent of any hypothesis concerning Adamic sovereignty, hence that property rights preceded royal prerogatives, hence that Parliament could crown William III; but though this anti-Hobbesian (and anti-Sartrean) vision of the pre-contractual world solves Locke's practical ideological problem, it raises another: what was the propulsive mechanism that drove the transition from stage (2) to stage (4) of property?

If the state of nature—the only human society that includes the whole human species—was one of equality, liberty, relative peace and plenty, indeed a time when "right and conveniency" merged, what "sin" forced most of the species out of this Edenic state into the exile of political society? Locke's text provides two inter-related causes: Criminals and Money. The efficient cause of political society was the "corruption and viciousness of degenerate men," criminals against natural law, but the final cause of crime is Money. It follows then that Locke's theory of crime and money is essential to understand the foundations of Government and its functions; for it is the existence of crime that calls for the creation of the state, though crime in turn presupposes the existence of monetary exchange: otherwise, as it were, crime would not pay. Yet, in the *Two Treatises*, Locke seems to neglect and marginalize the period of transition from the original state of property to the social contract stage (3). And he has been blindly followed in this neglect by his exegetes. Should we conclude, as they do, that Locke lacked a serious theory on these matters in the same way as, for example, he lacked a theory of the origin of languages?

This type of question forces us to consider, in a sociological vein, the various presuppositions of modern Lockean scholarship, which in my view are quite mistaken, because they do not properly take into account Locke's aims and environment.

One view takes it for granted that Locke's writings are scattered and incoherent for it is assumed that Locke was simply not interested in the consistency of his work. This view takes Locke's philosophical, economic, pedagogical religious and political texts as relatively isolated creations of a mind whose temper was non-systematic, and truly "empiric." He is, in effect, considered to be a predecessor of the discipline-bound and frag- mented approach to thought that has become habitual and institutionalized in modern scholarship.

In another, allied view, Locke is seen as deeply identified with and embroiled in "the history of ideas," and obsessively concerned about the relation of his ideas with those of his immediate predecessors (especially Descartes) and potential simultaneous discoverers; that is, he was something of a Newton.

The final view takes Locke as the "spokesman of the bourgeoisie" during the late seventeenth century, and claims therefore that he continued the debate which reached its climax in the Civil War, a debate that revolved around the relation of suffrage and property.

These views are by no means mutually exclusive, nor are they unsupported by textual and biographical evidence. Reviewing the matter even superficially, we see that the first view can point to the fact that he held an academic position in Oxford for decades, and that there is little cross-referencing in and among his works. Further, his frugal and extremely scrupulous references to other philosophers and "men of letters" are perhaps the sign of a hypersensitive academic ego and support the second view. And of course his long association with Lord Ashley (later the Earl of Shaftsbury), the positions he took in the central organs of state planning and power, as well as his well-known contempt for "idlers" and "criminals"—terms then synonymous with the "poor"—make him the exemplary "spokesman" of the third view.

Synthesizing these views, we might see Locke as something of a late starter and failure in academe (with an inferiority complex, perhaps), whose eyes were always returning to Oxford, but who history ironically placed in the center of ruling power, so that he produced his philosophical works outside of an academic setting and was even tainted by his surroundings.

But the facts that support these views are by no means unequivocal. First, Locke ended his real academic life in 1665; from then until he was thrown out of Oxford in 1684, his position there was something of a "cover." Further, Locke's environment was murderous; the political situation was always volatile, and exile or execution were common political experiences in public life. Textual camouflage and deceit were thus essential, even for "ruling class" writers, at least up until the eighteenth century, when political tension diminished and a different relation was created between the production and consumption of ideas. In the seventeenth century, publishing was always a very delicate enterprise, to cross-reference between anonymous and authored texts would perhaps trigger too many signals. The reading public was, however, quite conscious of the game (since many practiced it themselves); and if the devices of textual unification, footnotes and authorship were at times too dangerous and legally binding, there were other means—especially "word of mouth," for the reading public that counted was relatively small.

Second, Locke was not enamored of the "sweepstakes" conception of priority that obsessed Newton and—for different reasons—modern scholars. The long gestation of his works, their mostly anonymous publication make it clear that Locke was not interested in scoring points in an academic scramble for promotion and grant money (but for a death-bed letter, the *Two Treatises* could have been the only major work in modern political philosophy with a [?] beside its purported author's name). This is not to say that Locke was not concerned for the success or failure of his work, but rather that his measures were not rooted in the context of academic life. He was a creature of power after all; perhaps a cautious one, but once he entered the control room of world empire (for all its dangers and all his "complaints"), he never willingly left. As a consequence, his criteria of success inevitably included an element of political policy.

As for being a "spokesman of the bourgeoisie," what can one say but "of course," and it would be silly to deny it. Certainly Locke would not deny it, if anyone had the temerity to ask him the obvious. The problem is that in any recent century there have been many aspiring voices attempting to speak for the bourgeoisie; but most of them have turned mute, or stammered. It is not easy to "speak for" a social class, one must fight to do it. After all, "the bourgeoisie" is far from homogenous either materially or strategically. Moreover, to be a "spokesman" one must have something to say to the class, one must have some knowledge to convey; platitudes drawn from past class history will not do.

This is why I find the Macpherson tradition of Lockean commentary most sympathetic—for it does not deny the obvious—yet most mistaken. It continues to see Locke mired in Marsten Moor, concerned about a Hobbesian problematic forced upon him by the challenge of the Levellers, and so on. As a consequence, its interpretational battles still center on the relation of Locke's writings to the Putney debates or on the meaning of "the people." But while it is true that Locke's early thought was profoundly shaped in reaction to the Cromwellian experience, we must recognize that the *Treatises* are documents of the 1680s and 1690s, aiming at the problematic of the next century and not that of 1640–1660. A generation had passed, the "enemies of the people" had changed their form, and Locke was quite aware of this. Indeed, his project in the philosophical, economic and political texts he published was to impress this new awareness on the ruling circle. For to fight old battles in a new war is an invitation to defeat.

Thus, I argue that Locke's work is extremely unified and interdependent. The years 1690–1696 were a time of intense intellectual and political campaigns for Locke on many fronts, leading to the completion and publication of the *Letters Concerning Toleration, Two Treatises, Some Thoughts on Education, Considerations and Further Considerations,* two editions of the Essay, *The Reasonableness of Christianity,* as well as many replies to his opponents objections. These works are not separate entities; they create a "human cosmology" that, while directly responding to the decisive debates of the day, was to define the lineaments of a bourgeois mentality and practice for many centuries to come.

Thus, we should be cautious, when faced with problems in any of Locke's texts, and not blame them on his alleged "inconsistency." Rather we must insist on carefully searching for clues in his other texts. A good case in point is his theory of crime, which is "ignored" in the *Two Treatises* (though crime is a necessary condition for the existence of civil government), and expounded instead in the *Essay Concerning Human Understanding.* A similar move is required to understand Locke's monetary axioms, as will become evident when we investigate the dialectic of crime and money.

Chapter xxi of Book II of the *Essay* is appropriately titled "Of Power." According to Locke's analysis, crime flows directly out of what he defines as "active power." Active power is a power reserved for spirits only, and thus is an idea manifested in will and volition. Nature has no "active power," however violent its phenomena; thus, cyclones and earthquakes are purely passive. Locke's general psychology, a true anatomy of human "active power," postulates a continual criss-crossing of pleasure and pain, short-term and long-term, shaping our choices in life. Formally put, desire, for either the easing of present pain or for an absent pleasure, determines the will. "The greatest positive good," even if consciously acknowledged, does not usually determine our decisions. Though we are all "free," "conscious" and we all desire happiness ("the most pleasures we are capable of"), we make quite different, and often evil, choices, since our immediate experience can have a much greater effect on us than "the greatest good" that can be achieved, if we let it. The decisive element in Locke's theory of decision is the capacity not to decide, for we all have (more or less) the power to suspend decision and action until we can use our knowledge and reason to determine whether any particular course of action leads to "true happiness."

This capacity is crucial if Locke is to solve the paradox of crime: if all choose for the good, at least as far as our immediate desire is concerned, how can anyone do evil or be punished? The essence of crime is hasty judgment, that is, choosing immediate pleasures or the easing of immediate pains over a future and better good. Thus, the dialectic of present/future is the source of crime and the justification of punishment.

> And here we may see how it comes to pass that a man may justly incur punishment, though it be certain that, in all the particular actions that he wills, he does and necessarily does, will that which he then judges to be good. For, though his will be always determined by that which is judged good by his understanding, yet it excuses him not; because, by a too hasty judgement of his own making, he has imposed on himself wrong measures of good and evil; which, however false and fallacious, have the same influence on all his future conduct as if they were true and right. He has vitiated his own palate, and must be answerable to himself for the sickness and death that follows from it.
>
> (Locke 1823a: II, xxi, 57)

There are two great sources of Crime, from "bodily pain" and from "wrong judgements," according to Locke. This type of distinction echoes through the debate on crime to our day;[22] the "external," "environmental" source is defined as "the pain of the body from want, disease, or outward injuries, as the rack, &c." The "internal," "psychological" source is specified in the following way:

> *[W]hen we compare present pleasure or pain with future ...* we often make wrong judgements of them; taking our measures of them in different positions of distance.
>
> (Locke 1823a: II, xxi, 65)

Thus, with Defoe's heroes, Locke prays, "Lead us not into temptation,"[23] but he lays the chief blame for crime and evil on "the weak and narrow constitution of our minds":

> Objects near our view are apt to be thought greater than those of larger size that are more remote. And so it is with pleasures and pains: the

present is apt to carry it; and those at a distance have the disadvantage in the comparison.

(Locke 1823a: II, xxi, 65)

Locke runs through the standard "excuses of crime" and rejects them as crude forms of self-deception, for neither ignorance nor inadvertency are acceptable when important decisions are to be made. If you do not know, or if you suspect your judgment, you need not decide to act, but many do not recognize their situation, though they should:

Judging is, as it were, balancing an account, and determining on which side the odds lie. If therefore either side be huddled up in haste, and several of the sums that should have gone into the reckoning be over looked and left out, this precipitancy causes as wrong a judgement as if it were a perfect ignorance.

(Locke 1823a: II, xxi, 69)

To cap off his discussion, Locke resorts to a version of "Pascal's Wager":[24]

Who in his wits would choose to come within a possibility of infinite misery; which if he miss, there is yet nothing to be got by that hazard?

(Locke 1823a: II, xxi, 72)

When stretched to infinity, Locke says, the structure of evil and crime shows its fundamental irrationality and lack of measure.

Thus, Locke's concept of "the corruption and viciousness of men" essentially lies in an unrestrained *temporal myopia*, an inability to suspend judgment and re-educate one's self into making that which is conducive to our happiness pleasing as well.[25]

Impulsive, Immediate and Irrational: the criminal chooses his crime, yet what created the conditions of his choice? What led to his "temptation" in the first place? In the "original" state of nature, the attractions of theft were greatly attenuated: there was plenty of untilled land and a relatively low-level but even distribution of wealth. If one was in need, a little labor on the commons would satisfy, while the bounded wealth of those around stimulated neither envy nor inordinate risk. Scarcity, for Locke, is not natural.[26] It was only with the invention of money that wealth stopped being defined and bounded by use. With money, a man could own more land and produce more than he needed for his own necessities. While still abiding by the natural law, he could accumulate wealth in a quasi-eternal form that he need not share with others. In such circumstances, the temporal vectors of crime and money collide. The existence of money stimulates the "ambitious" and "industrious" to shunt aside immediate consumption for the purpose of amassing wealth. But money also stimulates those prone to evil and crime to see within short-term action the definitive solution either to their immediate pain or the satisfaction of an absent pleasure. As Locke writes so poignantly:

> [T]he abstinence from a present pleasure that offers itself is a pain, nay, oftentimes a very great one, the desire being inflamed by a near and tempting object, it is no wonder that that operates after the same manner pain does, and lessens in our thoughts what is future; and so forces us, as it were blindfolded, into its embraces.
>
> (Locke 1823a: II, xxi, 65)

Moreover, with the coming of money, the *object* of theft is logically transformed from particular to general. In the state of "original" property, if one stole something, one was largely "stuck" with that *thing*, like it or not. But since "money answers all things," it appears as the key to *all* possible pleasures, and thus as the solution to a multiplicity of desires. Unlike the street urchin who lifts a loaf for his belly,[27] the thief of coin can pick and choose his pleasures. Money trains its possessor, whether legal or illegal, in abstractness as well as in the potential infinity of satisfaction. The accumulation of money is thus the exercise of our power to suspend our determination, which is for Locke the highest expression of our liberty, before an infinity of choices, while for the thief it is the door to Paradise Now.[28]

Though these psychological contrasts could be multiplied, it is crucial to see that the invention of money created a new *social* polarity between accumulation and scarcity, between the rich and the dispossessed. Money created scarcity:[29]

> Since there is land enough in the world to suffice double the inhabitants had not the invention of money and the tacit agreement to put value on it, introduced (by consent) larger possessions.
>
> (Locke 1823a: II, 30)

Men, at first, for the most part, contented themselves with what unassisted nature offered to their necessities; and though afterwards, in some parts of the world (where the increase of people and stock, with the use of money) had made land scarce, and so of some value…

(Locke 1823g: II, 45)

Thus, in the beginning, all the world was America, and more so than that is now, for no such thing as money was anywhere known.

(Locke 1823g: II, 49)

But money is the precondition and justification of accumulation:

And as different degrees of industry were apt to give men possessions in different proportions, so this invention of money gave them the opportunity to continue and enlarge them.

(Locke 1823g: II, 48)

With scarcity and accumulation comes the division into rich and poor:

[I]t is plain that men have agreed to a disproportionate and unequal possession of the earth, they having by a tacit and voluntary consent found out a way, how a man may fairly possess more land than he himself can use the product of…

(Locke 1823g: II, 50)

This "state of money"—our stage (3)—is transitory and transitional. Unlike the state of nature, which has its own equilibrium in the nature-given equality of effort and use, a situation of great inequality of land and wealth arrived at *by consent* but *without compact* is fragile. One who consented or tacitly agreed one day to accept money as a universal equivalent would wish to renege on his agreement if he found himself hungry and hedged out of the commons. He would then want to claim his natural rights. Another driven by Envy or Desire might want to take part of the stored-up stock of a rich farmer or merchant, saying that the rich have violated natural law by keeping more than they need.

Who is to reason with hunger, what is to disarm envy? Certainly not the memory of a "tacit agreement" made under radically different circumstances. At this point the social conditions of mass crime are at hand: scarcity, the breakdown of any obvious relation of labor to property, an unbounded accumulation further widening the distance between rich and poor ... "Ambition and Luxury" confront "Despair, Anger and Envy" in a permanent war and tension. A vicious circle develops in this state of money: the very conditions of the accumulation of property vitiate the results of accumulation.

Something has to give: either the state of money collapses back into the state of nature, or a new "state" is originated, one which safeguards money, controls crime and guarantees accumulation. The impulse for the social contract is at hand.

True, Locke occasionally speaks of governments before the "state of money." These were, however, intermittent, in that they sprang into existence during a state of war against "foreign invasions and injuries," and dissolved afterwards. Locke takes as his model of these quasi-governments the American Indians (excepting "Peru and Mexico.").[30] They needed no governments in peacetime for "their possessions, or way of living ... afforded little matter for covetousness or ambition." These people were barely removed from the rule of the family, the first "natural society," where the kings are "little more than generals of their armies." What Locke is trying to explain here is not the original *cause* of government—Property, Crime and Money. It is rather the original *form* of government—Kingship.

The *causes* of civil government and their development are parallel to the development of the *forms* of rule. Thus, societies that felt "the want of people and money" accordingly "wanted not variety of rulers and abundance of officers."

We find here the problem of the relation between synchronic and diachronic elements in Locke's explanation of the social contract, that is, the problem of assessing whether Locke connected the compact to a specific event or historical process. For our purposes, we need only point out that in Locke the *permanent* government is a creation of the *permanent* "state of war" within society; or, rather, one creates a contractual society in order to escape war in the state of money. This "state of war" is *crime*, or theft of property, life or liberty; and it is a battle unto *death* between the civil government and the criminal, who by the actual use of force violates the law at its roots, even if he merely steals my horse or coat.[31] Hence the definition of "political power" as "a right of making laws with penalties of death ... for the regulating and preserving of property" (Locke 1823g: II, 2).

Though the criminal be a "noxious creature" and "degenerate," he is at the same time, in the rhetoric of the day, "The Father of Civil Government." Were He to vanish "we" could all return to our pre-contractual state of nature[32] but He is not likely to disappear, however many are hung on the gallows or transported to the Americas ... Why? Because "The Mother of Civil Government" is Money, and those possessing the Mother are unlikely to relinquish her.

Locke's criminology easily explains the rise and permanence of the "crime rate" with the consolidation of a monetary economy. In the womb of money, with the increasing accumulation and duration of wealth, the "enjoyment of property" becomes problematic. Before the invention of money, the enjoyment of property was quite straightforward and time-bound; most property had to be consumed within a given seasonal cycle or else it would disintegrate. If a surplus existed, it would have to be given out in charity or consumed in feasts or potlatches, while property in land was simply the land one cultivated in order to satisfy one's needs. Neither one of these could be the source of problems of enjoyment; enjoyment was immediate or not at all.

With money, however, the novel question arises. "When can I enjoy my wealth?" Money preserves property, but puts a hiatus between appropriation and pleasure, a hiatus that can fill one with "fears and continual dangers."

The thief can just as well stoop to pick up the acorns as the gatherer, with less trouble and the same results; but coins in a chest or plate in a closet are another matter. By preserving property, money puts an end to the "natural" identification between the owner and the pleasure an object brings; and by its own nature makes anyone substitutable with the owner. For not only is money a universal equivalent, it is universally ownable—the thief can interpose himself between the moment of possession and the instant of satisfaction just like everybody else. Thus, though money preserves property from decay, it makes it more vulnerable, "very unsafe, very insecure"; it preserves it from Nature only to expose it to Crime. When Locke writes:

> The great and chief end, therefore, of men's uniting into commonwealths, and putting themselves under governments, is the preservation of their property.
>
> (Locke 1823g: II, 124)

he really means: the preservation of their property.[33] Thus, the state's function is to annihilate the criminal, but its existence presupposes him. Here is a vicious circle indeed.

However, our inquiry into the Lockean theory of the origins of civil government has answered one of the questions we asked at the end Chapter 1: why are the clipper's and counterfeiter's activities elevated to the level of treason? We see, in fact, that if money is for Locke the generating cause of the social contract, then to undermine the state's regulation of the money supply is to literally degenerate the state. If the social contract entrusts basic representative functions to the officers of the state, then to destroy that symbolic trust is to nullify the general operations of the state.[34] This is why, while justifying the death penalty for both the highway robber and the counterfeiter, Locke views them in a different light. The violence of the robber in trying to get my horse or coat is a violation of natural law, an act of unreason that can take place either before or after the origin of civil government. But the act of a clipper or a counterfeiter presupposes the existence of civil government. Hence, it is *par excellence* a crime against the state. By creating a general semantic violence, monetary crime posits itself on the existence of money, but, by sapping the monetary system, it disposes of itself by its very action. It is parasitic upon the state regulation it destabilizes. Thus, in its paradoxical unreason, it threatens the life of the state, from the inside. This was a "heinous" enough crime for the thanatocratic magistrates of the day to call for the Tyburn tree.[35]

The recognition of the importance of money for explaining the social contract forces us to consider the paradox of the second of the *Two Treatises*: the apparent arbitrariness of the invention of money. We are first given the idyll of a global subsistence society, with the human species living in equality, liberty, mutual assistance and simple natural law. Money changes all this. But then we must ask, "Why was this Pandora's Box opened at all?" Consider again Locke's text:

> [T]he invention of money, and the tacit agreement of men to put a value on it, introduced (by consent) larger possessions, and a right to them; which, how it was done, I shall by and by show more at large.
>
> (Locke 1823g: II, 36)

Locke shows us, indeed, "how it was done," but not *why*:

[I]n the beginning, before the desire of having more than man needed had altered the intrinsic value of things, which depends only on their usefulness to the life of man; or had agreed, that a little piece of yellow metal, which would keep without wasting or decay, should be worth a great piece of flesh or a whole heap of corn...

(Locke 1823g: II, 37)

The greatest part of things really useful to the life of man, and such as the necessity of subsisting made the first commoners of the world look after, as it doth the Americans now, are generally things of short duration; such as, if they are not consumed by use will decay and perish of themselves: gold, silver and diamonds, are things that fancy or agreement hath put the value on, more than real use, and the necessary support of life.

(Locke 8123g: II, 46)

Locke seems to be tantalizing us, almost intensifying the paradox to the breaking point. We are compelled by the text to ask: Why did humans act so contrary to real use and "necessity" and, through "fancy" or "tacit agreement," invent something with such ambiguous consequences? They were driven into civil government by crime and its "state of war," but what drove them into the "state of money"?

The text responds with silence, passing on to other the forms of government and its dissolution—seeming to leave the matter as either self-evident or "just so." Locke simply repeats the axioms of *Further Considerations* in "Of Property," not specifically justifying them but giving them a new context.

Can we simply dispose of the problem of money in the way Hacking deals with the problem of the publicity of ideas in Locke's philosophy—by simply concluding that monetary as well as mental discourse was "taken for granted"?[36] Not likely, for Locke definitely puts money out of the light of natural law that shone during the "golden age" before gold; money was *invented*, the way government was. Its status is different from that of language, which was not only universal but of divine origin. Locke would not write of money what he wrote of language:

God, having designed man for a sociable creature, made him not only with an inclination, and under necessity to have fellowship with those of his own kind, but furnished him also with language, which was to be the great instrument and common tie of society.

(Locke 1823a: III, i, 1)

Not only is money an invention, but the context of its invention is quite elaborately sketched by Locke through a series of contrasts between money and the original form of property. These contrasts span the range from the mathematical (bounded/unbounded), the physical (perishable/durable), the psychological (real use/fancy), the social (natural law/tacit agreement) to the semantic (substance/mixed mode). They also provide definitive constraints for our problem of explaining and justifying Locke's monetary axioms. Along with the *Essay*, these contrasts found in Locke's economic and political writings will allow us to understand his conception of the complex of needs and ideas that led to the institution of money. Our method will be to weave these contrasts together, to let the image of money emerge.

The first contrast I will analyze will be the twofold semantic idea of money; that is, what kind of idea is it, and what do monetary words signify? According to Locke's categorical scheme, the original kind of property was a *substance*: Homer's cattle, wine and oil; the Bible's sheep, "corn" and bread … a stuff or a thing with powers to ease our pain and enhance our pleasure. But is *money* a substance? *Gold* is money and gold is a substance:

[T]he ideas that make up our complex idea of gold are yellowness, great weight, ductility, fusibility, and solubility in *aqua regia*, &c., all united together in an unknown *substratum*.

(Locke 1823a: II, xxiii, 37)[37]

But money is *not* gold, nor silver or diamonds. What transformed these substances into money is another idea. "Fancy or tacit agreement both put value on" the substance, and take it as "the universal barter, or exchange." Money is an *idea* of substance *plus* something else—a value men attribute to a substance that is not in it, a willingness to accept an equality between it and another object that is not *in* it either—*a mixed mode*. It is this non-substantial aspect of the complex of ideas that creates the mystery of money.[38]

Possessing gold *as* gold is quite different from possessing gold *qua* money. Mixed modes are not related to nature the way substances are, for mixed modes are

such combinations of simple ideas as are not looked upon to be characteristical marks of any real beings that have a steady existence, but scattered
and independent ideas put together by the mind…

(Locke 1823a: III, xxii, 1)

The nugget of gold and the side of beef are substances; the powers of each
substance in no way correspond—you cannot cook and eat gold. But they
are rendered comparable through a combination in the mind. Money thus
has a *double categorical character* for Locke: it is a substance *and* a mixed
mode. Those who speak of money independent of either idea abuse words
and reality. For example, Barbon & Co's attempt to detach the idea of money
from the idea of substance was as flawed as speaking of the pyramids of
Egypt as if they were purely mathematical structures and not made of huge
blocks of stone requiring physical as well as mental labor to construct. One
must understand the duplicitous nature of money in order to understand
the laws of its behavior. Since mixed modes are so bound up with the phenomenon of language, we must now turn to Locke's theory of language,
which is largely to be found in the *Essay*.[39]

3
Abused Words

I never saw so much money in my life, nor did I know how to tell Money. Why, *says he*, Don't you know that they are Guineas; no, *I told him*, I did not know how much a Guinea was.

—Defoe, *Colonel Jack* (1722)

Locke's *Essay Concerning Human Understanding* has a structure that mimics its theme. The two central books appear as reiterated, parallel planes: a pressed gold leaf and its image folded together. "Of Ideas" followed by "Of Words," or rather, the second echoing the first, creates a sense of repetition Locke is at times apologetic for, while at other times he sees himself as something of an innovator. Locke carries the study of *ideas* and *words* into a third branch of the sciences—semantics—that was to be the foundation of "another sort of logic and critic than what we have been hitherto acquainted with." As we shall see, one of Locke's main contributions to the theory of money is the application of the categories of semantics to it. In so doing, he submits monetary discourse to another sort of "logic and critic," of the kind that he leveled against Lowndes and the "devaluationist" tendency.

The idea of money, according to Locke's taxonomy of ideas, is a twofold idea. It is a compound, joining an idea of mixed mode with an idea of substance. Consequently, monetary words and signs (a coin's stamp) must have as their immediate signification ideas of both sorts in the mind of the person who uses such words, if they are not to be abused. But given its double-categorical nature, money can be abused in at least two ways. Thus, to understand Locke's position on the recoinage debate and "solve" the "axiom conundrum," we must look into the duplicitous ways in which ideas and words can join, for here we find the ontological foundations of Locke's concept of money. Unfortunately, although central to Locke's position in the debate, it is exactly this ontological background that most commentators ignore.

The double character of money in Locke's taxonomy creates a central difficulty for understanding the idea and signs of money. Mixed modes and substances, while radically different, combine to form a very subtle idea. When little Colonel Jack, in the passage quoted at the beginning of the section, says "I did not know how to tell Money," he was not referring to an inability to count; rather, he implied that, though he had the idea of gold as well as the idea of exchange, he did not have any idea of the quantity of gold that should be in a Guinea, nor of the number and kinds of other coins that are equivalent to a Guinea, nor of the sign of a Guinea, and so he had no idea of a Guinea. The London street kid knew the word "Guinea" but it had no signification for him. Ironically, we have seen Locke suggesting that the merchant who shows little Jack the coins might be just as in the dark about the idea of a Guinea as the boy, though for different reasons and with less excuse. (Though this is true to a lesser extent for all of Defoe's work, Colonel Jack is a regular *bildungsroman* of money, and an almost self-conscious commentary on Locke's distinction between mixed modes and substances.)[1]

The controversy over what Locke meant by "substance" began with the printing of the *Essay* and still remains one of the most contested grounds of Lockean scholarship, while the notion of "mixed mode" generated no such scholarly dust.[2] This is strange, for the contrast between mixed modes and substances is a major theme in his work and one exhaustively, even minutely, analyzed throughout "Of Ideas" and "Of Words." This care is not accidental; the distinction marks a deep divide in Locke's "human cosmology."

The ultimate source of contrast between these two types of ideas lies in the different conditions of their generation. Mixed modes have a mark of arbitrariness in their birth, whereas substances "carry with them the supposition of some real being, from which they are taken, and to are conformable." Again, unlike substances, mixed modes may be "made, abstracted, and have names and so a species constituted, before any one individual of that species ever existed" (Locke 1823a: III, v. 5).[3]

To illustrate these points, Locke turns to the progenitor of both human words and the human race—Adam—and creation of the names of mixed modes *Kinneah* and *Niouph* to that of the name of a substance *Zahab*. One day Adam sees a neighbor melancholic, and guesses that his wife is being "disloyal" to him. In speaking to Eve about his conjecture, Adam coins two new words: "Kinneah" (conjugal suspicion) and "Niouph" (adultery). It seems Adam had never harbored these ideas about Eve, nor observed extra-marital affairs before. It turns out Adam was wrong about the cause of his neighbor's melancholia—the problem was that he had murdered a man—but somehow the new words hung on without any exemplars until they began to have "common use" in the more "wicked" post-Adamic world.

However, the story of the substance name "Zahab" was quite different. One of Adam's children, "roving in the mountains, lights on the glittering substance which pleases his eye" (Locke 1823a: III, vi, 46). He brings a piece home and Adam experiments with it to find it hard, of a peculiar bright yellow color and of great weight. Adam *then* baptizes all such substances "Zahab." Locke pauses to draw the moral from this Biblical take: in the case of "Kinneah" and "Niouph":

> [T]he standard there was of his own making. But in forming the idea of his new substance ("Zahab") he takes the quite contrary course; here he has a standard made by nature...
>
> (Locke 1823a: III, vi, 46)

Thus, Locke infers, a substance, unlike a mixed mode, must be discovered but can never be invented.

The lack of an external standard forces mixed modes to have a dependence on language that is not found in substances. Though both substances and mixed modes are ideas, that is, "free creations" of the human mind, and though both are simple ideas compounded and decompounded, mixed modes ideas *require a name* to preserve and unify the combination. As Locke, so frugal with metaphors, puts it,

> Though therefore it be the mind that makes the collection, it is the name which is as it were the knot that ties them fast together.
>
> (Locke 1823a: Ill, v, 10)

It is true that nominal essences, the only essences we can know with regard to substances, are "man-made" but at the same time names are "annexed," "signify" and are "marks for" already unified ideas of substance. The substance name does not unify but merely tags an already coalesced idea. Hence, the names of substances are passive and external, while the names of mixed modes are active, penetrating into the "breast" to knot together simpler ideas into the nominal essence of a modality.

71

One major consequence of this language-dependence of mixed modes is that their translation from language to language is extremely difficult compared to the translation of substance names. The name of a mixed mode develops a life of its own within each language, weaving together ideas rather than allowing the ideas, already united and homogenized by a common experience with nature, to dictate their own names. Since there is no external, nature-based standard against which to coordinate it and check it, the translation of a mixed mode name is more likely to be "indeterminate."

This "indeterminancy of translation" was bound to have immediate practical consequences for an empire that spanned four continents, dozens of peoples and hundreds of languages.[4]

Locke first thinks of the law and the translation of legal terms in this regard:

> The terms of our law, which are not empty sounds, will hardly find words that answer them in Spanish or Italian, no scanty languages; much less, I think, could any one translate them into the Caribee or Westoe tongues.
>
> (Locke 1823a: III, v, 8)

As a maker of constitutions for the imperial provinces and as a member of the Board of Trade and Plantations, Locke naturally wondered whether the "native" speakers of the "tongues" (though *not* "languages") of the empire could understand, with the best will in the world, the very law that was to govern them. He undoubtedly wondered what legal status contracts with Americans would have if the parties involved did not understand the very terms of the contracts in the same way (or did not have a similar notion of a contract).[5]

For Locke, the indeterminacy of the translation of mixed-mode names was not only a serious political problem, it was also an economic one. Consider the transcendental question: "How is world trade possible?" One part of the answer had to be that trade could not be completely based on mixed-mode ideas, for if the names of monetary units signified mixed-mode ideas, the world trade would have collapsed in a chaos of misunderstanding. Consider how hard it is, already, to translate physical measures:

> There are no ideas more common and less compounded than the measures of time, ex-tension and weight; and the Latin names *hora*, *pes*,

libra are without difficulty rendered by the English names, hour, foot, and pound: but yet there is nothing more evident than that the ideas a Roman annexed to these Latin names, were very far different from those which an Englishman expresses by those English ones.

(Locke 1823a: III, v, 8)

If this be the case for names of physical measure, imagine the Babel in the world of economic measures if all one had at hand in making deals across the Atlantic, down the coast of Africa, or in Madras, was merely mixed-mode names: *pesos, livres, larin, cruzados, zecchini, shera-fim, doubloon, dollar*, etc. Each of these names might be signifying continually fluctuating ideas in the local markets; for although they might be universal equivalents, there was reason to think that they were equivalent universally.

The existence of the world market depended upon determinacy of translation across many languages, societies and fashions; and surely Locke, operating near the center of the world power that claimed to steer that very market, was conscious of the implications of his "semantic" analyses. The only hope for the continuation of the world trade was that silver (and/or gold) continued to be an element of the idea of money, since this substance would provide a supra-social point of agreement necessary for the coordination of a huge variety of individual minds expressing themselves in a cacophony of tongues.

The contrasts multiply. Substances have imperfect significations, while mixed modes are perfect. "Mixed modes are commonly more compounded and decompounded than those of natural substance" (Locke 1823a: III, v, 13); mixed-mode names signify real essences, substance names never do. A most decisive difference, for us, emerges in the dimension of duration and particularity:

This is further to be observed concerning substances, that they alone of all our several sorts of ideas have particular or proper names, whereby one only particular thing is signified. Because in simple ideas, modes and relations, it seldom happens that men have occasion to mention often this or that particular when it is absent. Besides the greatest part of mixed modes, being actions which perish in their birth, are not capable of lasting duration, as substances which are the actors; and wherein the simple ideas that make up the complex ideas designed by the name have a lasting union.

(Locke 1823a: III, vi, 42)

Mixed modes are vaporous; their exemplars no sooner come into existence than they dissipate; logically, the particularity of a mixed mode merges with its universality. For example, the name of a play or a musical composition has a different relation to its performances than does the name of a substance and its exemplars. Or consider the mixed-mode name "battle." Though the "Battle of the Bulge" and the "Battle of Marathon" are two exemplars of the general term, they, as exemplars, can never exist again and be re-experienced; this is not true of the combatants (unless, of course, they are killed).

As a consequence, exemplars of mixed modes cannot confront language with reality, as we cannot re-experience the same "event" and thus confront our words with the thing in order to compare them again and again. At best, we must rely on memory when we try to judge concerning incidents and actions and—as Locke well knows—memory is always entropically drifting to oblivion.

Thus, we have a peculiar paradox in Locke's epistemology, or rather his semantics: our knowledge concerning mixed modes (as in mathematics and morals) can be more certain than our knowledge of substances (as in physics). For example, we may be sure that the sum of the squares of the lengths of legs in a right triangle in Euclidean space is equal to the square of the length of the hypotenuse, but we may be far from certain that there are any right triangles or even that there is a Euclidean structure in physical space. Or, to take the case at hand, we might know with certainty that the quantity theoretical relation holds for money *per se*, but it might not apply to any actual period in economic history. This mixed-mode knowledge is double-edged, although capable of certainty, it is not necessarily about any existing state of affairs, nor does its certainty require existence. By contrast, our knowledge of substances can never be certain, yet whatever knowledge we have about them is about existents.[6]

Since we create mixed-mode ideas, we can know more about them; this is Vico's axiom. But this knowledge is only of our own minds:

All the discourses of the mathematicians about the squaring of a circle, conic sections, or any other part of mathematics, concern not the existence of any of those figures: but their demonstrations, which depend on their ideas, are the same, whether there be any square or circle existing in the world or no. In the same manner, the truth and certainty of moral discourses abstracts from the lives of men, and the existence of those virtues in the world whereof they treat.

(Locke 1823a: IV, iv, 8)

Substances, for all the difficulty they pose to our knowledge, are capable of lasting duration and unity independent of our mental constructions. Substance names are more imperfect than mixed-mode names, for the standard they try to achieve lies in a naturally objective realm not open to human tampering. It is only with substances that we attempt to "speak of things really existing."

The different relations mixed modes and substances have to changes in our knowledge and society had crucial consequences, in Locke's view, for contracts and the circularity of economic life. Let us remember that the "turnover time" of capital during that period of world trade was calculated in years.[7]

For example, our Colonel Jack, the petty-criminal turned Virginia planter-merchant, took a business voyage to Vera Cruz in Mexico that brought him back to Virginia a year and a half later.[8] These time lapses were by no means unusual; agricultural leases of "three lives" (99 years) were quite common during Locke's time (cf. Wilson 1965: 143).

The orbits of commerce were therefore quite sensitive to the vagaries of the idea of money and monetary discourse. If money were purely a mixed-mode idea, any chance of harmonizing the beginning and end of a transaction cycle would be lost.

True, our knowledge of silver and gold might change over a decade or in "three lives," but this change will be both progressive and conservative. That is, we might discover new properties of silver and gold through "experience and history" (Locke 1823a: IV, xii, 10), but since these new properties, like the old, are based on a real (though hidden) constitution independent of human society, the idea will have an inherent continuity.[9] This is not the case with mixed-mode names, whose signification can change radically and quickly. These mixed-mode names are the reason why languages change constantly, why they take up new and lay by old terms. Because change of customs and opinions bring(s) with it new combinations of ideas...

(Locke 1823a: II, xxii, 7)

Contracts written in a terminology so sensitive to social "fashions, customs and manners" would never satisfy the temporal exigencies of late seventeenth-century economy.

To digress for a moment—in an extemporaneous (though not whimsical) mood—we can see the relevance of Locke's distinction between substance and mixed mode for a wide range of controversies in more recent philosophy: for example, determinacy versus indeterminacy of translation (cf. Quine 1969: 26ff.); realism versus factionalism (cf. Hempel 1966: Ch. 6); theoretical continuity versus incommensurability (see, e.g., the essays in Hacking 1981); "spatio-temporal thing" versus "event" ontology (see especially Davidson's essays, e.g., "The Individuation of Events" [1970: 216–234]); the scientific adequacy of counterfactual and modal logic versus standard first-order logic (for a discussion of the debate, see, e.g., Linsky [1971]); *Erklärung* versus *Verstehen* (for a pre-deconstructivist survey, see Radnitzky [1973]); and so on.

It is easy to see how Locke would have deployed his distinction to "solve" these "dilemmas":

Table 3.1   Comparison of the division of mental labor

Substance	*Mixed Mode*
Determinacy	Indeterminacy
Realism	Fictionalism
Continuity	Incommensurability
Thing	Event
First-order logic	Counterfactual & Modal logic
Erklärung	*Verstehen*

But this exercise" concerns the work of those molded by the contemporary division of "mental labor": the Quines, Davidsons, Kuhns, Gadamers and Kripkes of our era.

There is, however, another twentieth-century figure who better compares with Locke in his own time, a political agent and philosopher used to working at the highest levels of world power, namely, Keynes. The relation between Keynes and Locke is not merely one of social "role," for if Locke was the theoretical progenitor of the "gold standard," then Keynes was its theoretical executioner. Why did they play such inverse roles in the history of money?

Aside from a number of technical considerations, Keynes' criticism of England's return to the gold standard in 1925 stemmed from his different view of the relation of gold and silver *qua* money to the future and the state. For Locke, the main function of metallic currency was to stabilize and preserve a relation between present possession and future pleasure; and the state's function was to guard and guarantee this objective, nature-given connection for each individual. Gold and silver thus created the conditions for future accumulation, and the state was to assure the individual possessor the enjoyment of it.

For Keynes, on the contrary, gold creates the illusion of protection against the future:

> [T]he possession of actual money lulls our disquietude; and the premium which we require to make us part with money is the measure of the degree of our disquietude.
>
> (Keynes 1937: 215–216)

But why disquietude? It arises because the future comes toward us in two forms: events that have a definite probability and events whose probability cannot be estimated. The former presents us with the problems of *risk*, the latter with that of *uncertainty*.[10] Uncertain events are an essential and increasingly large aspect of the future, according to Keynes. For in his view, new historical developments had invalidated the assumption of the existence of stable reference classes, which are necessary for the calculation of risks.

Take, a life insurance company, for example, which estimates the risk of death by observing longevity over long periods for a large population.[11] On the basis of such estimates, it calculates the risk of death for the average individual in a given class, and from these calculations it determines a premium. What happens, however, with the sudden arrival of war or "acts of god"? All the estimates are invalidated, and the policies are declared void.

Keynes recognized that a simple inductive principle does not apply for an important class of economic events. For them, the economic sun will not rise tomorrow; the future will not be like the present; and there is no method to determine the extent of deviation.[12] For economic transactions and expectations are made in the context of wars, general strikes, anti-capitalist revolutions, counter-insurgency operations, riots, looting, military coups, confiscations and nationalizations:

> [A]bout these matters there is no scientific basis on which to form any calculable probability whatever. We simply do not know. Nevertheless, the necessity for action and for decision compels us as practical men to overlook this awkward fact and to behave exactly as we should if we had behind us a good Benthamite calculation of a series of prospective advantages and disadvantages, each multiplied by its appropriate probability, waiting to be summed.
>
> (Keynes 1973b: 114)

From this viewpoint, gold and silver money ("as a store of wealth") are an expensive and dangerous fetish, as they give the possessor the illusion that, in the final analysis, beyond any eventuality, he is in control. Such a conception, which places money before society, generates the insane belief that we can detach ourselves from the fortunes of the system and (through an act of "bad faith") preserve an equilibrium above the existential anxiety of a mortal class. Thus, gold deceives, with its promise of an impossible protection against a social "sickness unto death."[13]

Clearly the locus of madness had inverted in the two centuries between our state philosophers. For Locke, madness arises from confusing the coin with the gold, while for Keynes, the confusion flows from taking the gold for the coin. Keynes argues a mistake could be understandable in a ruined, subjugated "ruling" class—like the one he had found in India, where he worked for the Royal Commission on Indian Finance and Currency.[14] However, unless the capitalist classes of Europe wished for the same fate, they had to awaken from their golden trance.

Further, there is a complementary variable in Keynes' gold equation that does not feature in Locke's: "the labouring classes." In Locke's time, the question asked of the Poor (the propertyless, who appear on Locke's pages as servants, thieves, clippers, country lads and wenches, etc.) was put by Petty: how was the state to better [the Poor], "manage" [them], and "shape" [them] to its advantage (Furniss 1957: 17ff)? By Keynes' time, the question had shifted to: "How were they to be controlled?" Locke—through his "99% labor theory of value"[15]—joined his generation's paean to the contradictory importance of labor to national wealth, and he was as obsessed as any other "mercantilist" with schemes for "setting the poor to work" and combatting their notorious "idleness."[16]

But the Poor were irrelevant, for Locke, in monetary theory and policy. A comparison of two statistical studies will give us the immediate reason. On September 27, 1696 the Board of Trade "received" Gregory King's *Natural and Political Observations and Conclusions upon the State and Condition of England.*[17] Locke was sitting on the Board at the time. Whatever its merits, it probably contained the best socio-economic data Locke had available. According to King's estimates, although the Poor outnumbered the Propertied 2,825,000 to 2,675,520, their share of the annual income was about 20 percent. Taking into account that the bulk of the Poor's income was in-kind or in non-precious metallic form, we can understand why Locke saw them as irrelevant to substantive questions of monetary theory and policy. On the other side, C.H. Feinstein has estimated that income from employment in the UK between 1924 and 1930 was about 66 percent of the net domestic income (Feinstein 1964). We can thus see why Keynes made the question of wages a central element of monetary theory. Whatever the problems of inter-temporal comparisons over such a long period, we can safely conclude that Labor had Money by 1930.[18]

Thus, the Poor entered into Keynes's monetary theory as wage earners. Inversely, Locke believed the Poor should be barred from the monetary realm, and his control strategies centered on punishment, especially the death penalty. By Keynes' time, the wage relation had definitively become monetarized. For Keynes, the problem of class control then turned on the question: How is Labor's Money to be controlled?

For example, how could the average wage be reduced? Keynes saw two options for the employer class and the state: a "flexible *wage* policy" or a "flexible *money* policy."[19] The former seemed rather dangerous, now that the laboring classes had organized themselves and new non-capitalist possibilities were on the horizon. The latter policy, however, would bypass direct confrontation through monetary mechanics, and yet achieve the same result:

Except in a socialist community where wage-policy is settled by decree, there is no means of securing uniform wage reduction for every class of labour. The results can only be brought about by a series of gradual, irregular changes, justifiable on no criterion of social justice or economic expediency and probably completed only after wasteful and disastrous struggles, where those in the weakest bargaining position will suffer relatively to the rest. A change in quantity of money, on the other hand, is already within the power of most governments ... it can only be a foolish person who would prefer a flexible wage policy to a flexible money policy ... Moreover, other things being equal, a method which it is comparatively easy to apply should be deemed preferable to a method which is probably so difficult as to be impracticable.

(Keynes 1964: 267)

A flexible money policy depends upon the powers of the state to control the "quantity of money," but it also depends upon workers reacting only to monetary changes in their wages. This is the famous "money illusion" of the laboring classes, of which Keynes writes:

It is sometimes said it would be illogical for labour to resist a reduction of money-wages but not to resist a reduction of real wages ... But, whether logical or illogical, experience shows that this is how labour in fact behaves.

(Keynes 1964: 9)

It is indeed fortunate for the capitalist system that the laboring classes who have seen through its "bluff or deception" still succumb to the "money illusion,"[20] but such illusions are irrelevant unless the state is in a position to exploit them. Here gold comes in. The existence of a gold standard makes it impossible for the state to control "the quantity of money," for it introduces a fundamental rigidity into monetary policy. In fact, if it operates without hindrance, an economy ruled by a gold standard literally has *no* monetary *policy*. As Schumpeter wrote of the gold standard in his own "adieu to *laissez-faire*":

An "automatic" gold currency is part and parcel of a *laissez-faire* and free-trade economy. It links every nation's money rates and price levels with the money rates and price levels of all the other nations that are "on gold." It is extremely sensitive to governmental expenditure and even to attitudes or policies that do not involve expenditures directly, for example, to foreign policy, to certain policies of taxation, and, in general, to precisely all those policies that violate the principles of economic liberalism … It imposes restrictions upon governments or bureaucracies that are much more powerful than is parliamentary criticism. It is both the badge and the guarantee of bourgeois freedom—of freedom not simply of the bourgeois *interest* but of freedom in the bourgeois *sense*.

(Schumpeter 1954: 405–406)

And, Keynes might add, it would lead to bourgeois *catastrophe*. For the state's function is not the preservation of individual contracts and petty parcels of capital. Rather the state must function as a "directive intelligence through some appropriate organ of action over many of the inner intricacies of private business," preserving capital as a whole and on a social scale.[21] The state must be free to use the monetary mechanism and exploit the blindness of labor to bring about short-run adjustments in the system without continually provoking total class confrontation. Gold hinders this social freedom, hence gold must go.

It is ironic that Keynes should so invert Locke, even though he is so similar and sympathetic to his predecessor. Phrased in terms of Locke's distinction, Keynes' argument is that the substantial element in the idea of money is not substantial at all, but is a mixed mode. Keynes is suspicious of the category of substance in general, and not just in monetary theory. He shares with his philosophical cohorts (Moore, Russell, Wittgenstein and Ramsey), and his scientific milieu (relativity theory and quantum mechanics) a skeptical view of the substance-attribute ontology advocated by Locke as an analogue of Newtonian physics.[22]

For Locke, our sensory ideas are generated by a completely determined, quantitatively defined corpuscular world. Thus, our knowledge of substances in the world can at best be probable, since we have no organs capable of directly observing corpuscular motion and structure.[23] The existence of such a structure, that is, "the real and primary qualities of [a substance's] internal constitution," though certain, will always render our knowledge incomplete in details (Locke 1823a: II, xxiii, 37). But this deeper determinate world—which is the source of our secondary quality and dispositional ideas—is, at the same time, a guarantee of the objectivity of any claim to knowledge. This explains why, starting with Locke, for over two centuries, the faith in the final reality of a material, mathematically deterministic, absolute structure of Nature was linked philosophically with a defense of the gold standard. Newton's presence at the Mint at the decisive conjuncture, which led to the adoption of the gold standard and to its triumph in the nineteenth century, stands as the concrete embodiment of the deep ontological connection between physics and money in the bourgeois era.

But Keynes and his generation witnessed not only the collapse of the gold standard and the eclipse of Newtonian physics, but the demise of Lockean metaphysics as well. This trinity lived and died together. The "revolutionary" theories of physics and philosophy that dissolved this triumvirate had as their characteristic traits: uncertainty, relativity and functionality. Keynes' economic theory self-consciously employed the methodological style of quantum and relativity theory: propensities, expectations, disequilibrium, indeterminacy, temporal relativity, imperfect information, etc. With it, a new world begins, where God, in the form of the Walrasian auctioneer, is truly dead.[24]

The philosophy of language developed at Cambridge in the first quarter of this century also found expression in Keynes' theory. The work in that period of Russell, Ramsey and Wittgenstein followed from Frege's two *dicta*:

(1) sentences have a function-argument form, and
(2) never ask for the meaning of a word in isolation, but only in the context of a proposition.[25]

The doctrine that was definitively rejected was the Lockean one, namely, that words signify ideas (for a discussion of this doctrine, see Kretzmann 1977). The methodological shift from Locke (whose tradition goes down to J.S. Mill) is profound. Sentences, according to the new linguistic paradigm, are not mere concatenations of words signifying, one-for-one, ideas in the speaker's mind; rather, sentences *do* something: their functions map their arguments into truth values. Thus, in order to understand meaning, we have to see how the word functions in a wider context: there is no hidden idea in someone's mind that can tell us its meaning. The use of a word, its function in the system of relations, is the essence of meaning; no amount of introspection can unearth the meaning of a word or sentence. Its worth is to be found in its action.

Even without embarking on an extensive exposition of the *Principia Mathematica* and the *Tractatus Logico-Philosophicus*,[26] we can see that this new theory of language had deep affinities with Keynes' rejection of any substantialist element in money. He wrote in 1937, compressing three decades of research:

> Money, as is well known, serves two principle purposes. By acting as a money of account it facilitates exchanges without its being necessary that it should ever itself come into the picture as a substantive object. In this respect it is a convenience which is devoid of significance or real influence. In the second place, it is a store of wealth. So we are told, without a smile on the face. But in the world of the classical economy, what an insane use to which to put it! For it is a recognized characteristic of money as a store of wealth that it is barren; whereas practically every other form of storing wealth yields some interest or profit. Why should any one outside a lunatic asylum wish to use money as a store of wealth?
>
> (Keynes 1937: 215)

Here Keynes expresses his complete functionalization of money.[27]

One recognizes money by the unique role it fulfills in an economy, and not by what it is made of, or the ideas it calls up in the breasts of investors or workers. It is always one side of every transaction, stemming from the lack of a "mutual coincidence of wants" between employers and employees and between savers and investors. But what *is* it? How should money be defined? Here Keynes is characteristically functionalist and contextualist:

> [W]e can draw the line between "money" and "debts" at whatever point is most convenient for handling a particular problem. For example, we can treat *money* as any command over general purchasing power which the owner had not parted with for a period in excess of three months, and as *debt* what cannot be recovered for a longer period than this; or we can substitute for three months, one month or three days or three hours or any other period; or we can exclude from money whatever is not legal tender on the spot. It is often convenient in practice to include in money the time deposits with banks and, occasionally, even such instruments as e.g., treasury bills.
>
> (Keynes 1964: 167, n. 1)

The use of the word "substitute" clearly reveals the functionalist form of Keynes' definition of money, which is *nothing* in *particular* nor in *general* but a complex, temporally relative and context-sensitive relation.

True, Locke's idea of money is also complex, but its complexity is of a linear order while its modal possibilities are limited by the substantial element of gold or silver. For Keynes, money is *just* legal tender or command over general purchasing power; it is a *pure* mixed mode—to put it, paradoxically, in Locke's terms: it is an action without an agent. Between Locke and Keynes, we see the arch or trajectory money must follow in the bourgeois period.

Locke's distinction between mixed modes and substances gives his "human cosmology" two roots: Nature and Convention. Nature provides objective limits, while invention offers the possibility of transforming and manipulating human relations.[28] The tension and contrast between these two becomes clearer when observed in action, for example, in the process of communication. The function of words is to transport ideas and thoughts from a private to a public realm so that they can be reprivatized, and "the thoughts in men's minds be conveyed from one to another." Equally important for Locke is the function words perform in recording our own thoughts, and serving as a tool for storing and preserving ideas. This function of words (as a "memory bank") still relates to communication. The use of words as recording instruments implies a communication process between *past* and *present* selves. This inter-temporal communication is essential for the preservation of personal identity, as we saw in our discussion of the "labor (and memory) theory of property," for the "person" is constituted through the continual self-retrieval of the past self from oblivion. It is no coincidence that two of the most concrete embodiments of this function of words during Locke's time were the private account book and the diary.[29]

Locke would agree that any system of communication must satisfy certain criteria of accuracy and speed.[30] Yet this truism of communication theory shows the gap that separates us from Locke. When a modern communication theorist worries about accuracy and speed s/he looks to the *channel* and *code* used,[31] that is, to the mediators of the message; and s/he tries to find what characteristics of channel and code would maximize the accuracy and speed of communication within the limits imposed by the channel capacity and the entropy of the source code.[32] Locke's theory of communication looks not to the mediators of the process but to the problems of *possession*, that is, to the source. He is continually asking, "Does the conveyer really *own* the 'goods'—the ideas and thoughts—that he is conveying with his words?" If he does not, the function of communication breaks down. The imperfections and abuses of communication arise from negligence and fraud, not from noise or jamming, as in modern communication theory. Mistakes in knowing that one really has a proper title to an idea, or the deliberate misrepresentations of such titles, are the common problems of communication for Locke. Putting things schematically, and for our day conventionally, if we segment the communication process into:

Figure 3.1   The communication process

then we see that Locke is concerned largely with the source, modern communication theory with the channel, and much of modern philosophy of language with the receiver.[33] These are not, of course, mutually exclusive distinctions, but what appears as a cavalier disregard for modern technical and philosophical concerns about communication is simply, from Locke's viewpoint, putting first things first, if you do not know what you are saying, then even in ideal conditions of channel transmission and reception nothing is communicated and everything is noise.

Locke is not completely *blasé* about the receiver, as some modern commentators imply, since he is continually noting the opposition of language and words. Language is a *necessity* of human existence "furnished by God," for Man as been created *qua* "sociable creature" (Locke 1823a: III, i, 1), yet words "signify only men's peculiar ideas and that by *perfectly arbitrary imposition*" (Locke 1823a: Ill, ii, 8). Locke returns to this opposition—of language's necessity being accomplished through words' arbitrariness—again and again, and he invokes "common use" and "tacit consent" as only a partial solution.[34] His attitude to the problem of ideational coordination is typical of his stance throughout the *Essay*: try to fulfill your duty as a user of the instrument of language by being as precise, as clear and as patient as possible, while recognizing the limits inherent to the instrument itself.

This attitude is exemplified by the position Locke takes toward that most crucial source–channel–receiver relation, namely, the relation established between humans and God through the scriptural channel. Here his advice in detecting God's message is simple: be "more careful and diligent in observing" the precepts of "Natural Religion," and "less magisterial, positive, and imperious, in imposing our own sense and interpretations" on the scriptural clothes that God's will is expressed in (Locke 1823a: III, ix, 23).

Turning from the universal word to the universal equivalent, we can easily see that monetary words and signs suffer all the imperfections and abuses of words and signs in general. More specifically, since such words and signs are names of both mixed modes and substances, they are vulnerable to the ills of both categories. But, as we shall see, this very *mixture* can reduce the ills instead of intensifying them, because they are caused by different circumstances.

The imperfection of names of mixed modes arises from the "great number of ideas put together" and, further, that there is "no settled standard anywhere in nature existing, to rectify and adjust them by" (Locke 1823a: III, ix, 5). On the other hand, the imperfection of names of substances arises from the difficulty we have in knowing the nature-given *standard* and *real essence* of the ideas they stand for. The ideas that mixed-mode names signify are complex and arbitrary, while the ideas that substance names signify are based upon external standards whose micro-physical structure we largely ignore. But can the external standard serve to control not only our idea of silver and gold, but the mixed-mode ideas involved in the idea of money as well?

Let us look more closely at the imperfections mixed-mode names are marred by, while remembering that Locke carefully distinguishes "imperfections" from "abuses"—though, of course, one potentiates the other. We find that an average speaker can get so confused by the complexity of the ideas behind mixed-mode names that frequently s/he does not understand his/her own meaning from day to day:

> [S]ince one man's complex idea seldom agrees with another's, and often differs from his own—from that which he had yesterday, or will have tomorrow.
>
> (Locke 1823a: III, ix, 6)

As nothing exists outside oneself to appeal to in order to accurately determine the signification of such ideas:[35]

[S]uch voluntary collection should be often various in the minds of different men, who have scarce any standing rule to regulate themselves and their notions by, in such arbitrary ideas.

(Locke 1823a: III, ix, 7)

No rule of common use, propriety or authority is adequate to regulate the signification of mixed-mode names; for it is our liberty to create such words as we will, and no one can compel another to think or signify as they do:

And therefore the great Augustus himself, in the possession of that power that rules the world, acknowledged he could not make a new Latin word: which was as much as to say, that he could not arbitrarily appoint what idea any sound should be a sign of, in the mouths and common language of his subjects.

(Locke 1823a: III, ii, 8)

This semantic liberty applies with a vengeance to names of mixed modes, for all we have in order to regulate our usage is our self-discipline and linguistic conscience. But these, Locke very well knew, are weak regulators, that never would be able to provide a check for corrupted and desperate beings like those who populated London and its empire at his time—beings all too easily prone to semantic crime and anarchy.[36]

If monetary words and signs were merely mixed-mode names, then they would be susceptible to all the diseases thereof, namely, they would become extremely complex, arbitrary and confusing signs whose use would be impossible to externally regulate and check.

From Locke's semantic perspective, Lowndes' devaluation proposal *de facto* reduced the idea of money to a mixed mode, whether Lowndes was aware of it or not. On this point, at least, his views agreed with those of one of his opponents, a defender of Lowndes who, however, was quite conscious of the semantic consequences of raising the value of money: "Old" Nicholas Barbon.[37] In his *Discourse Concerning Coining the New Money Lighter*, he writes, "*Money* is the instrument and measure of commerce and not silver." But Barbon concludes:

If nothing in itself has a certain price or value; if gold and silver are commodities or uncertain values; If money has its value from the authority of the government, which makes it current, and fixes the price of each piece of metal; Then the money will be of as good value, to all intents and purposes, when it is coined lighter. For, the authority being the same, the value will be the same.

(Quoted from Vickers 1959: 88)

"But," one might imagine Locke's reply, "First, the authority is *not* always the same. Second, even when it is the same, if the value is a purely mixed mode, it is so complex, fluctuating, arbitrary and ambiguous that the very monetary authority may unknowingly differ from its own rule as it was yesterday and as it will be tomorrow. Third, even if it can be self-consistent, it cannot impose its idea of value on its subjects."

If the great Augustus could not coin a Latin word, how could William III impose his symbolic will on a Portuguese wine merchant? Moreover, the slightest crisis of confidence (brought on by war, succession difficulties, economic depression) would immediately lead his subjects to ask whether they did value Barbon's pieces of "brass, copper, tin or anything else" the way they were told to do. Locke would add, "There is no reason to assume that they will."

Barbon confused creation with regulation, from Locke's viewpoint. The civil government cannot by its authority create value any more than it can create the consent required for the social contract. (For it is this value and consent that creates civil government.) The function of government is to guard and preserve the foundations of value and consent: silver and property.

The semantic side of Locke's analysis of money makes it clear why he thought that Lowndes' and Barbon & Co.'s position was not only futile, but dangerous to government. Their proposals threatened the very foundations of the State, because fundamental mistakes with regard to money *qua* money not only jeopardize a particular government, they pave a way to the very "dissolution of society."

Locke's semantic theory helps us to understand why Locke thought Lowndes and Barbon erred in trying to impose a semantic tyranny on the English economy that would violate the very nature of money. The ideas signified by monetary words and signs must include an idea of substance. For Lowndes could signify by a "shilling" what *he* wished—that was *his* semantic liberty; the problem came when Lowndes turned to the millions of other signifiers:

A creditor ought to think the new light money equivalent to the present heavier, because it will buy as much commodities. But what if it should fail, as it is ten to one but it will, what security has he for it? He is told so, and he must be satisfied.

(Locke 1823c: 169)

But if the idea of a substance is an essential component of the idea of money, an objective, nature-given standard could take the place of a coercive thought police:

In our ideas of substances we have not the liberty, as in mixed modes, to frame what combinations we think fit, to be the characteristical notes to rank and denominate things by. In these we must follow Nature, suit our complex ideas to real existences, and regulate the signification of their names by the things themselves, if we will have our names to be signs of them, and stand for them.

(Locke 1823a: III, ix, 11)

True, there might be a wide variety of nominal essences that different people signify by a particular substance name, because our experience of the "several properties" of a substance can vary. But though it is impossible to experience *all* such properties, and though it is doubtful that we will ever know "the figure, size, texture, and motion" of the insensible corpuscles that are the active parts of matter and constitute a substance's real essence, still we can have real knowledge of substances based upon experience and sensory observation. The importance of this knowledge is that it is based on *archetypes outside of us*: "they must not consist of ideas put together at the pleasure of our thoughts" (Locke 1823a: IV, iv, 12). No one can *dictate* that certain simple ideas coexist to form the complex idea of gold. Your nominal essence of gold might include *yellow, heavy* and *malleable*, while mine might include *yellow, heavy* and *fusible*, but if you show me its malleableness in practice while I show you its fusibility, we could expand and coordinate our idea of gold.[38] Though I may not choose to accompany you into the workshop in order for you to demonstrate gold's malleability, once in the shop I cannot help but *see* its malleability. Sensory experience has an objective power that can literally "force one to know" in a way that another person—however powerful and persuasive—never can.

Moreover, the sense experience relevant to substances, by being produced in us by the substance's atomic texture, has a directness and universality that is not to be found in mixed-mode ideas. Think, for example, of explaining the idea of "lateness" to Whorf's Hopi Indians, or "adultery" to De Sade's libertines.[39]

Our knowledge of substances is only partial, but it is cumulative. The real essence of gold can never be captured by our nominal essence—that is, our present ideational definition of gold—which is continually changing in response to our experience of gold. This nominal essence (a combination of simple ideas expressing the active and passive powers of gold) arises from a corpuscular structure which undoubtedly has a radically different character from what we observe. Further, the principle of change of the ideas of substances is "experience and history," from which "we may draw advantages of ease and health, and thereby increase our stock of conveniences for this life" (Locke 1823a: IV, xii, 10).

This process of change, though always inadequate to the real essence of things, is *continuous* and *self-correcting*. Still, mixed modes and their names change with the customs and opinions of society, a process which for Locke gave no assurance of what would later be called "Progress."

Just as the imperfections of mixed modes and substances differ, so do the *abuses* their names are subject to. Abuses of words, Locke tells us, are

> the several *wilful* faults and neglects which men are guilty of in this way of communication, whereby they render these signs less clear and distinct in their signification than naturally they need to be.
>
> (Locke 1823a: III, x, 1)

The abuse of substance names arises from what we might call a "learned arrogance," namely, the pretense to know what cannot be known, or, on a linguistic plane, the pretense to signify what cannot be signified. On the one side, we have words being taken for things and, on the other, we have words signifying real essences. Locke's targets in the first case are undoubtedly the natural magicians in all their varieties, those who "are persuaded that the terms of [their] sect are so suited to the nature of things that they perfectly correspond to their real existence" (Locke 1823a: III, x, 14).

Think of the magus Paracelsus' claim:

And even though (GOD) has hidden certain things, he has allowed nothing to remain without exterior and visible signs in the form of special marks—just as a man who has buried a hoard of treasure marks the spot that he may find it again.

(Quoted in Foucault 1970: 26)[40]

Those who claimed knowledge of these "special marks" had had their hey-day in the sixteenth century, but even at the end of the seventeenth century, the quest to find and manipulate these "marks" was not unknown among Locke's accomplices. For example, Newton's endless numerological labors, as well as his alchemical efforts (leading to his *annus maleficus*), were definitely in the tradition of those who hunted "the signature of all things."[41]

The other form of error—the attempt to have our words signify not our ideas but Ideas themselves, that is, substantial forms—this too was not a rare form of abuse in Locke's day. The Cambridge Platonists were guilty exactly of such a misdemeanor, and one of their leaders, Richard Cudworth, was the father of Locke's long-time lover and housemate, Lady Masham.[42]

But the abuse of substance names does not anger Locke as much as the abuse of mixed-mode names. Whatever its subversive effects in the past, by 1690, natural magic no longer posed any threat. Locke saves his venom for the "learned ignorance," especially when the arts of affected obscurity," of "subtlety and acuteness" move beyond the confines of academe into the "real world."

Where before he dealt with the abuses of the natural magicians and the like, Locke now introduces us (in a remarkably "figurative speech," for him) to language's dens of robbers, or "holes of foxes" to uncover that clique of semantic criminals: the Lawyer, the Disputant, the Projector, the Philosophical Politician, the Visionary Divine and the plain con man.[43] For there are many ranks and varieties of linguistic counterfeiters, who use language not to go beyond it, but to go against it.

Their tactic is the "coining of new words, where they produced no new things to apply them to, or the perplexing or obscuring the signification of old ones, and so bringing all things into question and dispute" (Locke 1823a: III, x, 8).

Their motives are multiple: some simply want "glory and esteem" for their cleverness, some without right wish to acquire "authority and dominion," while others try to "gain admittance or give defense to strange and absurd doctrines" (Locke 1823a: III, x, 9). They gain their ends because—though the unscholastic statesman," "the illiterate and contemned mechanics, and the "men of business" create the wealth and peace of the world—it is easy to hold them "perpetually entangled in that endless labyrinth" of abused words (Locke 1823a: III, x, 9).

Their ultimate result is "to destroy the instruments and means of discourse, conversation, instruction and society, and this is especially crucial in those centers of mixed-mode ideas and names: religion, justice and morals (Locke 1823a: III, x, 10). For it is exactly in these areas that the lack of an external standard makes it easiest to coin illegitimate words and create chaos. You might think you understand a law, but spend five minutes with a lawyer worth her/his salt, and s/he will make "the words signify nothing at all, or what he pleases." This can become a serious social problem:

> Nor hath this mischief stopped in logical niceties, or curious empty spec-ulation; it hath invaded the great concernments of human life and society; obscured and perplexed the material truths of law and divinity; brought confusion, disorder, and uncertainty into the affairs of mankind; and if not destroyed, yet in great measure rendered useless, these two great rules, religion and justice.
>
> (Locke 1823a: m, x, 12)

The irony of mixed-mode names is that *in the abstract*, since each indi-vidual makes up for himself the real essences of the ideas, he should be able to give them an exact definition to such a point that "morality is capable of demonstration" just as mathematics. But the *lack* of an external archetype, while making our moral musings demonstrable, creates the notorious impression that "anything goes." Without an external, nature-given standard, individuals tend to have very different ideas signified by the same moral word, and even the same individual easily becomes inconsistent in his use of a word because the great complexity of the idea has no natural unity. Thus for some "foxes" abusing moral words becomes child's play, since they can rely on the inevitable "negligence and perverseness" of the average person.

Locke's greater concern for the abuse of mixed-mode names arises from his estimation of the greater damage they can cause, especially in social matters. The recoinage debate was a case in point. The "confusion, disorder and uncertainty" semantic criminals had brought into religion and law would be the fate of money, too, if it underwent the type of reduction to mixed-mode status advocated by Lowndes and Barbon. To rid money of its substantial basis would rob it of an external standard and expose it to the "subtle" logic of "learned ignorance." "Strange and absurd doctrines" about money would multiply; projectors, "learned disputants," and crooks would flock around the Treasury with their latest schemes; slowly the "instruments and means of monetary discourse" would clog, and, in the first crisis, collapse.

Putting together the *Essay* with *Further Considerations*, we better see how Locke viewed the field of his opposition. While the counterfeiters and clippers under religion and law would be the fate of money, too, if it mined the material foundations of the monetary system, the Barbons and the Lowndeses provided the "intellectual superstructure" of the criminal attack. The speeches and pamphlets of these worthy gentlemen slowly filtered down to make the common merchant, the country wench and the lad suspicious of the very meaning of monetary words and signs. This was particularly true in a situation where Gresham's law had operated so that the very natural standards—the full weight of crowns, so crucial in instructing the subjects in the proper use of monetary word—had been taken out of circulation. The counterfeiters and clippers applied Lowndes' and Barbon's logic directly, without parliamentary trappings and protection. There is doubt then that for Locke the recoinage debate was a decisive, a fundamental confrontation, with portentous consequences.[44]

The *Essay Concerning Human Understanding* is therefore not so much located in the "empiricist"/"rationalist" dialectic; rather its place is more central to the "metallist/"chartalist" debate.[45] The "human cosmology" Locke develops in the *Essay* creates the ontological framework for *his* "metallist" position, a framework that is essential for analyzing the basis for his argument against Lowndes' devaluation proposals.

Let us sum up. Locke is a "metallist" for two major reasons:

(1) The idea of money must have a substantial element, otherwise it would be a pure mixed mode, with all the attendant practical difficulties involved; and

(2) The pre-governmental character of money would be lost if the theoretical nature of money were completely "socialized."

As we have pointed out (following Locke, ad nauseam, I'm afraid), mixed-mode ideas in their application have an inherent tendency to be parochial, subjective and unstable in time. In the abstract, we might be able to reason about them demonstrably, but in practice their "vaporous," non-substantive exemplars immediately reveal their weakness. This is true of all mixed-mode ideas. But there is reason to think that in "political arithmetic" the problems are multiplied. For in "arithmetic" (as an example of mathematics) we have naturally given, universal, "clear and distinct" simple ideas, while in politics, morals and religion we have tenets of natural law and the certain proof of God's existence to guide us. But there are no such "back-ups" with money, which is a product neither of God nor of natural laws, and yet is not a simple idea. There are no separate *monetary intuitions* that might obviate the imperfection of monetary ideas *qua* mixed modes. Without such support, free-floating monetary ideas are susceptible to the shifting flux of "manner and opinion." They are easily pulled into a whirlpool of semantic tyranny, crime and anarchy created by an undertow of counterfeiters, clippers, smugglers and pirates combined with the high winds of "learned ignorance."

In addition to these immediate practical dangers, Locke saw other, theoretical ones. Money is the bond between Convention (mixed modes) and Nature (substances), which the Civil Government is there to preserve. But money is "pre-governmental" in more than just a historical sense; and it has a logical priority that in Locke's time was becoming all too apparent to him and everyone else in London (including Lowndes and Barbon). First, nations (*qua* individuals) were in a state of nature, and frequently in a state of war with respect to other nations.[46] Locke writes:

> For though in a commonwealth the members of it are distinct persons, still, in reference to one another, and, as such, are governed by the laws of the society; yet, in reference to the rest of mankind, they make one body, which is, as every member was, still in the state of Nature with the rest of mankind. Hence it is that the controversies that happen between any man of the society with those that are out of it are managed by the public, and an injury done to a member of their body engages the whole in the reparation of it. So that under this consideration the whole community is one body in the state of Nature in respect of all other states of persons out of its community.
>
> (Locke 1823g: II, 145)

Hence, one need not go to the Americas or try to decipher the Bible in order to see how life carries on in the state of Nature. A glimpse at the morning newspaper, so to speak, is enough. Second, though nations are in the state of Nature with respect to each other, a lively monetary trade goes on between them through the wars, the "controversies," the "injuries" and the "reparations." This trade did not—and, according to Locke, could not—be carried out by means of one nation's denominated currency; it had to be earned by a unit that had no need to be "governed by the laws of society," since no such laws existed in the world market.[47]

This, in the end, was Locke's *reductio ad absurdum* argument against the "chartalists." True, it was built on a fact, namely, the existence of international trade, but it was an incontrovertible *fact*, one which provided Locke a model of money *sans* state, confirming the logical priority of money over civil society.

Money operates outside the orbit of civil compacts, indeed, it creates them; therefore, it has the power to dissolve them. This was the decisive aspect of money in the recoinage debate (an aspect that would have been hard for a merchant like Barbon to deny). For any merchant could argue as subtly as he wished concerning the chartalist character of money. But the practical effect of chartalism on his business would be devastating—*bankruptcy*. For what Portuguese wine merchant would part with his wares just for a paper portrait of William III?

Given its pre- and para-governmental status, money must therefore rely on perception, understanding and knowledge capable of universal application. Lacking the sanction of God, unsupported by the state, to gain this universality Money must have its root in Nature. Locke's metallism did not result from the type of argument and considerations that were to become standard in the *laissez-faire* period, though some can be found in anticipation. It was neither the possibility of *limiting* governmental power nor the *automaticity* of a metal standard that impressed Locke. Rather it was the potential universality of gold and silver both in men's regard and thought.

In this sense perhaps, the impact of Macpherson's writings has not been completely justified (Macpherson 1962).[48] "Possessive individualism" fails to characterize Locke's position as it gives the impression of an "anal retentive," petit-bourgeois shopkeeper sitting atop his chest of crowns and guineas with a shotgun. There is, of course, *something* to this image, but one could equally emphasize a "possessive universalism" in the origins of bourgeois "social thought." For Locke and his contemporaries—with more or less knowledge, pleasure or pain—lived in the midst of a remarkable and, at the time, novel process: capital accumulation on a world scale.

This process posed real "contradictions" that preoccupied Locke as he sat on the Board of Trade and Plantations. The key contradiction might take this shape: how does the *universality* of the "commodity form" coexist with the *particularity* of the "state form?"

There was undoubtedly a tension between state and money then—as there is now. But Locke saw in the universality of money (not in the pretensions of domestic "projectors" or "divine monarchs") the driving logical and social force of his age. And he put himself at the service of this universality.

Let me suggest at this point that the discussion of the idea of money can throw some light on the *Essay*, in the same way that the *Essay* illuminates the recoinage debate. At the very least, it might rid us of the old copybook myth that the *opponents* of Locke were the "Rationalists": Descartes, Spinoza and Leibniz.[49] As a preliminary, we should note that the *Essay* is remarkably free of proper names of contemporary people, philosophers included. In a book whose standard edition exceeds 500 pages, one can count only about a dozen direct references to contemporary philosophers, and these are either simply laudatory or merely informative. Only one directly polemical citation is provided—referring to Lord Herbert, on the innateness controversy.[50]

Clearly, the book's intent is not to launch an *explicit* debate across the Channel, though we can find implicit criticisms of Descartes and Spinoza. But we can also find direct borrowings. Thus, Locke's attack on Descartes' claim of the impossibility of the vacuum is matched with an almost direct lifting of the *cogito*:

> [I]f I know I doubt, I have as certain perception of the existence of the thing doubting as of that thought which I call doubt.
>
> (Locke 1823a: IV, ix, 3)

And Locke's view that moral generalities are demonstrable, after all, would make him more of a rationalist than most rationalists. But such a game of labels is misleading. Suffice it to say that the "empiricist"–"rationalist" distinction was not of Locke's making, but rather was part of the great propaganda war between England and France in the eighteenth century. It does not apply to him; Locke undoubtedly felt more at home in Spinoza's Holland, Descartes' France or Leibniz' Germany than in Hobbes' England.[51]

Who then are the Others of the *Essay*? The lack of proper names should inform us that Locke was interested in *social types* rather than in individual "great minds."[52] His reticence was certainly not caused by fear of reprisals, for when he deemed it useful he was quite clear as to the polemical target of his work—for example, Filmer and his followers in the *Two Treatises*, or Lowndes in *Further Considerations*. Moreover, Descartes, Spinoza and Leibniz were figures one could certainly oppose—given a cautious soul like Locke without fear of much trouble.

Who then were these antagonists? The religious sectarian enthusiasts; the smooth-talking disputants, lawyers and projectors, the impulsive and hopeless criminal mob; the strewers of scholastic "rubbish"; skeptics, idlers and swindlers: this was Locke's *Dunciad*.[53]

The inverted spectrum of the *Essay* rests in the transition between the seventeenth and eighteenth centuries, with one eye on the Civil War and the other on the South Sea Bubble. Thus, Locke sees fit to devote a chapter to "Of Enthusiasm," which even by the time it first saw print already had an archaic ring, filled as it is with the shards of a half-century-old rhetorical battle. The "True Lights," the "glow worms," "Holy Spirits," the "extravagant actions," "violence" and "the Son of the Morning" illuminate this otherwise somber post-Settlement book with the discourse of the sects: the Ranters, Diggers, Fifth Monarchy Men. It is as if to answer these ghosts from the past Locke must let them speak with their own heat once more. But the reply from the author of *Letters on Toleration* is predictable: let them rant—so long as they do not riot and steal my purse.[54]

The threat arising from the future, however, was the opposite of that posed by the Enthusiasts. Politically, the cool tone of the *Essay* is a direct response to the poetic warmth of mid-century rebels like Winstanley, but the "precision" of words and the "sensible" rhythm of Locke's prose aims at the *semantic* criminals, whose *modus operandi* is the word and sign itself: those who "with great art and subtlety" are "employed to darken truth and unsettle peoples rights" (Locke 1823a: III, x, 13). Their great weapon lay in the *variability* of language on the orthographic, grammatical and semantic levels. Locke—quite consciously in both the form and content of the *Essay*—attempts to create a hedge against it.

Consider his five-point program of linguistic reform:[55]

(1) To use no word without an idea annexed to it (sec. 8).

(2) To have distinct, determinate ideas annexed to words, especially mixed modes (sec. 9).

(3) To apply words to such ideas as common use has annexed them to (sec. 11).

(4) To declare the meaning in which we use them (sec. 12).

(5) To use the same word constantly in the same sense (sec. 26).

(Locke 1823a: III, xi)

With this program, variability and unpredictability are outlawed, while conservatism and linearity are enthroned. One can see Locke as the first self-conscious theorist of the Great Transformation of the English language that started during this period, which would turn the peculiar pidgin of the European World into *the* computable language. A modern communications theorist would say that Locke *reduced the entropy of language.*[56] Most obviously, this was accomplished on the orthographic level, with the dramatic reduction of the diversity of script, multiple spellings and variable capitalization (all already well advanced in the *Essay*). But the gnarled, quizzical and surprising grammatical constructions of a Shakespeare, a Browne or a Milton were also reduced to a set of relatively limited prose structures, while the penchant for the couplet perfectly expressed this stratagem in poetry.[57]

Locke is most explicit on the semantic level: each word must be backed by a publicly recognized, temporally durable, conceptually distinct and determinate idea. This attempt—to impose an "idea standard" on language—was perhaps Locke's most successful effort, since it ultimately guided the development of English from Swift down to Cobol, with only few exceptions: Blake, Joyce and Burroughs.[58]

The *Essay* thus appears as a carefully wrought social machine for repressing the Subtle Disputer as well as the Wild Enthusiast. Locke saw his times as extremely vulnerable to the innovations of the post-Settlement period, which—if based upon half-baked projects and experiments—could lead to the undoing of the gains made possible by the "Glorious Revolution." This was especially true for an institution that undoubtedly haunts the *Further Considerations*: the newly formed Bank of England. With the Bank, the civil government slowly abrogated to itself the power of monetary creation. Would this lead to a catastrophe? It is with such questions that the *Essay* is fundamentally concerned.[59]

Conclusion: Weaving an Origin

I shall I think in the beginning of July have some money paid me in, and perhaps some sooner. Pray tell me whether I cannot refuse clipped money, for I take it not to be the lawful coin of England and Know not why I should receive half the value I lent instead of the whole.

(Letter from Locke to Clarke, May 17, 1695)

It is, however, quite in keeping with the bourgeois horizon, everyone being engrossed in transaction of shady business, not to see in the character of the mode of production the basis of the mode of exchange corresponding to it, but vice versa.

(Marx 1978: Chapter 4)

Our discussion of the idea of money led to a hypothetical conclusion: *if* there is money, *then* it must have a metallic (or substantial) element. With this conclusion, Locke could defend the first axiom of *Further Considerations*:

Silver is the instrument and measure of commerce in all the civilized and trading parts of the world.

(Locke 1823c: 139)

Since it is an incontrovertible fact that there is commerce and money, by *modus ponens*, it must be in the form of silver (or a similar substance). But what of the other axioms? For example, why does silver have an intrinsic value? Why has "common consent" made it the "universal barter"? Ultimately, why is there money in the first place?

To answer these questions, we must examine the contrasts Locke stipulates between money *qua* silver and the original kinds of property. Let us put these contrasts in a tabular form:[1]

Table 4.1 Locke distinguishes between money qua silver and the original kinds of property

Dimension	*Money* qua *Silver*	*Original Property*
Psychological	Fancy	Real Use
Relational	Dyadic	Monadic
Social	Tacit Agreement	Natural law
Physical	Durable	Transitory
Mathematical	Unbounded	Bounded

We will now weave these contrasts into Locke's extremely sketchy account of the origin of money to get a fully Lockean solution to the problem of justifying his monetary axioms.

As a preliminary, however, let us consider the problem of origins in Locke's work. In the *Essay* and the *Two Treatises*, the origins of two social institutions are explicitly considered—property and government—while the origins of two others—language and money—are left obscure.

Consider language. Locke "guesses" that words all had their beginning

in sensible ideas … which filled their minds who were the first beginners of language, and how nature, even in the naming of things, unawares suggested to men the originals and principles of all their knowledge.

(Locke 1823a: III, i, 5)

But Nature was simply the assistant of God in this regard:

God, having designed man for a sociable creature, made him not only with an inclination and under a necessity to have fellowship with those of his own kind, but furnished him also with language, which was to be the great instrument and common tie of society.

(Locke 1823a: III, i, 1)

This is hardly an adequate explanation even from the standards of late seventeenth- and eighteenth-century thought, for the question of the origin of language was elaborately discussed at this time.[2] It begs the most crucial questions and shows Locke at his weakest.

For example, if language is "the great instrument and common tie of society" and if man does have an "inclination" and "necessity to have fellowship," then why the need for contracts creating "commonwealths," "political society" and government? Why is contract necessary? Indeed, can one contract a necessity? Further, this account shows the tendentiousness of Locke's critique of "innate principles," for if speaking is just a "natural faculty" like seeing, then Locke's purported debate with Descartes and Leibniz vanishes. Locke, in effect, casts the question of the origin of language into a huge pit marked "I know not" or "It is folly to expect demonstration."

One may be tempted to think Locke did the same for money. However, paragraphs 45–51 of the *Second Treatise* actually contain a three-stage account of the origin of money:

Stage A: [T]he first exchanges were inadvertent; pleased with the color of gold or silver or the sparkling of a diamond a man exchanges perishable goods for them.

Stage B: [S]lowly there is a growing "mutual consent" or "tacit agreement" to take the gold, silver or diamond as payment in general.

Stage C: [A]n impulse to accumulation begins to take shape as some parts of the population "enlarge their possessions" while others, of course, find theirs diminished.

Stage A is based upon a simple contrast: fancy/real use. Consider the discovery of *Zahab* (gold). One of Adam's children goes roving in the mountains and "lights on a *glittering* substance which *pleases* his eye" (Locke 1823a: III, vi, 46). But let us say that on the way back to Adam's house someone who has recently picked up a kilo of acorns sees the chunk of *Zahab* and is also pleased with its color to such a point that "he would give his nuts for a piece of metal" (Locke 1823g: II, 42). Though the acorns have a real use (i.e., when consumed while hungry they give pleasure), the *Zahab* gives the child and the acorn gatherer a fancied pleasure. Consider again what is happening at the other end of the primeval valley. But to indulge himself, a shepherd exchanges "his sheep for shells, or wool for a sparkling pebble or diamond" (Locke 1823g: II, 42). Is he mad? Perhaps. Is it within his rights? Surely. But what is the source of such behavior? Fancy.

These actions are motivated by what would later be called "aesthetic" or "ornamental" desires. Locke calls it "fancy." What is "fancy?" It is an informal term in Locke's psychology (like "imagination") but it has a wide variety of uses, especially when modified by loud adjectives: "wild fancy," "extravagant fancy," "wanton fancy," "boundless fancy," *etc.* As an operation of the mind it is closely related to "wit," whose opposite is "judgement" in the category of "discernment":

> For wit lying most in the assemblage of ideas and putting those together with quickness and variety, wherein can be found any resemblance or congruity, thereby to make up pleasant pictures and agreeable visions in the fancy; judgement, on the contrary, lies quite on the other side, in separating carefully, one from the other, ideas wherein can be found the least difference, thereby to avoid being mislead by similitude, and by affinity to take one thing for another. This is a way of proceeding quite contrary to metaphor and allusion; wherein for the most part lies that entertainment and pleasantry of wit, which strikes so lively on the fancy, and therefore is so acceptable to all people, because its beauty appears at first sight, and there is required no labor of thought to examine what truth or reason there is in it. The mind, without looking any further, rests satisfied with agreeableness of the picture and the gaiety of the fancy.
>
> (Locke 1823a: II, xi, 2)[3]

Fancy is thus a mental capacity and an evaluative term, it is the capacity to bring together ideas at will (hence it is boundless fancy) without considerations of truth or probability (hence "wanton fancy"). It is the play of the mind, pleasing or terrifying, itself independent of external considerations, twisting and turning ideas under the rule of metaphor and resemblance; it is the poetry of thought. We might say it is the last, now degraded, remnant of Aristotle's concept of thought *qua* activity: a timeless process which is an end in itself.

For Locke, *real* thought is laborious: a hard, time-bound process, which is a means to something beyond itself. We do not think, according to Locke, for the pleasure of thinking; rather thinking is the work we must do to arrive at pleasure (Locke 1823a: II, vii, 3). Thought has no life of its own, it is suspicious of images and forms, beauty and mimesis. Here we find the bourgeois mentality at its most self-reflexive: thought too must labor to advantage, otherwise it is not thought.

But our immediate concern is with fancy contrasted with "real use" in the context of the origin of money. Surely the color and glitter of gold, the sparkle of diamonds give some pleasure in the way that food and raiment give pleasure, and pleasure is pleasure, is it not? Not exactly, according to Locke. One of the great proofs of God's goodness is his "annexing pleasure and pain to our other ideas"—that is, to *some* of our ideas. If God had not done his "annexing," we would be in sorry shape:

> And so we should neither stir our bodies, nor employ our minds, but let our thoughts (if I may so call it) run adrift, without any direction or design, and suffer the ideas of our minds, like unregarded shadows, to make their appearances there, as it happened, without attending to them. In which state man, however furnished with the faculties of understanding and will, would be a very idle, inactive creature, and pass his time only in a lazy, lethargic dream.
>
> (Locke 1823a: II, vii, 3)

Thus, God has created the world to keep us moving, busy, attentive, planning and above all *dissatisfied*. The world is organized as an infernal machine where pleasure is frequently mixed with pain, and where we can be sure we will get no rest until death. God has so devised our bodies and minds, as well as the objects around us, as springs, levers, gears, pulleys and inclined planes of pleasure and pain.

> It has therefore pleased our wise Creator to annex several objects, and the ideas we receive from them, as also to several of our thoughts, a concomitant pleasure, and that in several degrees, that those faculties which he had endowed us with might not remain wholly idle and unemployed by us. Pain has the same efficacy and use to set us on work that pleasure has, we being as ready to employ our faculties to avoid that, as to pursue this.
>
> (Locke 1823a: II, vii, 3–4)

The notion of real use stems from God's complex design, for he is not only anxious to keep us dissatisfied, but also wants to keep us at work. So the pain and pleasure connections that God set up between certain bodily organs and certain natural objects constitute real use. It is no accident that acorns satisfy hunger and fire can cause pain; our bodies, our minds, acorns and fires are necessarily so related. True, God provided many acorns and few fires, so that *if* we do work we can preserve ourselves. As we work and toil, we are therefore reminded of the enjoyment of Him in the afterlife. (In passages like these one is completely awed by the diabolical nature of the bourgeois God!)

God, however, is selective, and fancy is at work. For pleasure and pain are ideas also, and fancy can combine them with other ideas as long as God has not ordained the connection. Thus, some might find the idea of a sauna pleasant, but no one can find the idea of roasting one's hand pleasant. Fancy has a wide field of operation. Though food is necessary, we can take a fancy to fish and shun meat; though raiment is necessary we can take a fancy to black jump suits and wear nothing else. Moreover, there are wide areas of sensation and reflection where real use is completely absent, for example, no colors are intrinsically "offensive," nor are any ideal geometric figures necessarily painful or pleasurable. With fancy, we arrive at the realm of freedom, away from God's pleasure and pain machine, since we literally can choose to be pleased or pained by certain ideas.

But how free is fancy? Quite free, as a glance at the spectacle of human society shows us:

[T]he various and contrary choices that men make in the world do not argue that they do not all pursue good; but that the same thing is not good to every man alike ... for the mind has a different relish as well as palate...
(Locke 1823a: II, xxi, 55–56)

Locke has us envision an infinite space-time of desire, whose order and metric is continuously changing. For example, he tells us of two men, one fond of the pleasures of the table, the other only moved by knowledge, but it so happens that the first is urged by his mistress to study a bit, while the second is gripped by hunger pangs while musing on a Euclidean theorem ... presto, their desire field undergoes a mirror transformation! (Locke 1823a: II, xxi, 44).

Sex, food, warmth, etc. (the "necessaries") form the fixed points in this space-time, while the "horizon points" at infinity have the sense of the afterlife and God. But the rest is Heraclitean change: the last becomes first, the far is brought near, the perspective is redrawn. This is the kingdom of fancy, and within the limits of God and Necessity one can *reform* one's own fancy:

> Men may and should correct their palates, and give relish to what either has, or they suppose has none ... Though this be very visible, and every one's experience shows him he can do so; yet it is a part in the conduct of men towards their happiness, neglected to a degree, that it will be possibly entertained as a paradox, if it be said, that men can make things or actions more or less pleasing to themselves, and thereby remedy that, to which one may justly impute a great deal of their wandering.
>
> (Locke 1823a: II, xxi, 71)

Those twentieth-century reformationists—the existentialists, and especially Sartre—would take up this theme under the slogan, "We choose our passions ... no more excuses!" Comparable to the Sartrean "bad faith" is Locke's analysis of the apparent polarity of Common Custom and Madness. For there is an element of self-deceit in both that will not wash on the "Great Day, when the secrets of all hearts shall be laid open" (Locke 1823a: II, xxvii, 22). For one cannot excuse an action simply because everyone else did it, any more than one can be excused under the plea of madness. They are both forms of wrong judgment, and they arise from the same source: the association of a chance connection of ideas.

Common Custom can lead to immense uniformities of desire and behavior among many individuals who *appear* to be bound by necessity to desire and behave the way they do. But this necessity is an illusion. They seem blindfolded and captivated by their environment, yet they are neither really blinded nor compelled. The apparent confusion is due to the fact that:

> [S]ome independent ideas, of no alliance to one another, are, by education, custom, and the constant din of their party, so coupled in their minds, that they always appear there together; and they can no more separate them in their thoughts than if they were but one idea, and they operate as if they were so.
>
> (Locke 1823a: II, xxxiii, 18)

This sort of custom operates on the level of pleasure and pain as well, for though there are natural connections between our ideas and our sympathies and antipathies based upon our "original constitution," our sympathies and antipathies are largely a product of custom—especially when the connection is started in *childhood.*

Common Custom or common opinion is a form of collective madness, and reciprocally madness is the individualization of the association of ideas to extreme idiosyncrasy. This sort of perturbation is to be found in most men, and certainly does not arise from "losing one's senses or reason." On the contrary,

> For [madmen] do not appear to me to have lost the faculty of reasoning, but having joined together some ideas very wrongly, they mistake them for truths; and they err as men do that argue right from wrong principles. For by the violence of their imaginations, having taken their fancies for realities, they make right deduction from them. Thus you shall find a distracted man fancying himself a king, with a right inference require suitable attendance, respect, and obedience; others who have thought themselves made of glass, have used the caution necessary to preserve such brittle bodies.
>
> (Locke 1823a: II, xi, 13)

Thus, both in the madman and in the "average citizen" clinging to common opinion and conventional behavior, we find the same mechanism and the same self-deceit at work. Unnatural connections of ideas are taken as natural, and reason simply deduces the consequences therefrom. But since the connections are not natural, the understanding *could* have separated the ideas; thus *ultimately* neither madness nor common custom can be a defense against the final judgment and infinite misery!

However, Locke is by no means underestimating the power of the association of ideas; in fact, his theories of education and "psychotherapy" are based upon this power.[4] So is his theory of the origin of money.

Now we are in a position to fill out Locke's remarks about Stage A. God created the world as a machine to induce work, "booby-trapped" with natural connections of objects to pleasures and pains, yet with appropriate "escape hatches" which—*if* one was rational and industrious enough—would guarantee the preservation of one's life for a while. If one labored, one lived and naturally acquired a limited amount of useful property; if not, one died and was forgotten. Such was the "Goldless Golden Age," so to speak.

But God has not determined *all* possible connections. Fancy too is afoot, especially among the marginals (e.g., the children and the shepherds) who are more easily struck by the beauty and pleasure of a color, a glint, a sparkle. Hence the beginning of unnecessary, fancied, desires and the connection of objects with pleasures and pains not programmed into the original machine. But the child grows up and has children; the shepherd is alone, but travels far and wide with his flocks; each carries within him or herself the pleasures of gold, silver and diamonds. Slowly the idiosyncratic passion spreads, until it becomes a common custom and these substances become precious *to each individual.* It is not a necessary connection, true, but once it has seized an individual or area it can have the power of a natural sympathy. And once common custom and common opinion operates this "deceit," these now precious stuffs enter into everyday exchanges cheek-by-jowl with other *really useful* necessaries. There will be individuals, families and "peoples" either uncaptivated by this fancy or simply ignorant of it. But these will be treated by the party of gold and silver the way a madman, believing he is a king, treats someone who makes no such association: as a rebel or more likely—as a madman.

But common custom is not yet really social, and common opinion is not yet truly common. For at this stage we are still on the level of the individual, even though the affected individuals comprise the whole population.[5] For in the end, it is each one's *individual choice* to accept the unnatural connection, even though the immense power of education, custom and constant din is put at the service of the sympathy, to reproduce and widen it. No laws or compacts are violated if s/he remains unaffected.

Stage A brings into play a peculiar but necessary freedom for the unnecessary, the freedom of desire; it also points out that this freedom can become its opposite, creating false necessities. This, indeed, is Locke's version of the "fetishism of commodities," but he does not totally disown this fetishism. This particular "fetish" for gold, silver and diamonds *violates no natural laws* and is, for all that, an expression of freedom—the freedom to desire what one will. However one might doubt that the glitter of a diamond or the "eternal beauty" of a golden Macedonian crown is naturally pleasurable, one cannot deny that they produce pleasure.

With Stage B, the new logical and social level is achieved. Whereas before there was *individual* fancy, now there is "*mutual* consent"; while in the state of nature, *natural* law ruled, in the state of money there is "tacit *agreement.*" Still, the "deduction" of the axiom—"silver is that which mankind has agreed on to take and give in exchange for all commodities as equivalent"—requires us to understand something about Locke's conception of the historical development that is skewed to "our" notions. If one were to sketch the "average" twentieth-century conception of the historical development of some of the institutions under discussion, this sequence would be in order:

Society → Language → Government → Money

A good indication of our distance from Locke is to see his ordering of the same institutions:

Language → Money → Society → Government

For Locke, language is *not* a collection of social relations or rules; nor is it *qua* institution the least bit conventional—Locke is *not* David Hume.[6]

There are no Gricean other-centered intentions, no Lewisonian coordination problems, or Fregean senses and references here; if anything, Locke explicitly rejects whatever equivalent he might have known. Words can only signify ideas in the mind of the speaker. People might "secretly" either "suppose words to be marks of the ideas in the minds of other men, with whom they communicate," or "suppose their words to stand also for the reality of things," but they are mistaken in these suppositions. True, something called the "common acceptation" or the "common use of a word," or, in general, the "propriety of speech" is recognized by Locke. But they have the status of "standing regularities," that no one agreed upon either implicitly or explicitly and that nobody can enforce. Concerning propriety Locke writes:

> [T]he rule and measure of propriety itself being nowhere established, it is often matter of dispute, whether this or that way of using a word be propriety of speech or no.
>
> (Locke 1823a: III, ix, 8)

Despite frequent analogies to monetary phenomena in Locke's discussion of "common usage," there is a crucial difference between language and money: though monetary discourse is linguistic, language does not have an essential characteristic of monetary discourse. By violating the rules of money, one violates agreements and contracts and so may be punished; by violating the "rules of language," (sic) nothing is broken and no one is liable. However much Locke may rant (and eighteenth-century writers like Swift and Johnson may moan) on this point he is quite clear; since language is the product of my utmost liberty, it is ultimately a "relation or agreement between me and myself."

The practice of language is fundamentally monadic; appearances not-withstanding, it is not social, nor was it ever. Similarly, the law of the state of nature, the natural law, is asocial: the essence of that state is a

> perfect freedom to order their actions and dispose of their possessions and persons, as they think fit, within the bounds of the law of nature; without asking leave or depending on the will of any other man.
>
> (Locke 1823g: II, 4)

In a way, language is in a state of nature without a natural law, since we can signify ideas by the words we use "without asking leave, or depending upon the will of any other man."

The bounds of the state of nature—the natural law—are equally non-conventional, for the natural law "obliges every one," not because any one *else* is obliged. Even if no one else follows its dictates, you are obliged to do so—and will suffer the consequences if you do not, either in this life, or the other, or both. Thus, law is monadic since it arises from Reason:

> and reason, which is that law, teaches all mankind, who will but consult it, that being all equal and independent, no one ought to harm another in his life, health, liberty or possessions.
>
> (Locke 1823g: II, 6)

Being Reason, a God-given faculty, it has no dependence on society.

Natural law, of course, affects our relation with other people just as language does. It not only dictates how I am to behave, it also enjoins me to "punish the offender, and be executioner of the law of nature" (Locke 1823g: II, 8). However, once again this injunction is not based on any form of "mutual consent"; it is based only upon the reason placed in me, upon "that faculty whereby man is supposed to be distinguished from beasts, and wherein it is evident he much surpasses them" (Locke 1823a: IV, xvii, 1).

Locke here lays the basis for his justification of capital punishment ("the making of laws with penalties of death"); for in breaking the law of nature one demonstrates an inability to use the very faculty of abstraction and mediation that differentiates mankind from beasts, so that the criminal is equated with the beast. And if the criminal turns violent, he may "therefore be destroyed as a lion or a tiger, one of those wild savage beasts with whom men can have no society nor security" (Locke 1823g: II, 11).

This mortal action requires no agreement, consent or approval in the state of nature. We all can—nay, *must*—be executioners according to our *own* reason, so extreme is the monadic character of man in this state.

Looking at Locke's state of nature with Leibnizian spectacles, however, we would see it as a collection of "windowless monads" without a "pre-established harmony." For though Freedom, Law and Reason are absolute, they are limited and imperfect in their interaction.[7]

Locke's monads *require* windows, and it is interesting that the first quasi-social laws arise in the origination process of money. For in money we find the universalization of certain relations, compacts and promises of the *exchange process*, which is where the first "interactions" occur among pre-social human atoms. When Locke points out that: "Promises and compacts men may make one with another, and yet still be with the same state of nature" (Locke, *Treatise*, II, 14), it is not surprising that the first example that comes to mind is "truck":

> The promises and bargains for truck, &c. between two men in the desert island, mentioned by *Garcilasso de la Vega*, in his history of Peru; or between a *Swiss* and an *Indian*, in the woods of America; are binding to them, though they are perfectly in a state of nature, in reference to one another. For truth and keeping of faith belongs to men as men, and not as members of society.
>
> (Locke, *Treatise*, II, 14)

What differentiates the money agreement from other forms of "truck" is its universality and generality in two senses. First, the "promises and compacts of truck are between man and man, but the money agreement goes beyond one-to-one ties; it implicitly involves *many* men exchanging with each other; second, money agreements involve *all* commodities being trucked in a certain region. Hence, with money we find a law relating men and things that is not a product of reason and yet, in its original form, develops before the formation of society.

What kind of law do we have in the state of money? Locke nowhere in the *Treatises* makes it explicit. But by applying our methodological principle— we can find an answer in the *Essay* in a chapter titled "Of Other Relations." Locke here discusses three types of laws, two of which we have already come across: divine law and civil law. Divine law is natural law assisted by the "voice of revelation," while civil law is "the rule set by the commonwealth to the actions of those who belong to it" (Locke 1823a: II, xxviii, 9). Surely neither law applies to the origin of money: civil law comes afterward, and only an Ayn Rand would trace the source of money to "the voice of revelation." But the third type of law—which Locke calls variously "philosophical law," "the law of opinion or reputation," or "the law of fashion"—is the appropriate one. He writes:

> Thus the measure of what is everywhere called and estimed virtue and vice is this approbation or dislike, praise or blame, which, by a secret and tacit consent, establishes itself in the several societies, tribes, and clubs of men in the world: whereby several actions come to find credit or disgrace amongst them, according to the judgement, maxims or fashion of that place.
>
> This kind of law is informal and variable, for what is called "virtue and vice" does change as we go from one place to another,
>
> (Locke 1823a: II, xxviii, 10–11)

although piously and inconsistently Locke adds, "for the most part [they] are kept the same everywhere" (Locke 1823a: II, xxviii, 11).

Such a law is appropriate for money, because money is not a universal phenomenon like the law of nature. As in the case of the origin of money, the "law of opinion and reputation" arises out of "secret and tacit consent." It requires consent because not being a divine law it involves relations between men; yet at the same time such law is not like civil law, which is necessarily "public and spoken." For civil law involves "an established, settled, known law," "a known and indifferent judge," and "an executive power." The "law of opinion" has none of these features; since its laws are not settled, it has no specially marked off judge or executive body. Its method of operation is much less direct and obvious, but this is not to say that its results are any less powerful than the other forms of law.

Let us say I suddenly decide not to use money in my daily transactions. In doing so, I violate no natural laws nor, unless I am in debt, break any divinely blessed compacts. I simply drop out of the "club of money users." But if there are no consequences, how can we claim there is a law in effect? As Locke points out—and it is a lesson that modern philosophers of language should heed—unless there is reward or punishment accompanying our "conformity or disagreement," there is no law. However, "the law of fashion," which is "nothing else but the consent of private men, who have not authority enough to make a law," does have its ways:

> I think I may say, that he who imagines commendation and disgrace not to be strong motives to men to accommodate themselves to the opinions and rules of these with whom they converse, seems little skilled in the nature or history of mankind: the greatest part whereof we shall find to govern themselves chiefly, if not solely, by this law of fashion.
>
> (Locke 1823a: II, xxviii, 12)

Clearly if I am a businessman or merchant in a place where the tacit and mutual consent of using silver or gold as a universal equivalent is the law of fashion, then, by dropping out of the "universal equivalent users' club," I will quickly find myself bankrupt. In some ways, I would more quickly and surely fail than if I violated my divinely or civilly sanctioned business deals, for to be a cheat is to still remain in the game. But by dropping out of the club, I would not even be allowed to play the game.

Locke is referring to an important fact: once there are large-scale but private mutual agreements operating, the power of enforcement can be more relentless (and effective) than any police can conjure.[8] For to remain out of the club everyone else is in (especially when remaining in violates no natural law) is a "burden too heavy for human sufferance" (Locke 1823a: xxviii, 12).

Locke is not being ironic here. This is a likely model for the original law of money, whose relevance is striking to any tourist stranded in a city when the banks are closed. Spending five days in New York City without dollars—however much foreign exchange one has—would be an interesting philosophical experiment, if it were not so dangerous. True, there are no laws against not having dollars, and no law forbids others from trading with you—but they do not have to, either. No judge will condemn you to hunger. No police will force you to starve—but you likely will. Such is the rewarding/punishing power of the law of fashion, and one slights it only with the gravest hesitations and the best of reasons.

Thus, in our reconstruction of the origin of money, Stage B immediately follows Stage A. Once gold and silver have struck everyone's fancy and have become such that it is common custom to get pleasure from them, it could easily become a "law of opinion or fashion" that all transactions are to be carried out in gold or silver pieces through a multitude of "secret and tacit agreements." Once such a law is operating, the consequences of dropping out can be severe—even if one finds that the agreements are to his disadvantage. For by staying one might become poor, but to leave might mean death. This self-reinforcing, self-sustaining, irreversible character of informal systems, where an accidental fluctuation can become a structural principle, is quite remarkable; Locke would not be far wrong in tracing to them the origin of money. By discovering a common "fetish" with his fellows and creating a "secret society" upon it, Locke's monad (in the state of nature) can break out of itself.

Stage C depends upon two aspects of gold and silver that arise from their pure physicality: they are extremely durable (even quasi-eternal), and there is no inherent limit to their accumulation. These physical characteristics differentiate gold and silver from those substances and stuffs that God thought fit to be of real use to us, which are continually spoiling and rotting. Perhaps this corruptibility is part of God's gigantic make-work scheme, as is perhaps the fact that they provide pleasures which are intermittent and non-cumulative. That one has eaten 40,000 meals in a lifetime will have no conditional effect on the fact that one will have to eat a 40,001st some time soon. Or, as the old saw put it, however many beds you may own, you can only sleep in one at a time.

To put Stage C in perspective with respect to the previous stages in the origination process of money, we might use a more modern terminology. If Stage A was the "ornamental" stage and Stage B the "medium of exchange" stage, then Stage C is the "store of value" and "primitive accumulation" stage.[9]

Locke's theory of the origin of money, however, is in no way "modern," because Locke is completely indifferent to the myth of the "inconvenience of Barter" that has proven so popular from J.S. Mill's day through Jevons' down to our time. R.W. Clower in the early 1970s was still trying to convince us with cost-curve graphs that a money economy is more efficient and less socially costly than a barter one. Jevons, in the later part of the nineteenth century, tried opera singers, but Locke had other concerns (Clower 1971: "Introduction"; and Jevons 1926: "Barter"). He was not unfamiliar with the phenomenon, for in *Further Considerations* the inconveniencies of barter appear as something to be avoided in the recoinage transition. But there is no hint in Locke's writings that this was the original "cause of money," nor even that it was its primary purpose or consequence.

Indeed, it is likely that the primary consequence of the origin of money remained unknown to Adam's child, who first got a fancy for gold, or even to the first "private men," who created the law of fashion that first made gold and silver universal equivalents. For it took time to reveal itself. The quasi-eternal durability of the precious metals and the potentially boundless desire for them lead to a new historical possibility:

> And as different degrees of industry were apt to give men possessions in different proportions, so this invention of money gave them the opportunity to continue and enlarge them.
>
> (Locke 1823g: II, 48)

Locke, of course, does not add, "or diminish them." In the last section of "Of Property," however, he spells out, the main consequence of the use of money:

> [I]t is plain, that men have agreed to a disproportionate and unequal possession of the earth; they having, by a tacit and voluntary consent, found out a way how a man may fairly possess more land than he himself can use the product of, by receiving in exchange for the overplus, gold and silver, which may be hoarded up without injury to any one; these metals not spoiling or decaying in the hands of the possessor. This partage of things in an inequality of private possessions, men have made practicable out of the bounds of society, and without compact...
>
> (Locke 1823g: II, 50)

Now we see how "tacit consents" can add up to become a "law of fashion," and, in effect, "found a way" to a seemingly paradoxical situation. People whose possessions were proportionate and equal could slowly and imperceptively find themselves on the one side dispossessed and on the other rich. It is not that some tacitly "consented" to be poor (which would be foolish), but by a previous series of consentings stretching back before their birth—perhaps concerning gold and silver—they found themselves in this state. Once this happened, however, they could not easily call the game off, or simply "leave the club." As we saw, systems of fashion and opinion are quite irreversible and once established, they exhibit a remarkable tenaciousness.[10]

Consider what this means in practice. If at the end of a growing season, either because of luck or skill, I find myself with an "overplus," in the state of nature I would have had to give a potlatch; but in the state of money all I need do is find someone to sell the surplus crop to for gold or silver. If I do that, I am in a radically different position than in the state of nature, for now I can accumulate; I can use the money to hire "servants" to till more land ... and perhaps next season! an even larger "overplus" and more servants and yet more land...

Though he gives us no reason for thinking that there will be "servants" and that money can give title to land,[11] Locke is convinced that necessarily there will follow a stage of primitive accumulation after the introduction of money:

> Thus in the beginning all the world was *America*, and more so than that is now; for no such thing as *money* was any where known. Find out something that hath the *use and value of money* amongst his neighbours, you shall see the same man will begin presently to *enlarge his possessions.*
> (Locke 1923f: II, 49)

Again Locke does not mention the "primitive losers" along with the "primitive winners," though undoubtedly—if they survived—they went into the category of "servants." But one might wonder why Locke was so sure an "instinct of accumulation" was to be found in Everyman.

His *immediate* certainty rests on the extrapolation of pre-monetary behavior and instincts into a monetary environment. After all, God ordained that we labor:

He gave [the world] to the use of the industrious and rational (and labour was to be his title to it), not to the fancy and covetousness of the quarrelsome and the contentious.

(Locke 1923f: II, 34)

Locke thought as highly as Filmer of the injunction to Adam, (though he interpreted it differently): "to multiply and people the earth and subdue." But Locke added, "So that God, by commanding to subdue, gave authority so far to appropriate" (Locke 1923f: II, 35).[12] This the rational and industrious did, in the state of nature, up to the bounds of use. But this did not mean that *they* could not go further; it simply meant that they did not in accordance with the natural limits placed on them. If the limits were erased, the Biblical injunction would continue to apply.

But with the invention of money, the "overplus" need not be feasted away, the fetters to accumulation are broken, and a new possibility opens up, the scale of progressive enlargement becoming unbounded. By simply following God's injunction planted in their breasts, if the environment proved propitious, the rational and industrious inevitably accumulated, and even in unpropitious periods they burned with the desire to accumulate. For once money overcomes the natural impediments to accumulation, then there is no limit inherent in the process of subduing and appropriating.

What of those of less rational and industrious types, who were living comfortably on the common, or even living off the "overplus of others," which the Old Testament explicitly allowed? (For how else are we to read verses like, "When thou comest into thy neighbor's vineyard, then thou mayest eat grapes thy fill at thine own pleasure"? Deuteronomy 23:24[13])

Well, the less industrious were in serious trouble! For now that the "overplus" of grapes could be used to make that famous marginal bottle of wine, the owner of the vineyard could claim that they were of use and could not be eaten to anybody's fill. These "grasshoppers" would have either to become rational and industrious "ants," and enter into the ranks of the accumulators, or simply become poor. And to be poor while remaining alive required either that they sign on as "servants" of the accumulators or that they live off the accumulator's charity, which was now purely gratuitous (and all the more Christian, since it did not have to be given—as it was in the Old Testament state of Nature.[14]) If the new poor did not accept this choice, they could try their luck on the highway.

Thus, the "instinct to accumulate" was hibernating during the period of the state of Nature, and with the first heat of a golden spring it stirred and began to feed.

But Stage C did not just depend upon an original instinct. It expressed itself in two definite mechanisms that were non-existent in the state of Nature: Interest and Inheritance. Locke does not mention them directly in the crucial final sections of "Of Property," but they are essential elements in his philosophy of money, for they both amplify through years and generations the accumulative effect of the introduction of money.

Let us consider Interest first. Locke is at the other end of that great debate on the legitimacy of "usury," which raged in the transition from feudalism to capitalism. In Locke, Genesis i: 28 definitely takes precedence over Deuteronomy xxiii: 19. Only a few fragments of the old battles lay scattered in his writing.

For example, his argument concerning the nature of interest begins with a hoary "paradox" from the then-archaic polemical literature: land is naturally fruitful and productive but "money is a barren thing." Locke intensifies even this apparent paradox with an aphorism that could easily have been found in a typical anti-usury tract:

> [Money] by compact transfers that profit, that was the reward of one man's labour, into another man's pocket.
>
> (Locke 1823f: 43)[15]

But Locke dispels the paradoxicality by turning the "natural profitability of land" against itself. After all, if you own land and you let another farm it (instead of getting your "servants" to), you expect and are justified in expecting a return—rent—even though you are vacationing in Bath. True, your tenant is using his skill and labor, but without your land, it would have been "wasted" in the tavern. Moreover, he too expects something: "to produce more fruits than his rent come to." Now the precondition of rent is a very unequal distribution of land, especially at the edges. There have to be some who have so much that they cannot farm it themselves, even if they wanted to, and there have to be many who have none at all to farm; hence, the landlord and the tenant. (This is how Locke speaks to his country cousins, who were apt to be suspicious of the London money men.)

Granting all this for land, Locke points out, the same logic applies to money. First, there is just as unequal distribution of money as there is of land. Second, some have more money than they can use, while others do not have enough to carry on their business; hence there are borrowers and lenders. But why not Interest?

> [A]nd the same unequal distribution of money (I having more than I can or will employ, and another less) brings me a tenant for my money; so my money is apt in trade, by the industry of the borrower, to produce more than six per cent to the borrower...
>
> (Locke 1823f: 43)

If my money-tenant uses my money to make money, do I not deserve a "rent" as well?

> [I]t follows, that borrowing money upon use is not only, by the necessity of affairs, and the constitution of human society, unavoidable to some men; but that also to receive profit from the loan of money is as equable and lawful as receiving rent for land, and more tolerable to the borrower, not withstanding the opinion of some over-scrupulous men.
>
> (Locke 1823f: 37)

It also follows that with the existence of interest, the accumulation and unequal distribution of money becomes a self-perpetuating mechanism without any new effort required on the part of the possessor of the money (in any sense of "effort" or "labor," unless you count "waiting"—in Bath—as labor). Would it be better if the "overplus" money were simply hoarded away in chests or shaped into plates and eaten off? Or, perhaps, "thrown away" to supply the feeding and drinking of the "quarrelsome and contentious"? The answer for Locke is self-evident.

Biblical restrictions notwithstanding, once a monetary economy begins to "take off," a completely new way of accumulating possessions is created that is autonomous from the original labor-title to property. But it is just as legitimate, since in the end it can trace itself back to the tacit consent of all money users (Locke 1823f: 45). Through interest, the "barrenness of money" shows itself to be the greatest of ironies, because land, while inherently fruitful, is limited in extent. One cannot—unless you're Dutch—create more of it. But money unleashes a self-generative force in society that has the boundless, purely quantitative, serial character of numbers, and is variously called Trade, Commerce, Appropriation.[16]

One might object that there is only a finite (though unknown) amount of gold and silver on the planet, hence only as finite an amount of money as there is of land. A Lockean response would be twofold:

1. Silver and gold are precious substances that "tacit consent" has made "universal Barter." There is no reason to think that some other substances will not be found that have similar characteristics, which will strike someone's fancy, etc. The origin of money is not a one-time event, any more than is the "state of nature." Further, our knowledge of substance is forever growing and deepening, and as a consequence who knows what the limits are in the transformation of substances.[17]

2. Money is the "instrument and measure of Commerce," and as in the case of any instrument, what is crucial is the proportion of itself to its object. Consider that the lever, the absolute weight of the object to be moved and the moving force do not decide the result, but rather that the proportions between the lengths of the lever's arms do. Similarly, the same amount of money can "drive" very different levels of Trade when different institutional arrangements are in place. Locke, being one of the founders of the "quantity theory of money," was quite conscious of what was later called the "velocity of money." For example, in *Some Considerations*, he made a rather elaborate analysis of the "input–output structure of the English economy," and concluded that it was quite possible to drive much more trade with much less money. Time, of course, was of the essence:

> [W]e may observe that it were better for trade and consequently for everybody, (for more money would be stirring, and less would do the business) if rents were paid in shorter intervals ... less money could serve the trade of the country.
>
> (Locke 1823f: 27)

We see that, for a Lockean, the finitest objection would not be worrisome. But now let us turn to the second force, besides Interest, that amplifies the accumulation and unequal distribution tendencies of Stage C, that is, Inheritance. Inheritance preceded the state of money and society, but, with the origin of money, the process changes dramatically. One of the essential features of money is its durability (what I've called its "quasi-eternality"), whose ironic consequence is that money is more durable than its immediate possessor. The original form of property—being much less durable than its possessor—made the question of inheritance a trivial matter for Locke (though not for Filmer!). Since there could not be any extensive preservation of the "overplus," a father, at best, could bequeath to his children enough, say, for the next growing season ... after that, they were on their own. Could a father deed the lands he worked on during his lifetime to his children? Certainly not, because *his* deed would simply be a work-deed that would have to be revalidated each season by a new dose of work. Thus, the best the children could do was to be out in the fields the first day of spring. All this, however, changed with the origin of money.

Undoubtedly, property inheritance was not the only kind of inheritance crucial for the formation of society during Locke's time. Surely Locke's "Glorious Revolution" arose out of the matter of royal succession and inheritance. But for Locke, and not only for him, there was a close relation between the two. Many in our day unreflectively place the question of who will succeed the king into the pre-capitalist past, into medieval fairy tales or anthropological gossip. On the contrary, royal succession and property inheritance become decisive matters precisely with the dawning of capitalism. Indeed, much of the struggle around royal succession could very well have "reflected" the more widespread struggles about property inheritance that were taking place in the bedrooms, kitchens and halls of the realm.

Inheritance was the cornerstone of capital's identity in this period. For *capital*, up until the middle of the nineteenth century, largely remained *family* capital.[18] In interfamily inheritance lies the immortality of property: though inheritance is supposed to preserve the descendants, it also preserves the property (if it is money, and can be preserved). This makes possible an inter-generational accumulation process where the function of the descendants is to preserve the property and not vice versa. Property loses its status as a continuously re-affirmed, laboriously acquired, decomposing thing when it becomes money: it becomes that which continues beyond death, to such a point that the family capital will go on to embody the family.

Locke is clear as to the inter-generational transmission of wealth when it *can* last through the generations, as well as to its impact on accumulation. (Again, we must add, the process can go one of two ways from the initial state of Nature; for there can be dispossession as well as enlarged possession.) Without inheritance, one of the major motives of accumulation would disappear. Thus, Locke asks, when a father dies "why does [his property] not return to the common stock of mankind?" Is it simply a matter of fashion? His answer is that the basis of inheritance is not common tacit consent … but where the practice is universal, it is reasonable to think the cause is "natural." What is the basis of this natural practice? We might say, with Plato, "the desire of immortality expressed in generation," but Locke chooses a more "Christian" argument. God "planted" in us two basic desires: one is self-preservation.

> But next to this, God planted in men a strong desire also of propagating their kind, and continuing themselves in their posterity, and this gives children a title to share in the property of their parents, and a right to inherit their possessions.
>
> (Locke 1823g: I, 88)

There is, however, a missing premise in Locke's claim. For what relation exists between the *desire* for children and the *right* to possession? The missing premise can be supplied by the close connection between person and property that Locke argued for before. The desire to continue one's self in posterity necessarily involves one's property as well, since one's property is a part of one's self. To be a child, from the parent's point of view, is to be a continuation of the parent's self, so the child can claim the possessions of the parent, in the same way as the parent within his own life can claim and reclaim his own possessions: through identity.[19] If X is identical to X' and if X possesses O, then X' will possess O.

But there is another element in the equation that shapes the question of inheritance: the child is not the possession of the parent. For all his homilies about "honoring thy father and thy mother," Locke insists on the diversity of the child from the parent, to such a point that we might call him an early theorist of the generation gap. Though the desire for the propagation and continuation of the parent's self creates the child, when the child is out of nonage, he is free to go his way. Parental power is not civil power over another adult (no matter how the adult was generated). But do we have difference in identity *or* identity in difference—which shall it be? No logic can decide this.

Hence, the importance of the inheritance as a means of ensuring that the natural products of generation are a continuation of the generators' selves. With a sly Machiavellianism, Locke writes of the family:

> Yet there is another power ordinary in the father, whereby he has a tie on the obedience of his children ... and this is the power men generally have to bestow their estates on those who please them best ... yet it is commonly in the father's power to bestow [his possessions] with a more sparing or liberal hand, according as the behavior of this or that child hath comported with his will and humour.
>
> (Locke 1823g: II, 72)

Locke adds pointedly, "This is no small tie on the obedience of children."

Indeed, as Sol Yurick has taught us, this "small tie" is the essence of centuries of bourgeois soap opera.[20] Without this extra control over the behavior of the child *qua* adult, the whole point of propagating one's self, under the rubric of preserving one's self beyond one's self, would be lost. Thus, all the tensions of the bourgeois family (the poor have nothing to fear of them) are brought into existence with the creation of monetary wealth. With money, possessions as well as children live beyond one's self and embody one (more or less) beyond the grave.

But these two means of extending identity into quasi-immortality must be coordinated to function properly. For the family capital, having a profligate child can be worse than having no children at all! But in the process of making possessions and children match, the father's manipulation of the potential inheritance becomes a means of power and control over the natural freedom of the child. True, the parent must assure the bodily existence of every child, but with a large fortune the distance between a subsistence share and a full share could be astronomical.

Here we get material for the endless novels, plays, newspaper stories and courtroom proceedings of the bourgeoisie. The combinations are inexhaustible, though the plot remains the same: the struggle between control and freedom, age against youth, life versus death, identity and difference—all end in the *denouement*, "Who gets the money?"

Interest and Inheritance add their definite flavor to the natural law injunction to "Appropriate, Appropriate!" Once the overplus can be transformed into money, a new realm begins. An unbounded accumulation of quasi-eternal entities becomes the "unintended consequence" of Adam's child's roving. But once the process begins, it has an irreversible direction: the increasing disproportion of possessions ignites a chronic state of war that necessitates a compact among those who find it in their interest to protect and preserve their property. Money, indeed, is the Mother of civil government.

Thus, we end our Lockean reconstruction of the origin of money. If this account is correct, then we can see why Locke was so sure of the "axioms" of his *Further Considerations.* In conclusion, let us review them in turn.

- "Silver is the instrument and measure of commerce": for money must have a substantial element and must be a mixed mode;
- "Silver has a role in commerce because it has intrinsic value": for fancy and later common consent gave it a value dependent on its intrinsic character (Stage A);
- "Common consent made silver universal barter": for a law of fashion or opinion formed a use for silver as universal equivalent that was not based on any natural or civil law, yet the enforcement powers of that law are enormous (Stage B).

Finally, with our analysis of Stage C, we can understand the "sanctity" in which Locke held money, as well as the reason why he was anxious to see that it not be made the object of continual state intervention and manipulation. The accumulation process and the state are preconditioned on the monetary system; should it break down, so will they. Mistakes with money are fatal.

Let us return now for a moment to our starting point: the clipped crown of silver. The coin bears the physical markings of the struggle that brought the state into existence. See the almost faded royal impressions (caused by innumerable baggings). Feel the uneven edge (made by some awkward clipper).

John Locke saw and felt in these absences the sure sign of another presence in the world.

Postface

John Locke, *the* Philosopher
of Primitive Accumulation

*[Locke] even demonstrated ... that the bourgeois way of thinking is the
normal human way of thinking,*
Karl Marx, *A Contribution to the Critique of Political Economy.*

John Locke is the most famous philosopher born and raised in the vicinity
of Bristol. His birthplace was Wrington, Somerset about 12 miles from
Bristol on August 29, 1632 and he was brought up in the market town of
Pensford, about 7 miles south of Bristol. He was the scion of a West Country
lawyer and Puritan, who fought for the Parliament in the Civil War. Before
he went to Westminster School in London at age fourteen he undoubtedly
had exposure to the economic winds that were blowing across the Atlantic
(both from the west—British America, and from the south—West Africa).
For after all, Bristol and West Country merchants were a major source of
investment for the sugar, tobacco, slave and cod fishing trades in the early
seventeenth century (Horsby 2005: 28–30).

Aside from being a Bristol "home boy," Locke is also important for our
investigation of the commons. For his philosophy has been deeply impli-
cated in the enclosure of two of humanity's most important commons: the
North American Indigenous people's commons and the commons of intellectual production. In this book, I have shown the relationship between
Locke's philosophy and these two enclosures, which justified my claim that
this local wizard was indeed *the* philosopher of primitive accumulation.

In passing, I should point out that Locke is also not only the main intellectual founder of liberalism, but also of *neo*liberalism, the "ruling idea"
of the ruling class of today. I wrote the first edition of my book on Locke,
Clipped Coins, Abused Words and Civil Government, in Nigeria at the time of
nation-wide debates and discussions, riots and demonstrations, concerning
the imposition of structural adjustment programs (the political-economic

vehicles of neoliberalism) on the Nigerian people. So for me, the book is a critique of primitive neoliberalism (which, as we have seen, is not so different from its present version!)

In order to carry out my plan, a word should be said about the idea of primitive or "original" accumulation. The classical discussion of primitive accumulation is the last part of Karl Marx's *Capital*, Vol. 1. Like all the parts of *Capital*, it is a critique of an important idea of the political economy of Marx's day. As Marx points out in this chapter, capital presents itself to the mind as a seamless, hermetic system moving in a never-ending circle where each node presupposes another … forever. If we are to "get out" of the circle, we must first conceptualize an end to it, but to do this we must be able to conceptualize its beginning. The ultimate revolutionary vision of "the expropriation of a few usurpers by the mass of the people" requires rethinking primitive accumulation, which he describes as "the historic process of divorcing the producer from the means of production … And this history, the history of [workers'] expropriation is written in the annals of mankind in the letters of blood and fire" (Marx 1976: 874–875).

Marx's critique of political economy with respect to "so-called primitive accumulation" is not directed to the concept (which is a logical necessity for revolutionary thought and action) but toward the "nursery tale" or "theological anecdote" told of it (like original sin arising from Adam biting an apple from the tree of knowledge of good and evil). Marx critically substitutes a narrative of blood and fire for the euphemistic nursery tale of the industrious capitalist ant and the shiftless worker grasshopper. But Marx was being a bit too hasty and unhistorical here in his anxiety to get on with the job of revealing the "secret" of primitive accumulation that he does in the last sentence of the book:

> The only thing that interests us is the secret discovered in the New World by the political economy of the Old World, and loudly proclaimed by it: that the capitalist mode of production and accumulation, and therefore capitalist private property as well, have for their fundamental condition the annihilation of that private property which rests on the labour of the individual himself; in other words, the expropriation of the worker.
>
> (Marx 1976: 940)

Marx references Adam Smith's *Wealth of Nations* and the abhorrent Adolph Thiers' *De la Propriété* and that is that. However, there is a long and complex history of reflection on the origin of what was to be called in the nineteenth century "capitalism" that Marx might have reserved for another time and place (although he did not).[1]

Yet not all discussions of the presupposition and origins of capitalist accumulation were simply and blatantly "nursery tales." In fact, John Locke's philosophy as expressed in the *Two Treatises on Government* and *Essay Concerning Human Understanding* is a study of the origins of the accumulation of money, land, ideas and knowledge. These origins have as their common base *labor* that Locke ironically turns from the subject to the object of the accumulation process.

In this book, I argue that Locke should be considered *the* philosopher of primitive accumulation. This effort will have a semantically anachronistic character since Locke, of course, never uses the term, "primitive accumulation." But he was clearly concerned with the question: how can the accumulation process of land and ideas begin? As far as the accumulation of land is concerned, he was concerned with the practical aspects of colonization (a process that Marx believed revealed the "secret of primitive accumulation," which was "discovered in the New World by the political economy of the Old World" long before Wakefield in the nineteenth century). As far as ideas and words are concerned, Locke was concerned to create a notion of property in ideas and to defend an early version of copyright of texts (King 1971: 202–209).

The interplay of these original accumulations of land and ideas torn from the commons of the earth and mind lay the foundation of a self-sustaining (but always conflictual) process of accumulation.

THE ORIGIN OF PROPERTY IN LAND AND MONEY

At first glance, Locke's version of primitive accumulation of land can be characterized as a variant of Thier's "nursery tale." Locke divides humanity between the "rational and industrious" and the "quarrelsome and contentious." God was apparently (and inscrutably) inconsistent with respect to land, since, though he gave the land as a common to all, he was also committed to have the former own the earth and the latter to be their landless servants: "[God] gave [the world] for the use of the industrious and rational (and labor was to be his title to it); not to the fancy and covetousness of the quarrelsome and contentious" (Locke 1823g: II, 34).

According to a standard account, Locke is deploying in this passage the Puritan ideology concerning the "sanctity" and "dignity" of labor. It was an important addition to the conceptual armory of enclosure and expropriation. But he was also extending the Cartesian *cogito* into the political and legal sphere. Locke transforms Descartes' performative deduction of the self (by the very act of thinking of myself, I create myself) into a performative deduction for the creation of my property: "I labor on X, therefore X is part of me."

It is a clever argumentative move that has taken center stage in the assessment of Locke's influence on the development of property and on the historical course on primitive accumulation. But Locke was a much more sober and precise a thinker of primitive accumulation than the remaining "the nursery tale" aura in his writing on the topic suggests. He introduces two caveats to the tale that are often passed over in silence by commentators.

First, he distinguishes between the commons in America and "the commons in England, or any other country, where there is plenty of people under government, who have money and commerce." The common land in England cannot be treated like the common land in America. In England, "no one can inclose or appropriate any part, without the consent of all his fellow-commoners" for two logical reasons: mereological—"after such inclosure, [the part of the land remaining in common] would not be as good to the rest of the commoners, on the whole as when they could all make use of the *whole*"—and quantificational—"though [the English commons] be common to *some* men, it is not so to *all* mankind " (my italics).

Together these two reasons create a fundamental distinction in the notion of the commons and of "primitive accumulation." One kind of primitive accumulation involving common land requires the consent of the commoners (in England) while the other does not (in America). This consent is not immediately forthcoming in England because there is often an advantage in *using the whole*. The commons in America was altogether different because there were "plenty of people living under governments with money and commerce." America was a universal common that was open to settlement by all of humanity, without the consent of the present inhabitants. Title to land was given by "inclosure" and agricultural labor (not hunting and gathering!) that would provide for the subsistence of the possessor.

But there was the rub; although Locke's labor theory of property justified in an influential way the course of primitive accumulation in the British Americas, the land that could be appropriated was limited by subsistence and the ancient prohibition on spoilage:

> if either the grass of his inclosure rotted on the ground, or the fruit of his planting perished without gathering, and laying up, this part of the earth, not withstanding his inclosure, was still to be looked upon as waste, and might be the possession of any other.
>
> (Locke 1823g: II, 38)

This is a symmetric argument, however, since if a statement applies to all, then it applies to some. If the English, according to Locke's logic, are simply subsuming their actions under a universal maxim, then, in reply and equally logically, so can the American Indians. The English are welcome (according to this logic) to go to the Americas to gain their subsistence, but who would accept this invitation but those who could not subsist in England? Moreover, such poor beings would not be able to claim, under Locke's labor theory of property title, more than a miniscule part of the American land. Only if the English could logically break out of the subsistence trough, would the Lockean doctrine be of any use as the justification for the primitive accumulation of American land.

This is where Locke's second caveat is important and shows us that Locke was not providing a simple "nursery tale" account of primitive accumulation. Labor (=rationality+industriousness) is not enough to initiate a process of accumulation. It is only enough to provide for subsistence. Hence, up until this point in his origin story, Locke could be considered the philosopher of the subsistence. Money is the *deus ex machina* that makes it possible to put the "accumulation" in "primitive accumulation." Locke's conceptual addition of money to labor creates the equation that will set the stage for the accumulation process. Money, not labor, is what creates the stimulus for surplus labor and hence accumulation. As Locke noted:

> Thus in the beginning all the world was America, and more so than that is now; for no such thing as money was any where known. Find out

something that hath the use and value of money amongst his neighbors, you shall see the same man will begin presently to enlarge his possessions.

(Locke 1823g: II, 49)

Thus, money is the real "secret" of primitive accumulation for Locke, since it (not labor alone) makes accumulation (hence capital) possible. In effect, the Lockean ideology of labor became something of a smoke screen for the real source of the accumulation process. In this, Locke is not unique. In the great seventeenth- and early eighteenth-century outpouring of sermons, judicial opinions, newspaper editorials justifying English land grabbing in the Americas that Barbara Arneil reviews in her *John Locke and America*, the key issue is always labor, agricultural labor, to be precise (Arneil 1996: 169–187). Their lament being, "we" (the English) labor on the land, "they" (the American Indians) simply live off it.

"Peopling" America with subsistence farmers was not the intention of colonization supporters. Their aim, for the most part, was to turn the "wastes" of America into "true original" zones of money and commerce that would justify the expansion of "productive" land and the investment (of both money and workers). Therefore, as Locke incisively recognized, there was a logical need for money that would set the conditions for surplus labor (and mere barter with neighboring colonists or Indians for necessities was not enough). His originality was to see past the smoke screen of labor into *terra firma* of money, the logical element of primitive accumulation. If American land was not linked to money, title to it would mean nothing. (This maxim echoes down to this day in the so-called sub-prime mortgage crisis.)

Indeed, Locke conceived of a "state of money" as a transition from the state of nature to the formation of civil society. This state of money had three stages and was based not on either natural law or civil law, but on "secret and tacit consent" and "the law or opinion or fashion." As I explained in my book, the three stages are as follows:

Stage A: The first exchanges were inadvertent; pleased with the color of gold or silver or the sparkling of a diamond, a man exchanges perishable goods for them.

Stage B: Slowly there is a growing "mutual consent" or "tacit agreement" to take gold, silver or diamond as payment in general.

Stage C: An impulse to accumulation takes shape as some parts of the population "enlarge their possessions" while others, of course, find theirs diminished.[2]

Stage C is a one of endemic class struggle that eventually led the propertied to gather together to create the laws, magistrates and police of civil society to defend their "enlarged possessions." Money, along with the introduction of Interest and Inheritance, amplified and eternalized differences between the "industrious and rational" versus "quarrelsome and contentious" of one generation to future ones. Indeed, Interest and Inheritance amplified and eternalized class war itself, since one can inherit debt as well as wealth!

The charging of interest makes clear that *money is not a common good* that is to be used by the community, that is, if you are not using your money, then the fellow member of the community who has need of it should have it without cost (like a tool that one borrows from a neighbor which is to be returned, but without payment of a rental fee). The Hebrew and later Christian prohibitions on interest were clearly intended to create and protect a common of money (or commonwealth) for the use of the community (as were the Jubilees that periodically canceled debts) and to discourage the excessive "enlargement of possessions." Locke clearly defended Interest as a part of his general critique of commons (in this case, the commons of money) and as a tool for inclosure as well.

Inheritance is another source of accumulation directed against the common. For why shouldn't the accumulated money a person owned and used in life not become part of the common wealth on his/her death? As Locke asks, when a father dies, "why does [his property] not return to the common stock of mankind?" This question is especially telling when capital still existed largely in family capital units:

In inter-family inheritance lies the immortality of property: though inheritance is supposed to preserve the descendants, it also preserves the property (if it is money, and can be preserved). This makes possible an inter-generational accumulation process where the function of the descendants is to preserve the property not vice versa. Property loses its status as continuously re-affirmed, laboriously acquired, decomposing thing when it becomes money: it becomes that which continues beyond death, to such a point that the family capital will go on to embody the family.[3]

Locke's contribution, then, to the discussion of primitive accumulation was the recognition that without money, there cannot be accumulation (primitive or otherwise). The paths he took to this insight, for example, through the anti-spoilage prohibitions of Leviticus, are often uncomfortably bizarre for neoliberal commentators today. But the logic is impeccable. The state of money is a crucial preliminary for the formation of civil society, otherwise one is stuck with imputing to humanity an innate sociality or an innate hostility, and Locke, as we shall see, was vitally interested in rejecting any innate ideas or passions.

ENCLOSING THE COMMON OF IDEAS

The intellectual territory of Locke's labor theory of land ownership has been the object of a huge political and scholarly discussion that goes down to this day. My contribution to it has been simply to point out that Locke's introduction of money into the analysis of primitive accumulation of land is not an idiosyncratic move, it is, rather, an essential logical presupposition of primitive accumulation. But there was another aspect of the accumulation process that Locke was also involved in that is just as crucial as that of land today—the accumulation of capital on the basis of the production of ideas and knowledge. This too has been another aspect of Locke's impact on contemporary politics. Selling "intellectual property" as a major source of capital accumulation and imposing copyright and patent requirements in all the major international "trade agreements" (NAFTA, WTO and dozens of SAPs) in the last twenty years is an important part of the neoliberal program. Locke set up the intellectual framework for the creation of "intellectual property" although, as we have seen, he was not yet able to found the accumulation of capital on the property claims to ideas and knowledge.

Just as with the barriers against usury (i.e., the commodification of money), the barriers against commodification of ideas and knowledge began to tumble with the rise of capitalism in the sixteenth century. As money became again the universal mediator, a new relation between ideas and knowledge and the commodity form was inevitably posed and the ancient Sophists (who demanded a monetary exchange between the owners of ideas and knowledge and those who would use them) were given a new hearing. Perhaps the most decisive legal sign of this change was the Statute of Queen Anne (8 Anne c. 21) of 1710 that is often dubbed the first true copyright law in history. The Statute gave copyright to authors in Britain for a period of at most twenty-eight years. It is no surprise that this law was crafted under a new discourse on property and thought that was decisively influenced by John Locke. The impact of John Locke's "labor theory of property" in his *Second Treatise on Civil Government* on modern concepts of property has been widely noted by historians of economics and politics. Less well known was how Locke's work in the *Essay Concerning Human Understanding* meshed with his views on property to challenge the Platonic separation between knowledge and property. For Locke argued for two distinctly anti-Platonic positions: (1) the non-existence of innate ideas; and (2) thought was a labor process.

The animus behind Locke's rejection of the doctrine of innate ideas (which constitute the common of thought, since they are available to all equally) lay in his suspicion that the doctrine tended to make people lazy and "collectively inclined" in intellectual matters. "If everyone believes X from birth, then so should I, even if the only evidence I have is the others' beliefs," is a kind of reasoning Locke rejected. In trying to explain why there was such a long adherence to the existence of innate ideas from Plato to Leibniz, Locke wrote:

> When men have found some general propositions that could not be doubted of as soon as understood, it was, I know, a short and easy way to conclude them innate. This being once received, it eased the lazy from the pains of search, and stopped the inquiry of the doubtful concerning all that one once styled innate. And it was of no small advantage to those who affected to be masters and teachers, to make this the principle of principles—*that principles must not be questioned*.
>
> (Locke 1823a: 116, I, iii, 25)

Or, as A.C. Fraser, his editor glossed this passage: "[Locke] protests the indolence which thus blindly reposes on the opinions of the community, and which grudges the private judgment by which each man is detached from the community and becomes *himself*" (Locke 1959: II, 116, n. 1).

Locke not only hoped to enclose humans from the common of ideas and knowledge, he also developed the view that thought was labor (or it was worthless). This view was diametrically opposed to Plato's or Aristotle's who both categorized thought as an activity that is an end in itself. As I wrote in the Conclusion to *Clipped Coins*:

> For Locke, real thought is laborious: a hard, time-bound process, which is a means to something beyond itself. We do not think, according to Locke, for the pleasure of thinking; rather thinking is the work we must do to arrive at pleasure. Thought has no life of its own, it is suspicious of images and forms, beauty and mimesis. Here we find the bourgeois mentality at its most self-reflexive: thought too must labor to advantage, otherwise it is not thought.

Instead of collective products of thought, internally available with no labor, Locke only recognized products of thought as being an individual's property, just as the physical labor in gathering acorns from the common ground transformed them into the gatherer's private property. As Mark Rose pointed out in his essay on the genealogy of modern authorship, Locke's labor theory of property discourse when "extended into the realm of literary production ... with its concern for origins and first proprietors, blended readily with the aesthetic discourse of originality" (Rose 1994: 30). Locke's conception of property and thought was a remarkable intervention in the field and justified the claim that the author of a text, the inventor of the design for a machine, the creator of a theory are proprietors.

Locke, however, was not involved in earning a living from the book trade (the way Hume was later to be). But he was familiar with the international book trade, especially due to his long stay (in exile) in Holland. His main writing on the trade was his "Observations on the Censorship" in 1694, which is a list of objections to the "Act for preventing abuses in printing seditious, treasonable, and unlicensed Books and Pamphlets, and for regulating Printing and Printing-Presses" (King 1971: 202–209). Locke was extremely critical of the Act and was probably a force behind its eventual demise in 1694 (at the very time of his work on his monetary pamphlets). In the conclusion of his observations, Locke refers to property in texts in the following words:

That any person or company should have patents for the sole printing of ancient authors is very unreasonable and injurious to learning; and for those who purchase copies from authors that now live and write, it may be reasonable to limit their property to a certain number of years after the death of the author, or the first printing of the book, as, suppose, fifty or seventy years. This I am sure, it is very absurd and ridiculous that any one now living should pretend to have a propriety in, or a power to dispose of the propriety of any copy or writings of authors who lived before printing was known or used in Europe.

(King 1971: 208–209)

Locke is here laying down a common of texts, a permissible enclosure, and something of a no man's land. Texts of authors from ancient times to the fifteenth century are definitely part of the common of texts, while property in texts would be limited to fifty or seventy years after the death of the author or the printing of the book. There is a bit of laxness here concerning private property, whereas the claims of the commons are clear: Tully is in the commons, Shakespeare's plays are in the no man's land (after all, they were written and produced more than seventy years before 1694 and Shakespeare himself died in 1616).

In the sixteen years between the demise of the so-called Printing (or Censorship) Act in 1694 and the Statute of Anne of 1710, Locke's framework became the basis for the claims of those who wish to totally commodify intellectual life. Indeed, the Statute of Anne of 1710 was something of a compromise between the full blown application of "freehold" or "full ownership" notions of property to texts, inventions and theories and the older Platonic "commonist" conception of ideas that rejected property claims and payments for the use of things that we were all born with and merely had to be stimulated to remember (as Socrates did for the slave boy in the *Meno*).

This compromise was decisively tested in the case of Donaldson versus Becket that was tried before the House of Lords in 1774. It was a celebrated and widely followed case, even among schoolboys. As Rose observes:

Having been reprimanded for stealing an old woman's gingerbread cakes baked in the form of letters, a cheeky schoolboy was supposed to have defended himself [in 1774] by explaining that "the [House of Lords] had lately determined that lettered Property was common."

(Rose 1994: 24)

The London booksellers, represented by Thomas Becket, brought Alexander Donaldson to court because the latter published a cheap reprint of James Thomson's *The Seasons*, a work composed more than twenty-eight years before. Becket and his supporters claimed that copyright was "a common law right" and hence should be perpetual. The House of Lords decisively rejected this claim and their decision has stuck for almost three centuries. But they did not entirely reject the property claims of the author:

> ... the Lords' decision did not touch the basic contention that the author had a property in the product of his labour. Neither the representation of the author as a proprietor nor the representation of the literary work as an object of the property was discredited.
>
> (Rose 1994: 45)

We might say that the complete victory of Locke's enclosure of the commons of ideas and knowledge is still in doubt and as is the enclosure of the common of land. These enclosures are tremendously contested throughout the planet. One need only see that the anti-Lockean commoners of the present are rejecting the enclosure of both the earthy as well as the airy commons.

Notes

INTRODUCTION TO THE NEW EDITION

1. I owe a debt of gratitude to Nicholas Beuret, David Harvie, Bue Rubner Hansen, Eoin O'Cearnaigh and George Caffentzis for commenting on drafts of this essay. Thanks also to Arlen Austin and Camille Barbagallo. An earlier version was published as "Cogito Ergo Habo," in C. Barbagallo, N. Beuret and D. Harvie (Eds.), *Commoning with George Caffentzis and Silvia Federici* (London: Pluto Press, 2019).

2. For an overview of Caffentzis' work in the critique of political economy, see the collections *In Letters of Blood and Fire: Work, Machines and the Crisis of Capitalism* (Oakland, CA: PM Press, 2013); and *No Blood for Oil: Essays on Energy, Class Struggle and War 1998–2016* (New York: Autonomedia, 2017).

3. The Locke literature has only very recently begun to focus on this debate in earnest. See, for instance, Daniel Carey, "Locke's Species: Money and Philosophy in the 1690s" (2013); Douglas Casson, "John Locke, Clipped Coins, and the Unstable Currency of Reason" (2016); and Patrick Kelly, "'Monkey' Business: Locke's 'College' Correspondence and the Adoption of the Plan for the Great Recoinage of 1696" (2009). Rather outrageously, this literature rarely cites Caffentzis' pioneering work.

4. I draw here on a series of studies of the relationship between accumulation and the concept of waste in Locke. See, in particular, Onur Ulas Ince (2011), Mark Neocleous (2011), Jesse Goldstein (2013) and Ellen Meiksins Wood (2002; 2012).

5. This is a point made especially clearly in Goldstein (2013). On the criminalization of "idleness," see Duff (2017).

6. John Locke writes: "for though I may kill a thief that sets on me in the highway, yet I may not (which seems less) take away his money, and let him go: this would be robbery on my side" Locke 1823g: II, 182. The protection of property seems to trump human life here.

7. On common law and the concrete person, see also "On the Scottish Origin of Civilization," Chapter 1 in Caffentzis' *Civilizing Money: Hume, His Monetary Project and the Scottish Enlightenment* (2021).

8. Marx makes an analogous claim in *Capital, Volume 1* where he argues that in order for commodities to be exchanged

> their guardians must place themselves in relation to one another as persons whose will resides in those objects, and must behave in such a way that each

does not appropriate the commodity of the other, and alienate his own, except through an act to which both parties consent. The guardians must therefore recognise each other as owners of property.

(Marx 1976: 178)

9. I owe the methodological insight in part to Jonathan Martineau, "Ellen M. Wood and the Social History of Political Theory," paper delivered to Historical Materialism Conference, London, November 2016.

10. The phrase "deep coherence" is used by Caffentzis to refer to the relation of philosophy and money in Berkeley's work but it applies equally to his reading of Locke. See Caffentzis (2000: 3).

11. The claims made here are largely reproduced from Paul Rekret and Simon Choat, "From Political Topographies to Political Logics: Post-Marxism and Historicity," (2016). It deserves mentioning that Sohn-Rethel's claim here is echoed by Silvia Federici, who has suggested understanding the Cartesian institution of an ontological division between the mental and the physical domains along with the mechanical conception of the body it implies, in terms of the suppression of pre-capitalist social relations. From this perspective, the central accomplishment of the age of reason entailed posing the body as intelligible and thus, as an object that could be subordinated to uniform and predictable modes of behavior (see Federici 2004: 138–155).

INTRODUCTION

1. For the "paradox," cf. Edmund Whittaker (1940: 652) and Douglas Vickers (1959: Chapter 4). For a classic discussion of the debate surrounding the recoinage legislation, see Karl Marx (1970: 76–82). Marx sums up Locke's contribution in the following way:

John Locke, who championed the new bourgeoisie in every way—he took the side of the manufacturers against the working classes and the paupers, the merchants against the old-fashioned usurers, the financial aristocracy against governments that were in debt; he even demonstrated in a separate work that the bourgeois way of thinking is the normal way of thinking—took up Lowndes' challenge. John Locke won the day and money borrowed in guineas containing 10 to 14 shillings was repaid in guineas of 20 shillings. Sir James Steuart gives the following ironical summary of this operation: "the state gained considerably upon the score of taxes, as well as the creditors upon their capitals and interest; and the nation, which was the principal loser," was pleased; because their standard was not debased.

(Marx 1970: 78)

For a discussion of the financial side of King William's War, cf. P.G.M. Dickson and J.G. Sperling, "War Finance, 1689–1714" (1970: 284) and the "streetwise" article by D.W. Jones (1972); Horwitz's *Parliament, Policy and Politics in the*

Reign of William III (1977) is an almost day-by-day description of the monetary crisis of 1695.

2. All references to Locke are from *The Works of John Locke in Ten Volumes* (London: 1823), reprinted by Scientia Verlag Aalen Germany in 1963. *The Essay Concerning Human Understanding* is in Vols. 1–3; the *Letters Concerning Toleration* are in Vol. 6; *Some Thoughts Concerning Education* is in Vol. 9; *Considerations, Further Considerations* and the *Two Treatises of Government* are in Vol. 5; *Fundamental Constitutions (of the Carolinas)* and *The Whole History of Navigation from its Original to this Time (1704)*, prefixed to Churchill's *Collection of Voyages* are in Vol. 10. Reference to the *Essay* is by book, chapter and section; reference to the *Two Treatises* is by book and section; reference to *Some Thoughts* is by section number; however, reference to the other works cited above will be by page number in the mentioned volumes of the *Works*. This is an obscure edition, but consider that, as I write, it is exactly 300 years since Oxford expelled Locke from his Studentship in 1684, and they have only begun to make amends by sponsoring a definitive scholarly edition of his works, beginning with Peter H. Nidditch's 1975 edition of the *Essay*; perhaps they will finish by the 300th anniversary of Locke's death in 2004.

It was inevitable that Oxford's rival would be the publisher of Peter Laslett's definitive scholarly edition of the *Two Treatises*, rev. edn (Cambridge: Cambridge University Press, 1967) and that we would find in Laslett's "Introduction" a passage of the following sort:

> It is ugly to see those who sat with him at table (in Christ Church) teaching. So little can Oxford and the House justly claim him as their own that he was a power over the whole learned world before they would recognize him.
>
> (Laslett 1963: 24)

Laslett is a Fellow of Trinity College.

3. Locke's famous obsession with anonymity is discussed in Maurice Cranston's biography, *John Locke* (1957). For example, he was quite willing to break with life-long friends (like Tyrrell and Limborch), who compromised his anonymity. The publication of the *Two Treatises* was the most problematic and Locke had quite justified fears concerning his authorship.

Laslett notes two such fears: fear of repression and fear of criticism. Locke's fear of repression was quite real, as Laslett notes:

> [W]hen [Locke] returned in 1689 and made up his mind to publish what he had written, it was not to a country whose political future seemed stable. The return of James II was a possibility throughout the 1690s: if he had returned, it would have meant exile for Locke, and perhaps, he must have argued, a harder fate for the known writer of this book. His own experience and the treatment of his friends and associates made it clear to him that a Catholic Stuart monarch would not hesitate to use anything found in his private papers against him.
>
> (Laslett 1963: 66)

Locke's purported "fear of criticism," however, is a bit far-fetched. Laslett again:

> But there may be another reason, much more interesting for political thinking and for its relation with philosophy. It is possible that Locke was unwilling to let it be known that the same man who wrote the *Essay Concerning Human Understanding* also wrote *Two Treatises of Government* because he was quite well aware that it was no simple matter to reconcile their doctrines. We have described a man who disliked criticism and shrank from controversy. There can be no doubt that he would have had to face both of these things if his contemporaries had been invited to compare the assumptions of his theory of knowledge with the assumptions of his political principles.
>
> (Laslett 1963: 66)

This example of academic *realpolitik* requires some response. First, Locke—like most non-masochists—did not bask in criticism and did feel the need to spend most of his last years replying to criticism both in a voluminous correspondence and in five published works between 1695–1699. Second, the apparent "inconsistencies" and "lack of connecting links" between the *Essay* and the *Two Treatises* that Laslett makes much of (and with which we will deal in detail) might be difficult to resolve. But should we conclude that Locke, who gestated both these works for almost two decades, could not even attempt to resolve them? Third, if that is Laslett's conclusion, one must assume a cynicism on Locke's part that rivals Iago's, and that Laslett's intensity of "suspicion" would put any Marxist to shame.

My methodological premise, however, is to assume that Locke was not a "thinker of difference" and that he did try to think consistently throughout the totality of his works. This principle of charity should especially be applied to authors of this period, even to "champions of the new bourgeoisie," given the repressive semantic condition of the time, which Laslett dismisses as less interesting to us. Indeed, the history of the relation of philosophical writing to political repression is a chapter of thought that is only beginning to be read again.

This repression had a definite legal character, for during the period Locke published his main texts, the Licencing Act was in force. In *The English Book Trade*, Marjorie Plant writes:

> The Licencing Act of (1662) provided that no book should for the future be printed unless it had been duly licenced by the appropriate authority ... Owing to the ill-feeling aroused by the Act it was allowed to lapse after three years, but it was renewed by James II in 1685 for a period of seven years, after which it was extended for one year more. This was the end of the attempt of complete state control.
>
> (Plant 1974: 144)

This Act not only dealt with books but with their printers as well, for example, it put a restriction on the number of printers allowed to operate in England as well as geographical restrictions on the location of printing plants, mostly London, probably for the convenience of surveillance.

Further, the general atmosphere of pseudonymity and anonymity penetrated into the skin of all authors of the period. So much so that the "material conditions" of writing became part of the form and content of the texts, in eternal condemnation of "formalist criticism." As Maximillian E. Novak's "Introduction" put it: "to ignore the concept of disguise in the writings of the Restoration and the eighteenth century is to disregard one of the distinguishing aspects of the age" (Novak 1977: 6). Novak mentions that "Anthony Collins (an intimate of Locke's last days), following Shaftesbury, maintained that irony was the inevitable product of repression—that through irony the unspeakable might be spoken" (Novak 1977: 6) Thus, Defoe, who was imprisoned for his writings and became a master of literary disguise, wrote ironically in *A Letter to Mr. Bisset*: "This Sir is an age of Plot and Deceit, of Contradiction and Paradox … It is very hard under all these Masks, to see the true Countenance of a Man" (Defoe 1710: 2). Let us not forget that Defoe worked as a spy for a number of employers during our period.

Certainly, these self-reflexive devices of camouflage can become tiresome and degenerate into a play at playing, a mirror of mirrors, ad nauseam more than ad infinitum. Especially when the need for them disappears, as we see in Dr. Johnson's excuses:

> The seeming vanity with which I have sometimes spoken of myself, would perhaps require an apology, were it not extenuated by the example of those who have published essays before me, and by the privilege which every nameless writer has hitherto been allowed. "A mask," says Castiglione, "confers a right of acting and speaking with less restraint, even when the wearer happens to be known."
>
> (Johnson 1969: 5, 317)

Locke was not as nonchalant as Johnson was concerning identity, for the conditions of authorship and repression began to change in the first decades of the eighteenth century. So that a disgust for a degenerate masquerade led to monsters of sincerity like Rousseau.

However, the authors caught in the height of this period's semantic repression, and who acted like *dei abscondi* with respect to their works, do cause us serious interpretational problems. Christopher Hill—who is familiar with a more recent period of semantic repression—sums up its implications for Milton, as well as Locke and Newton:

> Newton and Locke, who shared many of Milton's secret heresies and tensions, were of a younger generation, and lived on into the world of triumphant Whiggery. But they still, like Milton, censored themselves before publication. Milton concealed his views so successfully that in the eighteenth and nineteenth centuries he came to be regarded as the orthodox Puritan poet.

Newton—secret anti-Trinitarian and millenarian—was seen by Blake as the personification of rational science; Locke—anti-Trinitarian and millenarian, Arminian and mortalist—as the personification of rational philosophy. Against them Blake looked upon Milton as a potential ally. But in fact all these were furtively attracted by many of the ideas of the radical underground which were not to survive the triumph of "Newtonian" science and "Lockean" philosophy and politics. There are many ironies here to be incorporated in the history of English popular culture when it comes to be written.

(Hill 1977: 465)

Although, we must not assume, as Hill occasionally does, that those who "borrow" thoughts feel indebted to or even sympathetic to the "lenders."

We may conclude these initial reflections on Locke's publishing career by saying (with the late Michel Foucault in "What is an Author?" [Foucault 2000]) that the "author-function" between Locke's time and the time of Hume changed dramatically. We cannot apply the same methods to the ascetic, nervous and paranoiac Locke that we apply to the age of "the philosophers of the double chin." The Lockean "author-function" has many more variables and non-linearities than the Humean one; but we cannot, on that account, say with Laslett that no such function exists.

1. CLIPPED COINS

1. On Henry Morgan, see George Clark, *The Later Stuarts 1660–1714* (1955), 238–239. For a discussion of piracy as part of the "hidden" continuity of "English class struggle," see Peter Linebaugh's "All the Atlantic Mountains Shook" (1982). Linebaugh writes:

    Among the "lobster backs" of the New Model Army that captured Jamaica there were radicals. Some of these stayed on, joining the intensely egalitarian (and cruel) buccaneers who had established among themselves and the areas they influenced like Tortuga, Northern Hispaniola, and the Mosquito Coast (Nicaragua), an autonomous and mutualist tradition. After Henry Morgan sold out to work for Charles II and the Duke of York, the zone of these freebooters moved north and east to the Carolinas and the Bahamas. Until the cycle of repression initiated by Walpole in the early years of his administration put an end to them, the men and women (Mary Read, Ann Bonney) who sailed "Under the Banner of King Death" created a social existence that was, as Marcus Rediker has convincingly shown, collectivist, egalitarian, anti-authoritarian, comparing itself to Robin Hood, and venerating the memory of the Revolution. Christopher Hill hears echoes of Milton and Winstanley in Defoe's *A General History ... of the Most Notorious Pyrates* (1724) which besides emitting these sounds was dead-set against the slave-trade.

Thus, the defeated, the victims, Irish tories, and Scottish covenanters, Quakers, sectaries, Ranters, seekers and radicals—an antagonistic conglomeration of widely different linguistic, geographic and cultural origin—found themselves sharing an experience of valiant resistance to the English Adventurers and Grandees who had flung them to the edge of the map. There they shared an experience of survival in a strange ecology, a new kind of cooperation on the plantation, as well as the possibility of creating a life where, in Winstanley's words "There shall be no Tyrant Kings, Lords of Manors, Tything Priests, oppressing Lawyers, exacting Landlords, nor any such like pricking bryar in all this holy Mountain of the Lord God our Righteousness and Peace."

(Linebaugh 1982: 104)

I think that it was the combination of necessary violence, egalitarian adventure, absence of prolonged ideological discourse, and abounding hope which attracted Jack Kerouac and William Burroughs to this period.

2. William S. Jevons, in *Money and the Mechanism of Exchange* (1926), points out that "the intermixture of coinages of different states" was quite common in England until the mid-nineteenth century, and that even by the end of the nineteenth century:

> There are many half-civilized nations which have no national coinage, but employ the coins which happen to reach them in the course of trade. On the West Coast of Africa the Spanish dollar is the best known coin, but Danish, French, or Dutch coins also circulate. In several of the South American states the currency is in a state of complete confusion, consisting of a mixture of American eagles, gold doubloons, silver dollars, English sovereigns, piastres, etc., together sometimes with several different issues of coinage of the South American states variously depreciated. Even in British possessions we find the same state of things ... but it should be added that in most cases the Spanish dollar is treated as the standard of value, and other coins are quoted in terms of it.

(Jevons 1926: 92)

3. It is interesting to note that both Locke and Lowndes, his theoretical opponent, were both simultaneously suspicious of the Bank of England and yet actively involved in its creation. Of course, the immediate cause that drove them on to support the bank was "war finance" (cf. Horwitz 1977: 73) but there were deeper reasons. Georg Simmel's analysis of the form of money in *The Philosophy of Money* would see the formation of the bank as a decisive moment in a large-scale "historical development of money from substance to function":

> The broad cultural ramifications of the nature and significance of money are to be seen in the movements that lead money towards its pure concept and away from its attachment to particular substances—even though it never attains the goal that determines its course of development. Thus, money is

involved in the general development which in every domain of life and in every sense strives to dissolve substance into free-floating processes.

(Simmel 1978: 168)

Marx's view of the founding of the Bank differs from Simmel's perspective. He sees it as a moment in the progressive "alienation of the state":

> The Bank of England began by lending its money to the government at 8 per cent; at the same time it was empowered by Parliament to coin money out of the same capital, by lending it a second time to the public in the form of bank-notes. It was allowed to use these notes for discounting bills, making advances on commodities and buying the precious metals. It was not long before this credit-money, created by the bank itself, became the coin in which the latter made its loans to the state, and paid, on behalf of the state, the interest on the public debt. It was not enough that the bank gave with one hand and took back more with the other; it remained, even while receiving money, the eternal creditor of the nation down to the last farthing advanced. Gradually it became the inevitable receptacle of the metallic hoard of the country, and the centre of gravity of all commercial credit. The writings of the time (Boling-broke's, for instance) show what effect was produced on their contemporaries by the sudden emergence of this brood of bankocrats, financiers, rentiers, brokers, stock-jobbers, etc.
>
> (Marx 1976: 920)

4. But not all silver coins were the same:

> For the silver circulation was divided into two species by the new fashion. On the one hand, the machine-made article was uniform, deeply struck, compact, for it had been necessary to increase its thickness and therefore to reduce its diameter. Above all, its ornamented and perpendicular rim defeated the clipper. But the previous hand-struck coins were poor in comparison, with ill-defined periphery, thin, broad and soft, and a little worn and rubbed with age. Except for a handful struck after the Restoration none was more recent than the Civil War, and quite a large proportion had been issued by Elizabeth, and some even by Edward VI. Consequently, the new coins came to be used for savings, or export, or melting down for bullion, while the old had to bear the wear and tear of daily use. As the old coin deteriorated further, the practice always endemic, of snipping and filing a scrap of silver off any better preserved specimens and reducing them to a common level, flared up about 1686, into a widespread trade in which respectable bankers joined, while the blurring of the money let in a flood of counterfeits and foreign imitations. On top of distrust came inflation, begotten on the new system of credit by an expensive war. When people not only lost confidence in their currency but began to link its weakness with the change from James II to William and Mary, something had to be done.
>
> (Craig 1946: 8)

5. Why the distinction between "civilized" and "trading"? Here Locke refers to his doctrine that money antedates civil government.

6. The reference here is to Christopher Hill's works, especially *The World Turned Upside Down* (1970). For a discussion of the London working class, its relation to the past Civil War and the present forms of crime, cf. Peter Linebaugh's *The London Hanged* (2006), especially Chapter 2, "'Old Mr. Gory' and the Thanatocracy."

7. Here we must pause to tell a tale that might have been written by Jorge Luis Borges, but is actually to be found in a sober little volume: Sir John Craig's *Newton at the Mint* (1946: 17–19). It has to do with Isaac Newton, then Warden of the Mint, and a "versatile person" named William Challoner. Challoner first surfaces as an author in the pamphlet literature around the recoinage debate, with an anti-Lockean tract titled *Reasons humbly offerd against passing an Act for raising £1,000,000 for making good the deficiency of the Clipt Money*. During the first phase of the recoinage in 1696, there was much criticism of the performance of the Mint, and a Parliamentary committee was formed to investigate its operations and personalities, including the then Warden. Challoner appeared before the Committee on Mint Miscarriages, claiming that the Mint made counterfeit coin and worked in collusion with counterfeiters. Further, he submitted plans for two inventions to stop counterfeiting and offered his services to the Mint.

The Committee was clearly impressed, and demanded that Newton allow Challoner a chance to demonstrate his claims. But Newton refused, saying that on the basis of his own secret tests Challoner's devices would not work. The Committee finished up its Report in 1697, criticizing Newton's intransigence and recommending Challoner's inventions for adoption.

In response, Newton threw Challoner into Newgate. And then he began a "thorough" investigation of Challoner's past (which apparently cost him £9 10s.). Let Sir John give the details:

> Seven years before (1691), he had been but a poor workman in the new trade of japanning, a career of crime had raised him to the dignity of a residence in Kensington, a dinner service of plate and the clothe of a gentleman. Challoner had become the most accomplished counterfeiter in the kingdom of English and foreign coin; an inventor of better ways of casting and moulding; so nice an artist of dies that it galled him to spoil their perfection by use. As sidelines, he had stolen horses to furnish capital for a coiner's headquarters in the country; £200 had been obtained from the Bank of England for information about the forgery of their documents; the Exchequer had been robbed of £1000 by an elaborate trick. This sum had been offered by the Government for betrayal of the source of propaganda which was being spread about London on behalf of James II. Challoner got hold of a copy of the objectionable circular, had forty more copies printed, informed on the printers and pocketed the cash. And, dog eating dog, he had also sent a fellow false coiner to the scaffold.

A living paragon of disguise was William Challoner, but was he bested by an even deeper master of "the strange loop"? Challoner was convicted of counterfeiting and was hung at Tyburn on March 4, 1699. "Newton ran the prosecution," is Sir John's end to the tale.

Adequate reflection on this tale would take a volume, but taking Challoner as exemplary a few points relevant to our work should be made. First, the technical ability of the money forgers could be quite high. Second, their self-confidence was for some reason increasing. Third, they had a rather elaborate theory of money. Fourth, they had "friends in high places" (whether willing or not is another matter). Fifth, they had begun to master the new symbolic forms of money. In a word, Newton and his friend Locke had to confront the fact that the "underworld" included quite formidable figures like Challoner, as well as even more formidable ones that were wise enough to remain unknown.

8. William Stanley Jevons writes of false coining:

> The use of money creates, as it were, an artificial crime of false coining, and so great is the temptation to engage in this illicit art that no penalty is sufficient to repress it, as the experience of two thousand years sufficiently proves. Thousands of persons have suffered death, and all the penalties of treason have been enforced without effect. Ruding is then unquestionably right in saying, that our efforts should be directed not so much to the punishment of the crime as to its prevention by improvements in the art of coining. We must strike our coins so perfectly that successful imitation or alteration shall be out of the question.
>
> (Jevons 1921: 58)

Here Jevons is caught between the costs of detection and the efficacy of punishment. Speaking roughly, if "S" is an abbreviation for the proposition "A batch of false coins pass without detection" and "C" is "I am caught" while "p( )" and "d( )" are the probabilities and desirabilities of various states of affairs, then a "rational" forger will operate if and only if:

$$\frac{d(S) \cdot p(S)}{p(C)} > -d(C)$$

Therefore to "discourage" forging the "authorities" must do one of the following: (1) make $d(C)$ extremely negative, hence "punishment"; (2) make $d(S)$ as close to zero as possible by, for example, making the transactions of large sums difficult; or (3) make the $p(C)$ as close to 1 as possible by using a reliable detection system.

But each of these paths have an attendant cost for the monetary authorities. If number (1) is used and there is a good possibility of "false alarm," (i.e., people punished who were not forgers) then there will be a general disinclination to involve oneself with the money system at all. Number (2) will dramatically affect the circulation and velocity of money. Number (3) will involve not only the cost of better technical methods of striking coins but also the whole system of policing and surveillance. Indeed, as the costs of the detection system approach the costs of "false alarms" or "misses," the whole point of the exercise breaks down. On the "Bayes Criterion," cf. Ivan Selin, *Detection Theory* (1965: 11–12); for a general discussion of Bayesian decision theory, see Richard C. Jeffrey (1965). Thomas Bayes was an eighteenth-century English mathematician.

9. For more on pirates, see Daniel Defoe, *A General History of the Pyrates* (1724) and, more recently, Marcus Rediker, "'Under the Banner of King Death': The Social World of Anglo American Pirates: 1716–1726," (1981). For a good example of the pirate's differing conception of money and the state consider some verses that were current during Locke's time:

> Come all ye young sailors of courage so bold
> That venture for money, I'll cloath you with gold.
> Come resort unto Corney, and there you will find
> A ship called the Fanny, shall pleasure your mind.
> Bold Avery commands her, and calls her his own
> And he'll box her about, boys, before he is done;
> French, Spaniards, Portuguese, and Heathen like wise
> He's made a war with them 'till the day that he dies.
>
> …
>
> Farewell to Plymouth, Catwater be damned
> For once I was owner of part of this land
> But since I'm disowned, Adieu, I will take
> My person from England, my fortune to make.
> I'll cross the south sea, with courage so bold,
> For my men I resolve to cloath thee with gold,
> 550 brave boys of courage,
> Resolv'd the first ship we see to engage.
>
> …
>
> No quarter I'll give, nor no quarter I'll take
> There's not one man living, one glass is too late.
> For we are sworn brothers, and 'tis my design
> I'm bound for the Indies, the gold shall be mine.
> Now this course I intend for to steer
> My hard-hearted nation to you I declare.
> I have done you no wrong, so you may me forgive,
> For my sword shall maintain me as long as I live.
> My commission is large, for I made it myself.
> My capstan may stretch it wider by half,
> 'Twas dated at Crancy, believe me, my friend
> In the year ninety-two boys, unto my life's end.

The reference to Crancy is to Avery's seizure of the "Charles II", apparently not in 1692, but in 1694. The whole ballad may be found in John Holloway and Joan Black, *Later English Broadside Ballads* (1975: 37).

10. On the problematics of a world-economy without a world-empire, see Immanuel Wallerstein (1974: Chapter 7). As Marx points out:

> [A]s international money the precious metals once again fulfil their original function of means of exchange: a function which, like commodity exchange itself, originated at points of contact between different primitive communities and not in the interior of the communities. Money functioning as world money reverts to its original natural form. When it leaves domestic circulation, money sheds the particular forms occasioned by the development of exchange within particular areas, or the local forms assumed by money as measure of price—specie, small change, and token of value.
>
> (Marx 1970: 149)

It was this "original natural form" that Locke argued for as an essential precondition for international English rule.

11. Who was Lowndes? He first appears as an assistant to Henry Guy, the Secretary to the Treasury in 1689 and again in 1691, whom Horwitz includes in the "courtier" faction. When Guy was imprisoned for "corruption" charges, he was allowed to name his successor, and Guy named Lowndes. Locke's praise for Lowndes' abilities was not ironic; he appears to have carried out his dues with competence and energy. J.G.A. Pocock, in *The Machiavellian Moment: Florentine Political Thought and the Atlantic Republic Tradition*, describes "Court ideology" hence:

> Its attitude to historical change was one of pragmatic acceptance; it denied that government was based on principles to which there could be a return; and its moral and philosophical theory affirmed that the mainsprings of both motivation and perception in human beings were pride and passion, fantasy and self-interest, which it tended to describe in Mandevillean and Hobbesian terms.
>
> (Pocock 1975: 467)

In other words, Lowndes was someone who in more modern parlance could be called a "technocrat."

12. Analogies between thermodynamical and economic reasoning are quite extensive in the period between 1690 and Carnot's time. Locke (and Petty) initially show an economic *perpetuum mobile* is impossible. For the paradox of wealth is that its source, labor, is a curse but its result, value, is a blessing. There is no way one can make value out of ingenious alchemic or mechanic transformations of an economic nothing.

13. Indeed, even the officially minted coins were not up to Locke's "unvarying standard." Newton's job as Master had as a high priority the restoration of "the old strict accuracy to coining practice." Newton wrote:

> When I first came to the Mint and for many years before, importers (sc., persons who brought bullion to be coined) were allowed almost all the remedy, and the money was coined unequally, pieces being two or three grains too heavy and others as much too light, and the heavy Guineas were called "Come again Guineas" because they were culled out and brought back to the Mint to be recoined (as was the common opinion).
>
> (quoted in Craig 1946: 37)

14. Clipping is an epistemological crime since it robs one of knowledge.

15. On this complex of ideas, see Chapter 3, "Abused Words."

16. It is worth noting that though Locke and Newton were concerned about "unfairness" to creditors, Newton's solicited advice on the recoinage was on Lowndes' side. However, he proposed the creation of a Price Control Board, "with apologies for a restraint in trade," that would limit the price inflation that would follow the devaluation and hence protect the creditor class (especially the public credit). Cf. Craig (1946: 8–9).

17. Standard discussions of Locke's views on personal identity include: M.W. Hughes "Personal Identity: A Defense of Locke" (1975: 169–187); Henry E. Allison, "Locke's Theory of Personal Identity: A Re-Examination" (1977: 105–122); Richard I. Aaron, *John Locke* (1965: 148–153); and Antony Flew, "Locke and the Problem of Personal Identity" (1951). All these works see Locke's views on personal identity as a more or less important way-station on the Descartes-to-Kant highway. But there are other—subterranean and aerial—paths passing through Locke linking Hobbes and Nietzsche, Pascal and Wittgenstein. Consider Nietzsche's process of creating an animal that can make promises, in *The Genealogy of Morals*. He uses Locke's conceptual machinery: memory and oblivion, happiness and misery, consciousness as the will to power and appropriation; the main difference lies in their relations between memory and misery. Locke writes:

> And therefore whatever past actions it cannot reconcile or *appropriate* to that present self by consciousness, it can be no more concerned in than if they had never been done: and to receive pleasure or pain, i.e., reward or punishment, on the account of any such action, is all one as to be made happy or miserable in its first being, without any demerit at all.
>
> (Locke 1823a: II, xxvii, 26)

But Nietzsche perversely points out that "being made miserable stimulates memory" and literally creates "demerit" (or guilt). Hence, according to Nietzsche, the millennia of cruelty that have gone into making an animal that is even capable of making a contract, or a being like Locke, who sees contract-making as an inherent human characteristic.

18. This was not an idle possibility, for, according to D.W. Jones: "[H]ad the currency crisis, with its dislocative effects, come earlier—in 1693 for instance—there could well have been a Stuart Restoration and an abject peace ... [for] economic

resilience was far more important than military or naval successes" (Jones 1972: 314).

19. On the dramatic fluctuations of the world-economy (and their concrete embodiments), see Wallerstein (1974).

20. Who was Nicholas Barbon? We might call him a proto-Keynesian for his views on employment, for example, "The more every man earns, the more he consumes, and the kings revenue is the more increased." But, at the time, there was a word current for a type like him: "projector." Readers of Swift's *Gulliver's Travels* will remember the Grand Academy of projectors in Lagado and some memorable projects:

> The projector of this cell was the most ancient student of the Academy; his face and beard were of a pale yellow; his hands and clothes daubed over with filth. When I was presented to him, he gave me a close embrace (a compliment I could well have excused). His employment from the first coming into the Academy, was an operation to reduce human excrement to its original food, by separating the several parts, removing the tincture which it receives from the gall, making the odour exhale, and scumming off the saliva. He had a weekly allowance from the society, of a vessel filled with human ordure, about as the bigness of a Bristol barrel.
>
> (Swift 1726: Part III, Chs 5–6)

By the time of the publication of *Gulliver's Travels* in the 1720s, projectors were already becoming *passe*, for their hey-day was in the decades that straddled 1700. During that time, they besieged Parliament and ministers with plans, schemes and proposals to "get the job of government done." Indeed, some projectors passed into Parliament and the ministries, and some of their projects came to fruition. Horwitz writes:

> [S]ome of the most striking departures of the "financial revolution," including the creation of the Bank of England, seem to have originated in projectors' proposals. Sometimes, individual projectors were summoned before Commons to explain their schemes, as, for instance, Edmund Hemming was called before a committee of the whole on 18 December 1695 to speak to his plan for raising £8,000,000 by laying a tax on feather beds! Then, too there were other, more eminent practitioners of the trade, particularly Thomas Neale and Dr. Barbon, who were able to exploit their membership in the Commons to press their projects, and in late 1695 the Bristol M.P.s reported to their brethren back home that they had been given copies of one of Neale's schemes by the author in St. Stephen's Chapel.
>
> (Horwitz 1977: 207)

Barbon's most famous project was the creation of a National Land Bank, which in fact received royal assent in 1696, but the project failed within a year. Roughly, Barbon's idea was to use land instead of precious metal as the basis for issuing bank notes. But when the crunch came in July 1696—in the form of a cash-strapped William on the battlefield—the land bankers were not ready. In negotiation with William's men, they initially offered £200,000, but later, on August 4, they "could only advance £40,000, and that upon onerous terms—a result that left [King William's men] in despair the bank in trouble."

21. Appleby's method is somewhat ambiguous. For on the one side she is quite critical of "Marxist analysis" that presumably leads to postulating "a vanguard class creating the coherent structure of ideas that forms the modern world view" (Appleby 1978: 10); but on the other her explanation of the failure of "the new men of banking and commerce" in the recoinage debate is "Marxist." Why is this so? Perhaps it is because there is one element that is lacking both in her views of "Marxist analysis" and in her own "Marxist" position, namely, awareness of the existence of other subjects outside the circuit of merchants, bankers, ministers, politicians and what we now would call social workers whose opinions she quotes. Appleby does not consider that these other subjects—what they said and what they did not say—had a "shaping" and "compelling" influence on the perspectives of her merchants, bankers, etc., whose views she takes as the only possible views. Thus, Appleby loses any way to transcend their perspective and *show* what they are *not* saying, and *cannot* say.

    Appleby sums up her method in the following slogan: "[W]e can say that men and women can not long conceive of ideas that suggest actions they do not want to perform" (Appleby 1978: 279). Thus, since the bulk of English employers did not want to raise wages, the ideas that suggested such an action were not long conceived. But there is a slight variant of this slogan that will make our point: "Men and women can not long conceive ideas that suggest actions they do not want others to perform." The truth of this would explain why history is full of stupidities; that is, others actually do manage to perform actions that were not conceived. To understand an ideology we must not only see the interests of the dominant class expressed in it, but also the *fears* that are *not* expressed. Thus, we must approach from the other side of the ideology's limit, and that is not achieved simply by living 300 years later.

22. In *Further Considerations*, Locke writes:

    > [T]he use and end of the public stamp is only to be a guard and voucher of the quantity of silver which men contract for; and the injury done to the public faith, in this point, is that which in clipping and false coining heightens the robbery into treason.

    > (Locke 1823c: 144)

23. For a powerful discussion of working-class mobility during the seventeenth and eighteenth centuries and the compulsion and freedom it expressed, cf. Linebaugh (1982).

24. Locke was definitely "frightened by clipping," at least enough to break his self-imposed ban on figurative language. He writes in *Further Considerations*:

Clipping is the great leak which for some time past has contributed more to sink us than all the forces of our enemies could do. It is like a breach in the sea-bank, which widens every moment till it must be stopped; and my timorous temper must be pardoned, if I am frightened with the thoughts of clipped money being current one moment longer at any other value but of warranted standard bullion.

(Locke 1823c: 198)

Locke was not alone in understanding the military implications of the coinage question. Horwitz writes: "Godolphin had informed William in early August 1695, while the siege of Namur was in progress, that 'the exchange had fallen so low' against sterling that 'the returns are become wholly impossible to be had'" (1977: 159–160).

25. D.W. Jones confirms Locke in the following passage:

Rising silver prices had a dangerous corollary however, of increasing the endemic incentive to clip the hammered silver coinage through which the bulk of retail transactions were affected.

Out of sheer necessity, tolerance of the clipped coin was long suffering, but a severe attack on the intrinsic content of the hammered coin could, and did, produce a divergence between the actual bullion content of the coin and its nominal face value too great for credence and trust ... In a very real sense, therefore, the strategic outcome was both improbably and problematically poised on a race between the achievements on the battlefield and the inexorable deterioration of the hammered silver coinage.

(Jones 1972: 317–318)

26. What did happen after the recoinage? The story is complex, and surely the actual process had little to do with Locke's proposal. On the one side, there were liquidity riots, see Albert Feavearyear, *The Pound Sterling: A History of English Money* (1963: 140–143); and on the other, recoinage indirectly lead to England becoming the home of the gold standard, see Vilar (1976: 220–231).

2. CIVIL GOVERNMENT

1. Much of the disruption and dislocation produced by the recoinage were caused by the mechanics of the process, rather than by the theoretical power of either Locke's or Lowndes' conceptual systems. Whatever one thinks of the debate around "the crucial experiment" in the philosophy of science, one can be sure that the recoinage operation was far from an ideal test for either theory.

[T]he administrative preparations at the Mint were grossly inadequate, at least until Newton was named master in April 1696. By mid-1696, the country mints were just beginning to function and the mills at the Tower had produced only 700,000 in new milled coin, even though the clipped coin to the nominal value of 4,700,000 had been brought by that time into the Exchequer.

(Horwitz 1977: 180)

As William J. Cameron, the editor of *Augustan Satirical Verse*, points out, the recoinage was the butt of many a verse, partly for its audacity:

And what no Nation before did dare,
The coin is changed in time of war

(Cameron 1971: 489)

But this was mostly because of the hardship and uncertainty it caused for most money holders. Thus, Thomas Brown wrote "A Prophesy Found in a Football in Spittle Fields by a Weaver" in 1696:

[W]hen chalk pays for cheese, and gold dwindles to wood, The Bank rather lets in than keeps out the flood,
When Grocer's Hall fears to be sent to the Compter,
And faith public's so light that a feather will mount her.
When the coin scarcer grows by a war in hopes of a peace. When justice is found to abandon the land,
Though most people are seen with scales in their hand…
Then England, I tell thee, thou art cursedly shamed;
'Tis too late to repent—sin on and be damned!

(Cameron 1971: 486–487)

2. By "social Other," I refer to the image that Locke and the ruling circle constructed of the subversive forces in society. Inevitably, this image only partially intersects with the actual proletariat. For a thorough discussion of the class composition of the London and imperial proletariat during that period, cf. Peter Linebaugh (2006: Ch. 2).

3. Locke definitely rejected the views of his Massachusetts Puritan colleagues, who considered the Amerindians as devils. In his first *Letter Concerning Toleration*, Locke was called upon to answer the question, "What if a Church be idolatrous, is that to be tolerated by the magistrate?" Locke replies, "Not even Americans, subjected unto a Christian prince, are to be punished either in body or goods for not embracing our faith and worship" (Locke 1823e: 34).

Notice that Locke's "distinction" between "Americans" and "negroes" is built upon both theoretical and pragmatic assumptions.

4. The basic texts on the relationship between the witch-hunt and the development of capitalism are to be found in the work of Silvia Federici. She explains the witch-hunt as necessitated by the demographic needs of primitive accumulation, an imperative that was easing at the end of the seventeenth century. Cf. Silvia Federici, *Caliban and the Witch* (2004). For a relevant fact on the hunt:

[T]hroughout the [sixteen] seventies and eighties the trials and convictions were falling off and by the end of the eighties accounts of witchcraft were very rare. The last English judicial execution for witchcraft came in 1712 ... In 1736 the English laws against witchcraft were repealed.

(Clark 1955: 416)

5. One could almost hypothesize a "conservation law of death." For a detailed account of the state planning of death during this period, see Linebaugh's *The London Hanged* (2006) where a sound word is coined, "thanatocracy."

6. The war provided the immediate cause of the crisis, involving a large outflow of expenditure into foreign hands, through a foreign remittance mechanism described by D.W. Jones in "London Merchants and the Crisis of the 1690s":

The first move was always to issue government I.O.U.'s—or "tallies"—to the remittance contractors who were to deliver funds abroad at a fixed rate of exchange. Usually the remittance contractors instructed foreign bankers to make funds available to the army paymasters, and they then proceeded to purchase bills of exchange, which, after acceptance by the drawees abroad, could be cashed to reimburse the banks.

(Jones 1972: 321)

The connection between the war, taxes and liquidity problems was not a matter known only to the "experts." It was apparently the theme of many poems and songs, according to William J. Cameron (1971: 488–490). There is an especially insightful anonymous "anti-war" poem that brings together the war, the recoinage and the 1696 "assassination plot" that proved so useful to William III. Among other things, the poem has William speaking to his cronies, complaining of his Parliamentary opposition:

If we have not a care
They'll finish the war
And stop the new coin's exportation
And will rudely demand
That the tax on the land
Shall circulate now in the nation.
So that all our design Of new-making the coin,
Thus quite disappointed will be.
For had I not meant It abroad should be sent,
The devil should mind it for me.
(Cameron 1971: 477–478)

The *denouement* of the poem has William organizing his own "assassination plot," framing a whole set of dupes and winning over the hearts and minds of his gullible opponents.

7. Paper bank notes became "serious" only in the nineteenth century for Britain; it was only then that counterfeiting bank notes became a capital offense.

8. Rousseau's account of the cause of the social contract is in the *physicalist* tradition; in fact, it is a simple application of D'Alembert's Principle. In "The Social Contract," he writes:

> I assume men having reached the point where the obstacles that interfere with their preservation in the state of nature prevail by their resistance over the forces which each individual can muster to maintain himself in that state.
>
> (Rousseau 2018: I, vi)

Rousseau is merely pointing out the different impact a force has on a system of particles when joined together by constraints, compared to when they are mechanically free. If free they will likely scatter, if constrained they will move together in response to the impact. D'Alembert's Principle lays down the law of motion for constrained systems. Thus Rousseau can apply this law to social atoms facing a potentially annihilating natural force:

> Now, since men cannot engender new forces, but only unite and direct those that exist, they are left with no other means of self-preservation than to form, by aggregation, a sum of forces that might prevail over those obstacles' resistance, to set them in motion by a single impetus, and make them act in concert.
>
> (Rousseau 2018: I, vi)

It is interesting to note that Rousseau's—the proto-romantic's—account of human solidarity is much more mechanistic than that of the arch-mechanist Hobbes.

9. The offending clause is CX:

> Every freeman of Carolina shall have absolute power and authority over his negro slaves, of what opinion or religion so ever.

This document has been much criticized in the last century. Peter King, in *The Development of the English Economy to 1750*, writes: "John Locke drew up an astonishingly reactionary constitution in 1668 (for the Carolinas)" (1971: 403). Consider Michael Craton's two comments in *Sinews of Empire: A Short History of British Slavery*:

> The Carolinas, founded many decades later, owned their economic expansion more to the black than did the colonies to the north. Indeed, slavery was inherent to its foundation, for John Locke (more commonly remembered as a theoretical opponent of slavery) had found it politic to incorporate slavery into his "Fundamental Constitutions" in 1669.
>
> (Craton 1974: 48)

> At the same time John Locke was cynically drawing up a constitution by which white labourers in South Carolina would be tied to the land and their masters by a form of hereditary villeinage long eradicated in England.
>
> (Craton 1974: 162)

Or Clarence Ver Steeg in *The Formative Years, 1607–1763*:

> In the history of early Carolina, the Fundamental Constitutions, the articles of
> Carolina government drawn up by Ashley Cooper with the aid of John Locke,
> have attracted unusual attention. The customary point of departure is that the
> Fundamental Constitutions consisted of archaic, medieval ideas outmoded in
> England itself but which the proprietors, ignorant of New World conditions
> attempted to transplant to Carolina.
>
> (Ver Steeg 1965: 121)

But Richard Aaron, in *John Locke*, tried to exonerate Locke:

> [O]ne of [Locke's] first tasks was to help with the framing of a constitution
> for the new colony of Carolina, of which Ashley was one of the founders and
> lord-proprietors. (The whole constitution is attributed to Locke, since a copy
> of it in his hand was found among his papers, but it is very unlikely that he is
> the author of it.
>
> (Aaron 1965: 16)

However, Aaron gives no further explanation of his parenthetical remark.

Perhaps a little historical detail would be of help here. Locke's relations to
Carolina and to slavery antedated and continued after 1669. Apparently, the
first white settlers left for the Carolinas from Barbados in October of 1665,
to found "Charles Town," but by October 16, 1667 Samuel Maverick wrote to
Lord Arlington (a proprietor) that "the plantations ... are deserted, the inhabitants have come thither, some to Virginia." A few months before, Locke and
Ashley had heard about the growing desertions, and Locke was put to the task
of writing an appeal that would check the exodus, but it failed. Thus in 1669
another attempt at settlement, with a new batch of settlers, was launched. As
Charles M. Andrews writes, they left with:

> a new set of regulations covering government land-holding, the judiciary and
> social relations ... The body of law, known as the Fundamental Constitutions
> is believed to have been prepared by John Locke, at that time but thirty
> seven years old, with the assistance, perhaps, of Ashley himself, though the
> authorship is by no means certain.
>
> (Andrews 1964: 212)

Andrews points out that Locke's help was not a one-time thing; he was continually involved in drafting "instructions" for the colonial administration.

Informed contemporary opinion also placed Locke as the main drafter of the
Constitutions. Maurice Cranston, in *John Locke: A Biography*, writes:

> It is clear from other evidence, however, that Locke did have a considerable
> say in the framing of the Fundamental Constitutions. Notably there is a letter
> from Sir Peter Colleton, a man well informed in colonial matters, pleading

for "that excellent form of government in the composure of which you had so great a hand," to be put into effect.

(Cranston 1957: 120)

But Colleton's wish was never gratified; apparently the colonists never put the Constitution officially into operation, though they certainly took clause CX to heart. Locke himself invested in the slave trade a number of times and, for the era and his income, in substantial amounts. Cranston writes that "Locke bought £400 stock in the Royal Africa Co. in 1674 and £200 more in 1675" (1957: 115). He clearly thought that slavery had a future, and agreed with Smeal Wilson, who wrote a few years later in 1682 in "An Account of the Province of Carolina" for the Carolina Proprietors:

> But a rational man will certainly inquire *when I have land, what shall I doe with it?* What comoditys shall I be able to produce that will yeild me money in other countrys that I may be inabled to buy Negro slaves (without which a Planter can never doe any great matter) and purchase other things for my pleasure and convenience, that Carolina doth not produce.

(quoted in Higginbotham 1978: 167)

Wilson was echoing Locke's thoughts, at the very time when Locke presumably was working on the *Two Treatises*, when he stressed the uselessness of land in the absence of labor.

Other theoretical insights were to be gained from the slave trade as well. Although the much desired *Asiento* was not won until after Locke's death as a prize in the War of Spanish Succession, there was plenty of work for the English slave ships of the Royal Africa Co. in the triangle of the seventeenth century. This trade was the source of much education on the question of value, that is, the value of men, women and children. The practice of many exchanges (which we now participate in as if they were natural) had to be learned, for the transformation of money into labor power was only beginning to be mastered. Indeed the metamorphoses could be as baroque as Bach's. Basil Davidson writes: "Often the manner of payment was bafflingly complex. In one characteristic transaction a young woman was bartered against one roll of tobacco, two patches, twenty-four linen handkerchiefs, one gun, one jug, four-pint mugs and three 'garsets,' or textile measures" (1961: 90).

10. Was Locke a racist? Consider two passages: Book III, Chapter viii, sec. 1 and Book IV, Chapter vii, sec. 16 of the *Essay*. In the first passage, Locke is considering the relation between "abstract and concrete terms," while in the second he is involved in a critique of "Maxims." First let us settle the general points in each passage and then examine his examples, which revolve around the idea of whiteness and the relation between the idea of "negro" and the idea of "man."

Book III is "Of Words," and in Chapter viii, Locke is doing some mop-up work after dealing with most difficult questions concerning substance and mixed-mode names. After dealing with particles, he turns to "abstract and

156

concrete terms." Applying his general theory of what we would call nowadays "concept formation," he argues that a careful attention to language would have made this clear: "each abstract idea [is] distinct," and further there are "no ideas of the real essence of substances." It is important to keep in mind what Locke means by "abstract" versus "concrete" terms. "White*ness*," "animal*ity*," "sweet*ness*" "patern*ity*" are abstract terms, while "white," "animal," "sweet," "pater" are concrete. The first point he makes is that predicating one abstract term of another leads to odd, paradoxical or false propositions: Whiteness is sweetness. Humanity is whiteness. Rationality is paternity, etc. Thus, he implies that such propositions commit something of a category mistake.

His second point deals with the distinction between mixed modes and substances. For the former, we *qua* concept creators create the essences (definitions) of the terms, while for the latter we must wait on nature and experience to reveal essential properties, and this process is never ending. As a consequence, "[Mankind] has no ideas of the real essences of substances," while we can literally make up these essences for mixed modes. Hence we can have names for mixed-mode essences like Whiteness, Justice, Equality, etc. while attempts to create names for substance essences always have an odd ring: metallity, goldness, animality, etc. Of humanity, he writes:

Indeed, *humanitas* was a word in familiar use amongst the Romans; but in a far different sense, and stood not for the abstract essence of any substance; but was the abstracted name of a mode, and its concrete *humanus*, not *homo*.
(Locke 1823a: III, viii)

The second passage has a different focus. Here, Locke examines those maxims like "What is, is" and "It is impossible for the same thing to be and not to be." In the first book, these maxims had been considered not to be innate, but here Locke wants to show that, if we try to apply them to complex ideas like "man, horse, gold, virtue," then:

[T]hey are of infinite danger, and most commonly make men receive and retain falsehood for manifest truth, and uncertainty for demonstration; upon which follow error, obstinacy, and all the mischiefs that can happen from wrong reasoning.
(Locke 1823a: III, viii, 15)

The danger lies in our tendency to mistake words for things, and our assumption that our ideas are complete (especially about substances) when, in fact, they are products of quite limited experiences. Thus, Locke argues, though the Maxims are trivially true, their application can bring about "infinite danger."

How do these passages apply to our initial question? Let us start with the second. Here Locke points out that an English child would have formed the idea of man based upon his experience of English men, "whereof white or flesh-color in England being one." This child can, with the help of a Maxim, demonstrate "that a negro is not a man." How? Since white is always part of his idea of man, and given the Maxim that "It is impossible for the same thing to be and not to be," then a black man is impossible. The fallacy here, and Locke clearly believes a fallacy has been committed, is the transition from the child's idea of man to the substance man. It is clear that the context would make it difficult for Locke to agree with the child, but is it the fallaciousness of the argument, or the falsity of the conclusion, that Locke rejects?

Let us now turn to our first passage. The point here is to contrast a correct and incorrect way of making a general statement,

> For how near of kin soever they may seem to be, and how certain soever it is that man is an animal, or rational or white, yet everyone at first hearing perceived the falsehood of these propositions: *humanity is animality*, or *rationality* or *whiteness*: and this is as evident as any of the allowed maxims.
>
> (Locke 1823a: III, viii)

The proposition "Humanity is whiteness" is false because of its form, but what of "a man is white" or "man is white"? Are these true or false? From the context we must conclude that Locke would want them to be considered true, in order to show most clearly the impact that the change of form from concrete to abstract has.

What can we conclude? On the basis of Book IV, Chapter vii, sec. 16, we have reason for thinking that the English child's argument that "a negro is not a man" is unacceptable to Locke, while on the basis of Book III, Chapter viii, sec. 1, we can conclude that he certainly granted the likely truth of "man is white." Is this an example of Locke's alleged inconsistency? Or, perhaps, oversubtlety? Again, as always when we are baffled by Locke, we must broaden our investigation to obtain an adequate answer.

To do that, we must first consider the political-economic environment in which Locke operated, in its relationship to the question of slavery. Slavery and racism, especially with regard to black Africans, are now considered as nearly synonymous; ironically, a major reason for this synonymy lies in the impact of "homophonic" readings of Locke in the later part of the eighteenth century. In this period, a new configuration of relations developed between England, Africa and the Americas, a black community grew *in* England, the first major "slave rebellions" in the West Indies took place, etc. The debate around slavery therefore took a definite turn toward questions of human essence. The anti-abolitionist could use Locke to argue: if it is of the essence for humans to be free as well as rational, then the justification for slavery could be either that the slave is not human, hence not free (by a sort of modern Aristotelianism), or that the slave is not quite human and must be developed (slavery being a Hegelian training ground in rationality).

But this type of debate was not Locke's concern. Locke wrote clause CX of the Fundamental Constitutions (in his own "hand") and there is no reason to think that he considered it problematic. He did not need to worry because nobody was challenging him. The same Dryden, for example, who attacked his employer, Shaftesbury, for setting the people "in the papal chair" ("*The Medal*"), would not have dreamed of attacking him, or "the loudest bagpipe of the squeaking train" for being involved in the slave trade; cf. *The Poems of John Dryden* (1913). On the contrary.

To understand what Locke's associates thought of the "slavery question," let us turn to Davis and Anstey. David Brion Davis, in *The Problem of Slavery in Western Culture*, writes:

> We must conclude, then, that the thought of Grotius, Hobbes, Pufendorf, and Locke, while preparing the day for the secular theories of the Enlightenment provided little basis for criticizing Europe's policy of supporting and extending slavery in the New World ... For Locke ... original sin had been replaced by a supposedly willful act which required that the slave be forever excluded from the paradisial compact and worked, in the sweat of his brow, for the benefit of others. And from this secular hell there was apparently no redemption.
>
> (Davis 1966: 121)

Roger Anstey agrees with Davis: "[A]s the eighteenth century opened there was nothing in the work of the philosophical luminaries of the previous century to suggest other than continued acceptance of slavery" (Anstey 1975: 93).

Locke did have a theory of slavery, but it was not related to the late eighteenth-century debate. Rather, it was a development of his justification of the death penalty. If the other violates the law of nature of society so much so that s/he deserves to die, then such a being can rightfully be made a slave. A slave is thus a living dead person. But this theory, though useful for the organization of "white slavery" through the "transportation" of criminals from London to the American colonies could have little bearing on African slavery which patently involved non-criminals—children as well as generations born into slavery. That his theory did not apply in such a glaring way to an important source of his income again did not seem to upset Locke, and his nonchalance did not arise from lack of knowledge. His knowledge was, as some would say, "hands on," through his work for the Proprietors of the Carolinas and his various stints on the various economic advisory councils he sat on. He was also something of an early "armchair anthropologist," a type which the British ruling class would produce in abundance. At that time, anthropology was a branch of "travel literature," of which Locke was an avid reader. His interest is revealed by a peculiar document, *The Whole History of Navigation from its Original to this Time* (1704), prefixed to Churchill's *Collection of Voyages*. It is a book with an immense number of references not only to voyages but also to the climes, people and commodities of the worlds that the European voyagers "discovered."

The editor of the 1823 edition of Locke's works, in the face of some moot evidence, included it in the ten volumes with the following challenge: "[It] must be submitted to the public, and those who are styled proprietors." I am not so styled, but I do submit to *my* public that it is a good sign of Locke's involvement in such matters that it was thought possible to attribute such a vast catalogue to him.

Consider what the author of the *History* writes of Africa:

> The natives are for the most part black, or else inclined to it. All the commodities that are brought from thence are gold-dust, ivory and slaves; those black people selling one another, which is a very considerable trade, and has been a great support to all the American plantations. This is all that mighty continent affords for exportation, the greatest part of it being scorched under the torrid zone, and the native almost naked, no where industrious, and for the most part scarce civilized.
>
> (anonymous: 414)

This passage is part of a remarkable run-on paragraph that sums up the inventory of the African and Asian world, that is, as "a vast extent of land" and "the commodities it supplies us." I submit that the author of the summary was probably not far from Locke's thinking (if it was not him). We have here the *makings* of a racist defence of slavery, but no such defence is given. On the contrary, the prevailing attitude is remarkably matter of fact: Africa exports ivory and slaves. Slaves? Yes, they sell one another. Oh? Lucky too, for it has made the American plantations possible. Are they industrious? No, they are mostly naked, and have not developed most of the European arts and skills (including government). But ... it is damned hot down there after all! The author appears more interested in the *fact* of the trade than in its *justification*.

But though Locke did not seem concerned about justification, his views were to enter the debate around slavery and race both as a weapon of attack for the abolitionists and as an instrument of defense for the pro-slavery forces. The abolitionists read his remarks on slavery "homophonically as, indeed, many have done in the twentieth century": cf. Coupland (1964: 41); Grant (1968: 127–128); and Miers (1975: 2–3). They concluded that, on the authority of Locke, "Slave trading is immoral and unpolitic." However, pro-slavery eyes read in his remarks a strategic relation between the death penalty and slavery, concluding that Locke endorsed the right to transform a free person into a slave once it is demonstrated that s/he lacked reason. Thus their program: to prove that blacks were not reasoning creatures.

David Hume contributed decisively to the pro-slavery argument, giving it an "empiricist basis" by his observations on African technology and culture (of which, of course, he was blithely ignorant), as Anthony J. Barker notes (1978: 57). Just as Aristotle's nasty philosophy of slavery was prompted (while both developed from an ambiguous Plato), so too does the late eighteenth-century debate have its roots in Locke.

Having established that Locke had no need to identify slavery with either an absolute or relative lack of human essence—that is, he did not need to be a racist—we turn now to his conception of *man* or the human *species*. And here

160

we can see the source of the apparent equivocation noted at the beginning of this note. First, with respect to the notion of species, Locke had a general skepticism: "Wherein, then, would I gladly know consist the precise and unmoveable boundaries of that species? It is plain, if we examine, there is no such thing made by Nature and established by her amongst men" (Locke 1823a: III, vi, 27).

Since the real essence of a substance is based upon its atomic texture, which is removed from our immediate inspection, our definitions of species suffer accordingly from the lack of a total experience of Nature.

Locke's species skepticism was to have a profound effect on eighteenth-century biology, according to Arthur Lovejoy (1960: 229–231). But our main concern is its implications for the species "man." Here, his species skepticism applies with a vengeance:

> There are creatures … (*sit fides penes authorem*), but there appears no contradiction that there should be such), that with language and reason and a shape in other things agreeing with ours, have hairy tales; others where the males have no beards, and others where the females have. If it be asked whether these be all *men* or no, all of human species? It is plain, the question refers only to the nominal essence: for those of them to whom the definition of the word man, or the complex idea signified by the name, agrees, are men, and the other not. But if the inquiry be made concerning the supposed real essence; and whether the internal constitution and frame of these several creatures be specifically different, it is wholly impossible for us to answer, no part of that going into our specific idea: only we have reason to think, that where the faculties or outward frame so much differs, the internal constitution is not exactly the same.
>
> (Locke 1823a: Ill, vi, 22)

In other words, differences in quantity of hair or, perhaps, skin color might be "a mark of a different internal specific constitution," but then again they might not. At any particular historical point, we must make a decision (by the very fact that we use a word like "man"), but this decision must always be taken with a grain of salt. Thus, it is one of the major ironies of the *Essay Concerning Human Understanding* that the essence of human understanding is, in effect, its inability to really understand Humanity. For Locke concludes his discussion with these words:

> And I imagine none of the definitions of the word *man* which we yet have, nor descriptions of that sort of animal, are so perfect and exact as to satisfy a considerate inquisitive person; much less to obtain a general consent…
>
> (Locke 1823a: III, vi, 27)

Undoubtedly an element that would keep a "considerate inquisitive person" in doubt is exactly the fact that the typical item classed as "man" has an ontological complexity that one does not find in other species. A man can be a person or self (like our inquisitor) as well as be associated with an *immaterial, thinking, spiritual* substance. These different entity layers need not be identified or correlative; moreover, our knowledge of them arises from radically different sources. The problem, thus, intensifies to infinity on many different axes.

Indeed, there is a distinctly "existential" cast to Locke's notion of humanity: man makes *himself*, and all that. Thus, man can *un*make himself as well. There are monsters, drills, changelings, talking parrots, the Abbot Malotru and other curiosities galore in the pages of the *Essay*, but there are madmen, criminals, the lazy and contentious as well. The latter choose—it would seem—to be less than rational, less than human. For our freedom is perverse and can turn against its own foundations, condemning itself to slavery and death. The criminal declares "himself to quit the Principles of Human Nature and to be a noxious Creature" (Locke 1823a: II, 10).

It is in this self-reflexive fluidity of the human that Macpherson found reason to discover "class differentials in rationality" in the *Two Treatises* (Macpherson 1962: 238ff).

Locke recognizes a natural relation between rationality and "industriousness" determined by God, for "[God] gave [the World] to the use of the Industrious and rational (and Labour was to be his title to it); not to the Fancy or Covetousness of the Quarrelsom and Contentious" (Locke 1823g: II, 34). And, one can decide to be Industrious or quarrelsome, rational or contentious—intriguing contrasts, these—and hence one can decide to be more or less human, perhaps. The consequences of this original sin, for example, the choice to be quarrelsome instead of industrious, are unfortunately passed down the generations, however. Marx might have been thinking of Locke when he wrote the following:

> [P]rimitive accumulation plays approximately the same role in political economy as original sin does in theology. Adam bit the apple, and thereupon sin fell on the human race. Its origin is supposed to be explained when it is told as an anecdote about the past. Long, long ago there were two sorts of people; one, the diligent, intelligent and above all frugal elite; the other, lazy rascals, spending their substance, and more, in riotous living. The legend of theological original sin tells us certainly how man came to be condemned to eat his bread in the sweat of his brow; but the history of economic original sin reveals to us that there are people to whom this is by no means essential. Never mind! Thus it came to pass that the former sort accumulated wealth, and the latter sort finally had nothing to sell except their own skins. And from this original sin dates the poverty of the great majority who, despite all their labour, have up to now nothing to sell but themselves, and the wealth of the few that increases constantly, although they have long ceased to work. Such insipid childishness is every day preached to us in the defence of property.
>
> (Marx 1976: 873–874)

For Locke, one's humanity is naturally mysterious and perversely fluctuating. This is true for everyone, whites included. One must *always* be on one's spiritual toes; no one is self-evidently human.

But what is the outcome for black Africans in Locke's conceptual net? Let us consider their attributes, as listed in the Lockean passage from the *History*: "nowhere industrious," "scarce civilized," "selling one another." Surely lack of industry—even if excused by the climate—is a "bad sign," while "scarce civilized" is simply a sociological description referring to those "who have [not] made and multiplied positive laws to determine property"—which include the Biblical patriarchs. Thus, that would not have had any bearing on the matter. But "selling one another" is problematic, and could provide a Lockean "loophole" for slavery. For if "selling one another" was a general practice in Africa—for example, parents selling children—then such a fall from the natural law would allow for a different approach to the African slave. Thus, the very existence of the slave trade might constitute evidence for its justification in a Lockean perspective.

Now let us return to the two original passages we discussed, one in Book IV, Chapter vii, and the other in Book III, Chapter viii of the *Essay*. We now have reason for believing that what Locke found objectionable in the child's argument was not so much the *conclusion* "a negro is not a man" but its *modality*, that is, it is impossible for a negro to be a man. Locke finds such negative certainty unwarranted for any proposition involving substance terms like "man." Locke uses a child as a reasoner precisely to emphasize the limited kind of evidence that he has concerning the conclusion, and the intellectual megalomania that the Maxims lead to when employed badly.

In the passage that examines the abstract/concrete distinction, our previous discussion will help us focus on what might have appeared as gratuitous qualifications. Locke writes: "*[H]ow near of kin soever* they may *seem* to be, and *how certain soever* it is that man is an animal, or rational or white…*" (italics mine).

In the light of the Lockean doctrine of substance, we see that these qualifications are essential. Locke refuses to acknowledge any absolute certainty with respect to these propositions since their subjects are substances. Hence, "man is white" is open to his universal skepticism concerning species, and can only claim a high degree of belief.

So, was Locke a racist? Let us be Aristotelian about it: yes, potentially; no, in fact. We might conclude that Locke remained comfortably agnostic about the matter while the sharks of the Middle Passage feasted.

11. The political context of the *Two Treatises* spanned more than a decade, from the Popish Plot to the Settlement, as Laslett has shown (Locke 1963: "Introduction"). Locke only speaks about the events of 1688–1689 in his Preface. Referring first to the pages of the text lost in the years of exile and expulsion, he writes: "These, which remain, I hope are sufficient to establish the Throne of our Great Restorer, Our present King William…"

Apparently, however, Locke's initial version was hatched under Shaftesbury's wing. Perhaps it formed part of Architophel's temptation of Absalom. Certainly

Dryden, in another poem of the period. *The Medal*, has Lockean words spew from Shaftesbury's mouth:

> He preaches to the crowd that power is lent,
> But not convey'd to kingly government;
> That claims successive bear no binding force That coronation oaths are things of course.
> Maintains the multitude can never err.
> And sets the people in the papal chair.
>
> (Dryden, *The Medal*: 82–87)

12. A word on "Whig" and "Tory":

> It is not mere coincidence that the two party names Whig and Tory become current about this time (1679–1681). Both were originally terms of abuse: whigs were Scots presbyterian rebels and tories were Irish catholic bandits. The parties to which they were applied were on the one hand the exclusionists, who wanted parliamentary limitation of the Crown and toleration for protestants only, on the other hand the supporters of hereditary succession and the prerogative.
>
> (Clark 1955: 101)

13. Adam was refracted through many political prisms between the Civil War and the Settlement. Compare Filmer's with Milton's Adam. Cf. Hill, *Milton and the English Revolution* (1977).

14. In fact, a series of Jacobite plots (real ones, apparently, despite the skepticism of the poet in note 8) to assassinate William III between 1690–1696 were the outcome of Filmer's theory. Ironically, but that is how things go, a theory built to give absolute power to the monarch became the ideology of regicide. For a short description of the plots, cf. Clark (1955: 183–185); and Horwitz (1977: 168).

15. Locke was much closer to Descartes than to his immediate English predecessor, Hobbes. Histories of philosophy built along "empiricist/rationalist" lines impose an anachronistic nation-state rivalry on the immediate lines of influence. As Silvia Federici points out, the decisive element of the Cartesian model's success throughout Europe was the concept of "self-mastery," a theme very close to Locke.

    The relation of mental with physical appropriation reaches its absolute imperial end in Hegel's *Philosophy of Right*:

> A person has as his substantive end the right of putting his will into any and everything and thereby making it his, because it has no such end in itself and derives its destiny and soul from his will. Thus the absolute right to appropriation which man has over all "things."
>
> (Hegel 1952: sec. 44)

16. The inability to see the relation of Locke's to Descartes' political project is just one of a number of deep flaws in Hannah Arendt's *The Human Condition*

(1959). What is of special relevance for us is her use of Locke to create a rather contrived Weberian trichotomy of Labor, Work and Action. She makes much of Locke's passage: "The Labour of his Body, and the Work of his Hands, we may say, are properly his" (Locke 1823g: II, 27), in order to justify two ideal types: *animal laborans* and *homo faber*. But, after making so much of these ideal types, she recognizes that Locke makes no use of this "distinction." To overcome this difficulty, she creates a *deus ex machina* out of Locke's own purported *deus ex machina*:

> Thus Locke, in order to save labor from its manifest disgrace of producing only "things of short duration," had to introduce money—a "lasting thing which men may keep without spoiling"—a kind of *deus ex machina* without which the laboring body, in its obedience to the life process, could never have become the origin of anything so permanent and lasting as property, because there are no "durable things" to be kept to survive the activity of the laboring process.
>
> (Arendt 1959: 89)

But Locke is not interested in the type of property that Arendt's *homo faber* inspires: furniture, buildings, art works, etc. What he is interested in is property in land and property in money. Their quasi eternity far outdistances the chairs, tables and other heirlooms of the world. Further, if Locke were to have a view here, he would say that it is money that makes for the durability of *homo faber's* work, not vice versa.

17. For a very interesting discussion of the revival of "the art of memory" in the late sixteenth and seventeenth century, for very different purposes than the ancient's interest in memorizing lines in a speech, see Frances Yates, *The Art of Memory* (1968).

18. Indeed, since personal identity is based on memory (the present appropriation of the past) this conclusion should not be surprising.

19. Let me remind the reader of the old Lockean chestnut: the solitary acorn picker is an extremely atypical example of worker in any period of history; work is social in that it immediately involves many individuals "working together," or presupposes *past* work (as well as knowledge and thought).

20. A long line of what Marxists would call "petit bourgeois" anarchists do trace their intellectual pedigree back to Locke. The Libertarian Party in the USA and the work of Robert Nozick in political theory, *Anarchy, State and Utopia* (1974), revived Locke for the Reagan era.

21. Much of "Of Property" surprisingly sounds like a Diggers pamphlet, without the rhetorical flourish. The common is given its due, while labor is dignified, but all with a twist. The secret of Locke's strategy is to be found in Federici's work:

> [N]either the Diggers, nor Absolutism, but a well-calculated mixture of both, whereby the democratization of command rested on the solid shoulders of a

state always ready, like the Newtonian God, to reimpose order on souls who proceeded too far in the ways of self-determination.

(Federici 2004: 289)

Locke uses the "rights of labor" against the "rights of the common."

22. Hans Jürgen Eysenck gives an almost perfect Lockean exposition in his *Crime and Personality* (1977). Consider:

> The theory here advocated would say that all societies, as the price for survival, must insist on a certain amount of socialization, and in the renunci-ation of all citizens of flagrantly anti-social conduct. This is accomplished by a process of conditioning in which parents, teachers, peers, judges and others join. The outcome, in any particular case will depend upon two factors, one is the amount and kind of conditioning attempted by parents, teachers, peers and the other is the conditionability of the child.

(Eysenck 1977: 209)

23. Locke's *Necessitas cogit ad turpia* is obsessively echoed by almost all of Defoe's fictional heroes and heroines as well as by Defoe himself, no stranger to the truth of the adage and its consequences. Defoe writes in *The Review* of 15 September 1711:

> The Man is not Rich because he is Honest, but he is Honest because he is Rich … What shall we say?—Give me not Poverty Lest I steal, says the *Wiseman*, that is, if I am poor I shall be a Thief—I tell you all Gentlemen, in your poverty, the best of you will rob your Neighbor … Distress removes from the Soul, all Relation, all Affection, Sense of Justice, and all the Obligations, either moral or Religious, that secure one man against another…

Defoe's "social-democratic" solutions to the "crime problem" did not impress Locke however. As Peter King described it in a sentence in *The Development of the English Economy to 1750*: "John Locke claimed that brandy and beer were responsible for poverty in a report to the Board of Trade in 1697" (1971 444).

24. Ian Hacking is somewhat critical of Locke's handling of the wager:

> Locke, it is evident, had no conception of probability logic … Locke picked up Pascal's argument like much else, from the Port Royal Logic. (Indeed, it has regularly been conjectured that Locke was one of the "several hands" who translated one of the early English versions.)

(Hacking 1975b: 70)

25. Much of the "enlightened" prison reform in the late eighteenth and nineteenth centuries will take this theme to heart. Cf. Michel Foucault's now almost classic *Discipline and Punish: The Birth of the Prison* (1978).

26. Did the younger Locke ever meet that great opponent of scarcity, Winstanley? According to James Alsop in "Gerrard Winstanley's Later Life," it would have

been possible (1979). Apparently after his defeats on the common, Winstanley joined the 1660's version of the "Me" generation.

> Around 1657 he established himself as a minor landed gentleman in Cobham, the scene of his radical phase. Finally he returned to London and re-entered commercial life as a corn-chandler.
>
> (Alsop 1979)

If Alsop's take is true, it is a perfect illustration of that recent adage: "you can't always get what you want, but if you try sometimes, you'll find, you get what you need."

27. Apparently Grotius and Pufendorf condoned theft when hunger presses a man; this impressed Defoe, but not Locke. Cf. M.E. Novak, *Defoe and the Nature of Man* (1963).

28. The Americas offered Locke a direct glimpse at a "pre-monetary" world; they also provided him a stage for the working out of human experience in a "state of nature," especially English experience. The line between suspension and immediacy, accumulation and piracy, law and crime was filled with surprises that undoubtedly had a profound effect on Locke's theory of man in the "state of nature." The following incident in 1697 might not have amused Locke, but it certainly added to his experience:

> [King William's War] was followed by an outbreak of piracy by the seafaring men, whom the peace deprived of their employment as privateers. The home government's first attempt to suppress them was made by granting a commission to Captain William Kidd in command of a privateer, the *Adventure Galley*, in which some of the leading whig politicians were share-holders. Kidd turned pirate himself and, before he was hanged, the incident made much noise in party politics at home.
>
> (Clark 1955: 330)

For a more detailed version, see Horwitz (1977: 261). The conditions of space exploration are unlikely to provide a similar human X-ray for some time.

29. It is amazing to see that Locke is quite frank about the source of scarcity in the accumulation process, while Sartre—presumably a Marxist—defines scarcity as an ontological condition of the human species in *Critique of Dialectical Reason* (Sartre 2004).

30. The history of the relation between English anthropology and the British Empire has yet to be written but, when it is, Locke will undoubtedly prove to have been a seminal figure.

31. Locke sometimes appears to be arguing against opponents of the death penalty. But who were they? Figures like Winstanley, who wrote: "Did the light of Reason make this law, that some part of mankinde should kill and hang another part of mankinds that could not walk in their steps?" (*The New Law of Righteousness*

[1649], quoted in Linebaugh 2006: 42). But most figures like Winstanley were long dead or silenced. Linebaugh writes:

> This did not mean that other voices did not exist or were not remembered. Evidence of opposition arose from the hanged themselves. It can be found in their "Last Words." Or, evidenced in action, or expressed in ballad…
>
> (Linebaugh 2006: 42)

32. The famous "we" and "them" of the law-and-order politician would find some embarrassing confusions in Locke's time as well as the present. Certainly money created the temporal differentiation between the criminal and the legal businessman. It is only with money that the contrast between present behavior and future result could open a chasm between humans as well. For with money came the twin passions of Ambition and Despair, but these need not be essential characteristics. If money can make a man, it can also break him. The gap between the thief and the capitalist was *paper thin*, not only in the tried but true tradition of "honest workers versus capitalist bandits," but more importantly, in the continual cycle of bankruptcy, poverty, enterprise, bankruptcy which was a quite widespread personal expression of world-economic fluctuations. Furthermore, the criminal actually created forms of enterprise and behavior that legitimate capital was to appropriate. Indeed, what sly member of Barbon and Co. did not secretly recognize that the clippers and counterfeiters were servants of the nation's businessmen, who provided an expanded money supply at the risk of their own skins. The writings of Mandeville Gay, Swift and Defoe show that this point was becoming a commonplace at this time.

33. Michel Foucault, in his analysis of Locke in *The Order of Things* (1970), does not take seriously the accumulation aspect of the monetary relation. Exchange is not just for its own sake; that is why Barbon & Co. lose the debate with Locke. But Foucault, before he rediscovered Power, took much of the debate at face value (see 1970: 180–182).

34. For a discussion of the relation between "trust" in the state and credit during this period, cf. J.G.A. Pocock, *The Machiavellian Moment* (1975), Chapter 13, titled "Neo Machiavellian Political Economy."

35. One must remember that the counterfeiter is trespassing on the basic conjuncture of the new bourgeois state: that of representation and trust. Just as our ideas re-present experience in the creation of the self, so too does the state re-present the individual and his interests to himself. A loss of fidelity leads to dissolution in either case.

36. Hacking's importation of Foucault into anglophone philosophy brings a refreshing ease into historical analysis. However, he gives the wrong impression of Locke, whom he views as relatively blasé about problems of public communication due to his lack of interest in the question "Does 'violet' signify the same idea for you as it does for me?" Locke located the public problems of communication in different areas, perhaps, but he was vitally interested in the conveying of ideas from "breast to breast." He thought that difficulties arise from not

having any *ideas*, or *confused* ideas, as will be shown in the Conclusion. Cf. Ian Hacking, *What Does Language Matter to Philosophy?* (1975b: Chapter 5).

37. The *Essay Concerning Human Understanding* is obsessed with gold. Gold is used repeatedly, in dozens of different contexts, as an example. In fact, it would not have been far wrong to have titled the book, An *Essay Concerning the Understanding of Gold*. Perhaps the obsession arises from the fact that much of the book was written in exile, when financial difficulties were the source of much anxiety for Locke.

38. Vicker's and Appleby's critiques of Locke, by simply avoiding his semantic writings, are substantially invalidated.

39. In the last fifteen years or so, there has been a small revival of interest in Locke—inspired, ironically enough, by Chomsky's earnest critique of "empiricism" and espousal of "rationalism." Cf. Noam Chomsky, *Cartesian Linguistics* (1966).

3. ABUSED WORDS

1. The incident in *Colonel Jack* I refer to has the following background. Little Col. Jack goes out to the Customhouse on his first pick-pocketing venture with a young Rogue as his "Master." His Master lifts a little leather case with various Bills of Exchange (in English and French) as well as Goldsmith's notes, one for £300 the other for £12 10s. The Rogue manages to "cash" the £12 10s note but despairs of cashing in the larger one. He gives £5 to little Jack as his share.

   This begins Colonel Jack's journey into the anxiety-ridden world of money. Up until then he had never had *any* money, that is, he inhabited Locke's state of Nature in the middle of London. Thus, he did not know what to do with it or what it was. Foremost for him was the problem of carrying money, for his pockets were full of holes! He reflects:

   > And now as I was full of Wealth, behold! I was full of Cares, for what to do to secure my Money I could not tell, and this held me so long, and was so Vexatious to me the next Day, that I truly sat down and cried.

   But the Rogue puts together a scheme whereby the £300 note as well as the other bills could be recovered by their owners, and Col. Jack could get the reward, a common enough practice then (as now). The referred-to incident arises from the reward Col. Jack gets from the merchant. The verb "to tell" in this context is synonymous with "to count," as in bank "teller" (see Defoe 1970: 23).

2. Until relatively recently, this was true, with a few exceptions like the fine book by Roger S. Woolhouse, *Locke's Philosophy of Science and Knowledge: A Consideration of Some Aspects of An Essay Concerning Human Understanding* (1971). But since the Putnam-Kripke critiques of the standard theory of reference, new attention has been given to the distinction.

3. The philosopher of "modes" was, of course, Spinoza in the seventeenth century. Perhaps a definition of "mode" from the *Ethics* might be of interest:

By mode, I mean the modifications ("affectiones") of substance, or that which exists in, and is conceived through, something other than itself.

(Spinoza 1901: Part I, Definition V)

4. This was true not only for the rulers. As Linebaugh writes in "All The Atlantic Mountains Shook":

> The people packed in the slavers spoke many languages. To communicate they had to develop a language of their own, and as often as not this was the oppressor's language … A combination of 1) ("Jack Tar English"), 2) "sabir" or the *lingua franca* of the Mediterranean, 3) the canting talk of the underworld and 4) West African grammatical construction produced the "pidgin English" that became the language of the African coast … Pidgin became an instrument, like the drum or fiddle, of communication among the oppressed: scorned and not easily understood by "polite" Society.
>
> (Linebaugh 1982: 109)

5. This was and *is* especially true of land. In more recent times, the indeterminacy of translation has led, on a legal as well as political level, to an international aboriginal revolt (especially in North America) with demands for good translation and the return of land taken on the basis of null and void contracts. Locke's suspicions were thus prophetic; of course, Locke was neither the first nor the last to harbor such suspicions. Consider R. Meinertzhagen, writing in his diary in Nairobi, Kenya in 1902, of a conversation he had with the British High Commissioner, Charles Eliot:

> He is not my idea of a High Commissioner; he looks more like a university don or priest. He is a scholar, a philosopher, and a very able man with great vision. He amazed me with his views on the future of East Africa. He envisaged a thriving colony of thousands of Europeans with their families, the whole of the country from the Aberdares and Mount Kenya to the German border divided up into farms … He intends to confine the natives to reserves and use them as cheap labour on farms. I suggested that the country belonged to Africans and that their interests must prevail over the interests of strangers. He would not hear of it; he kept on using the word "paramount" with reference to the claims of Europeans. I said that some day the African would be educated and armed; that would lead to a clash. Eliot thought that day was so far distant as not to matter…
>
> (Quoted in Davidson 1964: 366)

But aside from the "echoes" of the initial European enclosure on non-European lands reflecting back on episodes like Wounded Knee a decade ago, there is a more pervasive and subtle effect that the indeterminacy we have been noting under Locke's influence has had. The land tenure in the legal systems of once-colonized nations appear filled with "anomalies" when there is an attempt to translate their rules in a European legal code. This is certainly the case of Nigeria where there are, in effect, three legal codes operating: traditional, English, Nigerian governmental. Gaius Ezejiofor writes:

> [B]efore the advent of the British all lands were held under customary law. Since some of them are now held under English tenure it means, therefore, that there have been conversions from customary to English tenure. The question is, given the feudal foundations of the estates, can they really be created in Nigeria, which has never experienced feudalism?
>
> (Ezejiofor 1980: 245)

6. Vico makes this point as part of his inversion of the sciences: *Geometrica demonstramus, quia facimus: si physica demonstrare possemus, faceremus* (literally, "we can demonstrate geometric entities because we make them, but if we were able to demonstrate physical entities, we would have to have made them.") Vico is referring here to the "constructivist" interpretation of geometry, which was the major interpretation until Hilbert's *Grundlagen der Geometrie* of 1899. After Hilbert, however, the *wonder* of Descartes' algebraicization of geometry became largely unexperiencable. However, it was in the work of Descartes, Fermat and Viete that we have one of the first great victories of the Moderns over the Ancients (with the help of the Arabs). Carl Boyer writes of this development in *The History of the Calculus*:

> The influence of [Archimedes] had been very strong for almost two centuries, but in the work of Viete and of Fermat we have evidence of the impression made by [Apollonius and Diophantus], as well as by the Arabic and Italian developments of algebra. Viete realized the facility to be gained in the handling of geometric problems by their reduction to the solution of algebraic equations ... an inversion of the Greek view, in accordance with which algebraic equations were reduced to geometric constructions for purposes of solution ... The work of Fermat and Descartes went much further than did either the algebraic solution of geometric problems by Viete or the graphical representation of variables by Oresme, for it associated with each curve an equation in which are implied all the properties of the curve.
>
> (Boyer 1949: 154)

We have here an example of the famous "linearization of thought" whereby a multidimensional mental activity is reduced to a code. But this activity persisted until Hilbert, so to speak, as on a reservation. In the twentieth century, mathematical pedagogy has seen persistent attempts to revive it, but like all attempts to resuscitate old folk practices one wonders at the result. For a recent discussion of Vico, cf. Leon Pompa, *Vico: A Study of the New Science* (1975).

7. As Marx points out there is much confusion over the notion of turnover time because of the many different time cycles in the process of capitalist reproduction. This confusion has not lifted to this day. Consider Marx: "For the capitalist, the turnover time of his capital is the time for which he has to advance

his capital in order for this to be valorized and for him to receive it back in its original shape" (Marx 1978: 236).

8. Col. Jack had the "good fortune" of being "shanghaied" (to use the jargon of the next century) to Virginia, where he went through a transformation the inverse of William Kidd's.

9. Hilary Putnam has revived a Lockean conception of substance in—Locke would be pleased—semantic theory, under the rubric "natural kind": "Natural kinds are classes of things whose normal distinguishing characteristics are held together or even explained by deep-lying mechanisms" (Putnam 1975: 139). Lovers of historical continuity would be pleased to note that Putnam cites "gold" as one of his examples of natural kind.

10. G.L.S. Shackle has made a career out of emphasizing this "existential" aspect of Keynes' thought, for example, "Keynes and Today's Establishment in Economic Theory: A View" (1973). Perhaps Keynes thought that Ramsey was moving toward the domain of uncertainty in his "human logic," for, in his eulogy for Ramsey, Keynes refers to Ramsey's nipped-in-the-bud attempt to create a "human logic" in contrast to "formal logic" and the "calculus of probability":

> Thus the calculus of probability belongs to formal logic. But the basis of our degrees of belief—or the *a priori* probabilities, as they used to be called is a part of our human outfit, perhaps given us by natural selection analogous to our perception and our memories rather than to formal logic. So far I yield to Ramsey—I think he is right.
>
> (Keynes 1972b: 339)

Keynes wrote this in October 1931 or before, that is, during the period when he was making the transition from the *Treatise on Money* to the *General Theory*. Wittgenstein lived to carry on in this domain, beginning the year of the Crash, 1929.

11. For an interesting account of the early history of "life insurance's" transcendental basis, cf. Ian Hacking, *The Emergence of Probability* (1975a). The following is a typical passage in his chapter on "Annuities":

> In 1692 the British government devised one of its characteristically unique annuity schemes. There had been public discussion of how it should go and this aroused the interest of Astronomer Royal, Edmond Halley. Since there were no adequate statistics in England, he enlisted the help of a German pastor, Casper Neuman of Breslaw. Leibniz acted as intermediary.
>
> On the basis of five years of exact records of mortality he was able to draw up the best table of mortality so far and then combine this data with his solution to problems in joint annuities (1693).
>
> (Hacking 1975a: 111–112)

12. One way to put the problem is to say that historical predicates, that is, terms referring to classes of human action are not *projectible*, in Nelson Goodman's terminology; cf. Goodman's *Fact, Fiction and Forecast* (1955: Chapter 4).

This, of course, is a source of serious problems for economics and especially for econometrics. Keynes was doing on the level of theory exactly what he saw capitalists (in their "best moments") doing in practice ... acting in the face of uncertainty. That is, he tried to do economic theory on the basis of "animal spirits" without the comforting "as if" fables of equilibrium. Or, to put it in Goodmanian jargon, projecting non-projectible predicates with the projectible hope perhaps that so projecting them would transform them into projectible predicates. It was, as they say, a gamble.

To put this point in Keynes' language:

> Our criticism of the accepted classical theory has consisted not so much in finding logical flaws in its analysis as in pointing out that its tacit assumptions are seldom or never satisfied, with the result that it cannot solve the economic problems of the actual world.
>
> But if our central controls succeed in establishing an aggregate volume of output corresponding to full employment as nearly as is practicable the classical theory comes into its own again from this point onwards.
>
> (Keynes 1964: 378)

Keynes' problematic was generalized by the "later Wittgenstein" into mathematics itself; for a forceful presentation of this point, see Saul A. Kripke, *Wittgenstein: On Rules and Private Language* (1982), with his grue-like "quus"-function.

13. Lawrence spotted "bad faith" in the young Keynes and his circle. He writes in a letter to D. Garnett on April 19, 1915: "I feel I should go mad when I think of your set, Duncan Grant, and Keynes and Birrell. It makes me dream of beetles" (quoted in D. Garnett's introduction to Keynes' memoir of his early life in Keynes [1972b]). Keynes' reply was more than two decades in coming, although one might say that the whole *General Theory* is a vindication of Lawrence's distaste. On September 19, 1938 Keynes spoke these words:

> If, therefore, I altogether ignore our merits—our charm, our intelligence, our unworldliness, our affection—I can see us as water-spiders, gracefully skimming, as light and reasonable as air, the surface of the stream without any contact with the eddies and currents underneath. And if I imagine us as coming under the observation of Lawrence's ignorant, jealous, irritable, hostile eyes, what a combination of qualities we offered to arouse his passionate distaste; this thin rationalism skipping on the crust of the lava, ignoring both the reality and the value of the vulgar passions, joined to libertinism and comprehensive irreverence ... All this is unfair to poor silly, well-meaning us. But that is why I say that there may have been just a grain of truth when Lawrence said in 1914 that we were "done for."
>
> (Keynes 1972b: 450)

14. This passage, written in 1913 or before, reveals much of what Keynes described in his *Memoir*:

> India, as we all know, already wastes far too high a proportion of her resources in the needless accumulation of the precious metals. The government ought

not to encourage in the slightest degree this ingrained fondness for hoarding hard gold. By the elimination of both precious metals, to the utmost extent that public opinion will permit, from amongst the hoards and circulation of the country they ought to counteract an uncivilized and wasteful habit. It is interesting to reflect that India's love of the precious metal, ruinous though it has been to her own economic development, has flourished in the past to the great advantage of Western nations.

(Keynes 1971b: 69–70)

The tone of Keynes' circle changed perhaps as a consequence of the war; a decade later E.M. Forster visited India and the product of his experiences describes the brewing of a nationalist struggle; see Forster, *A Passage to India* (1924).

15. But what happens to the remaining 1 percent, that is, Nature or Land? Marx, in an "uncharacteristic passage," explains:

[A]ll progress in capitalist agriculture is a progress in the art, not only of robbing the worker, but of robbing the soil; all progress in increasing the fertility of the soil for a given time is a progress towards ruining the more long-lasting sources of that fertility. The more a country proceeds from large-scale industry as the background of its development, as in the case of the United States, the more rapid is this process of destruction. Capitalist production, therefore, only develops the techniques and the degree of combination of the social process of production by simultaneously undermining the original sources of all wealth—the soil and the worker.

(Marx 1976: 638)

16. Locke was not alone, writes Charles Wilson:

The idea of public workhouses and charity schools was noted in many of the pamphlets of the [sixteen] nineties. John Bellers, the Quaker clothier, published his *Proposals for a College of Industry* in 1695; in 1697 his *Epistle to Friends concerning the Education of Children*. John Cary, the wealthy Bristol sugar merchant, touches on similar proposals in his *Essay* (1696). All these writers were "mercantilist."

(Wilson 1965: 232)

17. Gregory King's statistics, for better or worse, are the standard. King fully realized the etymology of the word "statistics." He prefaces his *Observations* with the following remark:

If to be well apprized of the true state and condition of a nation, Especially in the two maine Articles of its People, & Wealth, be a Piece of Politicall Knowledge, of all others, & at all times, the most usefull, & Necessary; then surely at a Time when a long & very expensive War ... seems to be at its Crisis, such a knowledge of our own Nation must be of the Highest Concern.

(Quoted in Wilson 1965: 229)

A digest of King's income statistics is printed in Wilson (1965: 239).

18. Of course, wages are as illusory as ideologies, aren't they? Consider the following:

    > In the expression "value of labour," the concept of value is not only completely extinguished, but inverted so that it becomes its contrary. It is an expression as imaginary as the value of the earth. These imaginary expressions arise, nevertheless, from the relations of production themselves. They are categories for the forms of appearance of essential relations. That in their appearance things are often presented in an inverted way is something fairly familiar in every science apart from political economy.
    >
    > (Marx 1976: 677)

    But if you received a wage increase would you refuse it as imaginary? Or a half million dollars is offered for a forgotten piece of property left to you by an uncle in Tennessee, would you laugh at the imaginary temptation? As with the moon illusion, knowing its causes does not reduce its power.

19. A "flexible wage policy" was tried in the USA during the first phase of the depression. Thus, the money wage-earnings of US workers in 1932 were 71 percent of the 1925–1929 level (whereas they were 110 percent and 95 percent in France and England respectively). But by 1938, even in the face of more than 20 percent unemployment, wages rose 20 percent higher than the 1925–1929 average (data taken from Phelps Brown 1968: 234, Table 20; and 258, Figure 45). E.H. Phelps Brown writes of the cause of this change:

    > In the USA, this was due to a revolution: a new unionism, recruiting new members, armed with new statutory powers and encouraged by a new purpose of government, obtained recognition and agreement from employers who had never dealt with unions before.
    >
    > (Phelps Brown 1968: 239)

    The Flint "sit down strike" or live-in came along a few months after the printing of the *General Theory* and made Keynes' point quite graphically.

20. Keynes writes that the working class sees through the deception that is presupposed by capitalist accumulation:

    > It was not natural for a population, of whom so few enjoyed the comforts of life, to accumulate so hugely. The war has disclosed the possibility of consumption to all and the vanity of abstinence to many. Thus the bluff is discovered; the labouring classes may be no longer willing to forego so largely and the capitalist classes, no longer confident of the future, may seek to enjoy more fully their liberties of consumption so long as they last, and thus they precipitate the hour of their confiscation.
    >
    > (Keynes 1971a: 13)

21. There has been much said about Keynes' "directive intelligence" and the social being it presupposes; the passage quoted comes from the 1926 essay "The End of Laissez Faire," in *Essays in Persuasion* (1972a: 272). To get a better sense of whom Keynes had in mind, a review he wrote in 1927 of H.G. Wells' *The World*

of William Clissold might be of help. There, he praises Wells' attempt to deal with the problematic of his hero, Clissold. At the beginning of the book, Clissold becomes disillusioned with Socialism because he found socialists to be sentimentalists and pseudo-intellectuals, but he still wants a "socialist revolution." Here is how Wells—and, with reservations, Keynes—sees a path for the solution of the dilemma:

> This is Clissold's "Open Conspiracy." Clissold's direction is to the Left—far, far to the Left; but he seeks to summon from the Right the creative force and the constructive will that is to carry him there … The remoulding of the world needs a touch of the creative Brahma. But at present Brahma is serving Science and Business, not Politics and Government. The extreme danger of the world is, in Clissold's words, lest, "before the creative Brahma can get to work, Siva, in other words the passionate destructiveness of Labour awakening to its now needless limitations and privations, may make Brahma's task impossible." We all feel this, I think. We know that we need urgently to create a milieu in which Brahma can get to work before its too late.
>
> (Keynes 1927)

The main difficulty Keynes finds with this "Open Conspiracy" is that businessmen are, in effect, nihilists:

> They have no creed, these potential open conspirators, no creed whatever … That is why they fall back on the grand substitute motive, the perfect *Ersatz*, the anodyne of those who, in fact, want nothing at all—Money.
>
> (Keynes 1927)

In the midst of this passage, Keynes makes one qualification: "Unless they have the luck to be scientists or artists." Following that, he regrets Wells' caricature of the universities, saying, "They may yet become temples of Brahma which even Siva will respect" (see Keynes 1927).

In these qualifications and regrets, we see what kind of social figure Keynes expects to solve the Crisis. It is not the capitalist, who could but won't, nor the proletariat, who could not, but wants to try. It is the scientist, artist and university don or—to put it more rhetorically—the synthetic, creative poet, the virtuoso scientist, the unmoved mover of thought *qua* politician, *qua* enlightened prince, *qua* directive intelligence. Yes, we find in Keynes the sorry tale of Plato's *Seventh Letter* all over again.

22. Keynes was officially and personally involved in the affairs of Cambridge University all his life, and his cultural antennae were extremely sensitive. He locates himself in intellectual space with these words, in 1920, in the "Preface" to *A Treatise on Probability*:

> It may be perceived that I have been much influenced by W.E. Johnson, G.E. Moore and Bertrand Russell, that is to say by Cambridge, which, with great debts to the writers of continental Europe, yet continues in direct succession

the English tradition of Locke, Berkeley, and Hume, of Mill and Sidgwick, who in spite of their divergences of doctrines, are united in a preference for what is matter of fact...

(Keynes 1973: xxv)

As for Wittgenstein, aside from being helped financially by Keynes when he first came back to Cambridge from Austria in 1929, it is interesting to note that in his "Preface" to *Philosophical Investigations* (1953) written in 1945, only two men are mentioned, Frank Ramsey and Piero Sraffa, the Cambridge economist who was part of Keynes' circle.

23. And its good that we can not see microscopically, Locke argues:

And if by the help of such microscopical eyes (if I may so call them) a man could penetrate further than ordinary into the secret composition and radical texture of bodies, he would not make any great advantage by the change, if such an acute sight would not serve to conduct him to the market and exchange...

(Locke 1823a: II, xxiii, 12)

24. As Axel Leijonhufvud put it in "Keynes and the Keynesians: A Suggested Interpretation":

To make the transition from Walras' world to Keynes' world, it is thus sufficient to dispense with the assumed *tatonnement* mechanism. The removal of the auctioneer simply means that the generation of the information needed to coordinate economic activities in a large system where decision making is decentralized will take time and will involve economic costs. No other classical assumptions need to be relinquished.

(Leijonhufvud 1967: 403)

The essence of Leijonhufvud's argument is like Nietzsche's; even though most people have heard that God is dead, they do not quite know what it means.

25. The fundamental principles of Frege are to be found in *The Foundations of Arithmetic* (1960: xxii).

26. Why this rage for Latin titles in the first two decades of twentieth-century English philosophy? (Apparently, Moore suggested *Tractatus* to Wittgenstein. Cf. W.W. Bartley III, *Wittgenstein* [1973: 52].) One can only speculate that it was part of a European-wide "crisis of the intellectual," whereby the use of Latin referred back to the ancient esoteric but international code of the "Dark Ages."

27. Two major pre-World War One theoreticians on money, Weber and Simmel, hesitated at the portals of this functionalization. Consider Weber's *The Theory of Social and Economic Organization* (1947), which was finished in 1919, at a time when post-war hyper-inflation was beginning to take off. Prices of wholesale goods between November 1918 and January 1920 went up approximately 140 percent. Cf. Tables 1 and 2 in Karsten Laureen and Jorgen Pedersen, *The German Inflation 1918–1923* (1964: 133). A communist insurrection had

just barely been crushed, and the Red Armies were marching in the East. In his debate with Knapp's "State Theory of Money," he grants the possibility of freeing the monetary system from any "mechanical limits," set by the technological availability of the precious metals, but this possibility opens up two related probabilities: (a) the dominance of the "purely personal interests of the members of [the monetary authority's] administrative staff, as was true of the use of the printing presses by the Red Armies" (Weber 1947: 307); and (b) inflation and depreciation. As for (a), he writes:

> The significance of metallic standards today lies precisely in the elimination of these interests from influence on the monetary situation, or more precisely, since it is always possible for the state to abandon them in favour of a pure paper standard, a check on such interests. In spite of the mechanical character of its operation, a metallic standard nevertheless makes possible a higher degree of formal rationality in a market economy because it permits action to be oriented wholly to market advantages.
>
> (Weber 1947: 307–308)

Putting it in Marx's terms, Weber's recommendation of a metallic standard is that it keeps the attention of both workers and capitalists on the commodity-form instead of the state-form, thus letting the logic of the commodity prevail.

Knapp, of course, recognized (b), but he argued that, on the basis of a form of Say's law, since every one is both a debtor and creditor on the whole the absolute value of money is irrelevant. Weber dismissed this argument as "a phantom" by pointing out that creditors, rentiers and "people living on fixed salaries or income" are ruined by inflation (and especially by hyper-inflation). That is, what is true of the whole is not necessarily true of the part. He concludes his critique with the following warning:

> The effect of this kind of radical alterations in the purchasing power of money is today to produce a chronic tendency toward social revolution in spite of the fact that many entrepreneurs are in a position to make unusual profits from the foreign exchange situation and that a few of the workers are powerful enough to secure increases in their nominal wages. It is, of course, open to anyone to welcome this revolutionary tendency and the accompanying tremendous unsettlement of the market economy. Such an opinion cannot be scientifically refuted.
>
> (Weber 1947: 308–309)

Weber would have agreed with that famous but historically inaccurate opening sentence of Keynes' 1919 article "Inflation": "Lenin is said to have declared that the best way to destroy the Capitalist System was to debauch the currency" (Keynes 1972a). At that time so did Keynes, but within a decade Keynes was to invert his position. For in the process of developing the *General Theory*, Keynes was to see that Lenin's purported technique of sabotage could be turned into the prime instrument for the survival of the Capitalist System. After all, what is a "flexible money policy" but a (controlled) "debauching of the currency"?

28. Locke's master, Shaftesbury, was a master of manipulation, as evidenced by this little piece of gossip concerning the Popish Plot in the memoirs of a contemporary, Roger North:

> A certain Lord, of his Confidence in Parliament, once asked [Shaftesbury] what he intended to do with the Plot, which was so full of Nonsense, as would scarcely go down with Idiots; what then could he propose by pressing the Belief of it upon men of Common Sense, and especially in Parliament? It is no matter, said he, the More Nonsensical the better; if we cannot bring them to swallow worse nonsense than that, we shall never do any good with them. This was a true politic Thought; For, when the Design is to drive Men upon changes that are to terminate in their own Confusion and Perdition, it is not to be attempted without an extreme insanity of mind, or Infatuation, in the Generality of people, by way of Postulation, to be well established by previous Experiments upon them.
>
> (North, quoted in Birrell 1963: 284)

29. Bertrand Russell ridiculed this obsession with self-retrieval in the Tristam Shandy paradox in *The Principles of Mathematics* (1937: 358). The paradox arises from the hero of the novel complaining that it took two years to record the events of his first two days of life. Russell pointed out that even at that rate, if Tristam had an infinitely long life, he would eventually manage to "record all of it."

30. Locke writes:

> The comfort and advantage of society not being to be had without communication of thoughts, it was necessary that man should find some external sensible signs, whereof those invisible ideas, which his thoughts are made up of, might be made known to others. For this purpose nothing was so fit, either for plenty or quickness, as those articulate sounds which with so much ease and variety he found himself to make.
>
> (Locke 1823a: III, ii, 1)

31. For two elementary texts on communication theory, cf. John F. Young, *Information Theory* (1971) and Elwin Edwards, *Information Transmission* (1969).

32. Roughly stated, if C is the channel capacity ("the amount of information transmitted over a given time maximally"), and if H is the entropy of the source ("a measure of the information emitted by a source"), and if R is the rate of transmission, then:

$$R \leq \frac{C}{H}$$

Clearly if you are interested in a high rate of transmission and the channel capacity is limited then the entropy of the source must be reduced. It is this relation, plus the previously mentioned constraints, that have led to the tendential reduction of the entropy of language. Hence, less surprise, fewer idiosyncrasies and greater standardization in orthography and in language generally.

33. Wittgenstein's work played a crucial role in the theoretical transition from private ("What do I mean by what I say") to public discourse ("What do the others mean by what they say"). Even Grice's attempt to reduce meaning to intentions posits those intentions as other-centered, cf. H.P. Grice, "Utterer's Meaning and Intentions" (1969).

34. This, of course, is a point of difference between linguistic systems *per se* and monetary ones.

35. Of course Wittgenstein would argue that there is nothing "inside" to appeal to either. His argument against "private language" employs a familiar Lockean prop, the diary, against the Lockean axiom that words signify ideas (in the mind). Cf. Wittgenstein, *Philosophical Investigations*:

> 258. Let us imagine the following case. I want to keep a diary about the recurrence of a certain sensation. To this end I associate it with the sign "S" and write this sign in a calendar for every day on which I have the sensation.—I will remark first of all that a definition of the sign cannot be formulated.—But still I can give myself a kind of ostensive definition. How? Can I point to the sensation? Not in the ordinary sense. But I speak, or write the sign down, and as it were, point to it internally.—But what is this ceremony for? For that is all it seems to be! A definition surely serves to establish the meaning of a sign.— Well, that is done precisely by the concentration of my attention; for in this way I impress on myself the connexion between the sign and the sensation. But "I impress it on myself" can only mean: this process brings it about that I remember the connexion *right* in the future. But in the present case I have no criterion of correctness. One would like to say: whatever is going to seem right to me is right. And that only means that here we can't talk about "right."
> (Wittgenstein 1953)

Where Locke despairs of finding any standing rule or criterion for the use of a word in the community of linguistic others, Wittgenstein locates here the only possible source. The internal "ceremonies" of Locke are empty; they do not constitute a Wittgensteinian "game."

From Locke's viewpoint, the transformation of the reflection on language and money between the 1690s and the 1930s is one of intersection and inversion: signs become things (language), while things become signs (money). The symbolic world becomes simultaneously more objective and more subjective after Keynes and Wittgenstein. As if to seal the signs/things relation, Wittgenstein ends Part I of the *Philosophical Investigations*:

And nothing is more wrong-headed than calling meaning a mental activity! Unless, that is, one is setting out to produce confusion. (It would also be possible to speak of an activity of butter when it rises in price, and if no problems are produced by this it is harmless.)

(Wittgenstein 1953: §693)

We might comment on this analogy from a Marxist tongue, or perhaps, trade another analogy with it. Just as there is a process of reification, so too there is a process of psychification, that is, social relations (price) can be transformed into the activity of things (butter-activity), and social relations (meaning) can be transferred into psychological episodes (mental-activities) ... and both can create "confusion."

36. Linebaugh analyses the philology of money as well as its many "deviant" uses among the London proletariat:

Many forms of money existed besides gold and silver—privately minted tokens, the tallyslicks of the public house or victualler's shop, clipped, coined and counterfeit monies, navy tickets, and the tickets of "mine uncle's" ... Each denomination had its own name: "Jack" (1/4 d.), "mopus" and "make" (1/2 d.), "winnings" (1 d.), "threpps" and "thrums" (3 d.), "kick," "sice," "simon," and "pig" (6 d.), "loon-slatt" (13 s. 1/2 d.) "slate" and "trooper" (2 s. 6 d.), "ounce" (5 s.) "smelt" (1/2 guinea), "heart's ease" (20 s.), and "yellow boy" (one guinea)...

(Linebaugh 2006: 56)

"Old Mr. Gory," the title of the chapter from which this passage was quoted, is another name for "gold."

37. Barbon, besides being a "projector," was a real-estate speculator, indeed one of the most active speculators in the London of his day. If we are to trust the delightful portrait drawn by Christopher Hibbert in *London: The Biography of a City*:

Barbon was the son of Praise-God Barbon (Bare-bones), the leather merchant and Fifth Monarchy man who, being nominated by Cromwell and his council of officers as Member for London, gave his name to one of the Common- wealth's Parliaments. Nicholas was born about 1640, studied medicine in Holland, and was admitted as an Honorary Fellow to the College of physicians in 1664. He was an ambitious, shrewd, persuasive and masterful man whose arrogant demeanor gave way on occasions to an insinuating charm. Although better known as the founder of fire insurance companies and as an economist quoted by Marx, he was also the most active and ambitious of all the property dealers of Restoration London ... Some of his schemes were successful, others not. Many of the houses his contractors built were sound, a few fell to pieces. His methods were questionable, on occasions actually criminal ... He was a humbug, dishonest and unscrupulous; but his flair amounted almost to genius ...

(Hibbert 1977: 89–90)

Barbon was something of an "urban pioneer":

> He "transformed Milford Lane" … from a squalid alley of brothels and tip-
> pling-roose into a respectable lane of handsome houses, cook-shops, taverns
> and vaulting schools, with a new wharf at its lower end for brewers and wood
> mongers.
>
> (Hibbert 1977: 91)

But his demise was typical of the age:

> The trouble was that Barbon had over-reached himself, and was in difficul-
> ties with his creditors. Unable to sell numbers of unfinished houses, he was
> forced to let the contractors keep them as payment for their bills. By 1694 his
> finances were strained beyond recuperation; and four years later he died. He
> left instruction in his will that none of his debts should be paid.
>
> (Hibbert 1977: 92)

38. This is where, for Locke, Φνδικη and Σημειωτηκη meet, whereas for us it is
the conjunction of semantics and the philosophy of science. But philosophical
parameters have shifted in the last decade from incommensurability (Kuhn)
and indeterminacy (Quine) to essentialism and realism (Kripke and Putnam),
scientific progress (Laudan) and an "end to fuzzy thinking" (Glymour). Indeed,
something of a Lockean tone is becoming apparent as we move to the end of
the century in this point of intersection. For some reading in the "counter-rev-
olution" in philosophy of science, cf. Larry Laudan, *Progress and its Problems*
(1977); Clark N. Glymour, *Theory and Evidence* (1980); and Saul A. Kripke,
Naming and Necessity (1980).

39. For Sade's libertines and their perverse way with mixed modes, see Roland
Barthes, *Sade, Fourier, Loyola*:

> The Family is defined on two levels: its "content" (ties of affection, society,
> gratitude, respect, etc.) at which the libertine mocks, and its "form," the
> network of normative ties—and therefore combinatory ties—with which the
> libertine plays, which he recognizes the better to fake them and on which he
> brings to bear syntactical operations; it is on this second level that for Sade
> the original transgression occurs, the one that produces the intoxication of a
> continuous invention, the jubilation of incessant surprises: "He says he knew
> a man who had fucked three children he had had with his mother, whence
> he had a daughter he had married to his son, so that by fucking her he was
> fucking his sister, his daughter, and his daughter-in-law, and he was making
> his son fuck his sister and stepmother."
>
> (Barthes 1976: 138)

Thus, Whorf contrasts SAE ("Standard Average European") languages with
Hopi:

The duties of our three-tense system and its tripartite linear objectified "time" are distributed among various verb categories, all different from our tenses; and there is no more basis for an objectified time in Hopi verbs than in other Hopi patterns...

(Whorf 1956: 145)

40. Foucault's chapter, "The Prose of the World," in which the passage is found, is a useful introduction to the kind of thinking Locke is criticizing. For a thorough study of the matter, the works of Francis Yates are essential.

41. Keynes comments on this aspect of Newton's work in "Newton, the Man," in *Essays in Biography* (1972b). After picking through Newton's trunk full of numerological calculations, Keynes concludes that "His deepest instincts were occult, esoteric, semantic...," he was indeed a magician:

Why do I call Newton a magician? Because he looked on the whole universe and all that is in it *as a riddle*, as a secret which could be read by applying pure thought to certain evidence, certain mystical clues which God had laid about the world to allow a sort of philosophers' treasure hunt to the esoteric brotherhood ... He *did* read the riddle of the heavens. And he believed that by the same powers of his introspective imagination he would read the riddle of the God head, the riddle of past and future events divinely fore-ordained, the riddle of the elements and their constitution from an original undifferentiated first matter, the riddle of health and immortality.

(Keynes 1972b: 366–367)

Here Keynes uncovers the "neurosis" hidden behind the marriage of mechanics and gold.

42. For the Cambridge Platonists, see Alexandre Koyré, *From the Closed to the Infinite Universe* (1957), Chapter 6, "God and Space, Spirit and Matter."

43. These types were continually hounding the state. Thus, in 1697, "self-confessed counterfeiters and other denizens of the London underworld" were making charges of infidelity against the Duke of Shrewsbury and causing his resignation from government.

44. Historical counterfactuals are notoriously dubious but there is no doubt that the historical conjuncture of the 1690s set the course for many subsequent developments. Had William III's regime collapsed, Locke s life would have been in danger and so too his "vision."

45. The term "chartalist" comes from Knapp's "State Theory of Money."

46. Indeed, F.A. Mann in *The Legal Aspect of Money* (1982) points out that official recognition of the "obligation of one nation to punish those who, within its own jurisdiction, counterfeit the money of another nation," was clearly enunciated by the U.S. Supreme Court in 1897, 200 years after Locke.

47. As we know, all this changed after Bretton Woods, under Keynes' guidance.

48. For an interesting discussion of "anality and money," as well as the basic essays on the matter, see Ernest Borneman, *The Psychoanalysis of Money* (1976).

49. We like to believe that we are "rid" of that myth, but it always returns "through the back door."

50. This count can be verified by looking at Nidditch's index in his edition of the *Essay Concerning Human Understanding* (Locke 1975).

51. Of more use would be a study of the development of this distinction.

52. If it is granted that *Two Treatises* was written for a specific political purpose, then why not the *Essay*? Is epistemology "above" politics?

53. Locke's influence on Pope is well known.

54. Christopher Hill sums up Locke and his age in the following words:

> Locke began as a political supporter of Shaftsbury and followed him into political exile. Yet he was no democrat, and happily accepted 1688 as the revolution to end revolutions. He and Sir Isaac Newton were the backroom boys of the Whig Junto ... Locke's *Reasonableness of Christianity* was followed by a series of books showing Christianity was not mysterious. The religious approach to politics ceased to predominate ... Discipline, and especially labour discipline, was felt by the non-working classes to be a natural necessity, preached now by economists with the same zest as by theologians.
>
> (Hill 1961: 295–296)

55. Swift and Johnson come immediately to mind. Cf. Swift's *Proposal for Correcting, Improving and Ascertaining the English Tongue* (1712) and Johnson's efforts "to stabilize the language" through his dictionary.

56. There is another way of increasing the rate of transmission of information, which is, for some, a new measure of the wealth of nations, namely, increasing the channel capacity. But this has always been done with great hesitancy, since it involves the possibility of giving access to a much wider audience than desired by the controllers of the information flow.

57. Pope captures in form and content the Lockean spirit. Consider the following lines from *An Essay on Criticism*:

> False Eloquence, like the Prismatic Glass,
> Its gaudy colors spreads on ev'ry place,
> The Face of Nature we no more survey,
> All glares alike, without Distinction gay.
>
> (Pope: 311–314)

With a little of Newton's *Optics* added.

58. Blake's response was vitriolic and unceasing. Consider the following lines from "Milton, Book the First," *William Blake: The Collected Poems*:

> If you account it Wisdom when you are angry to be silent, &
> Not shew it: I do not account that Wisdom but Folly.
> Every Mans Wisdom is peculiar to his own Individuality
> O Satan my youngest born, art thou not Prince of the Starry Hosts
> And of the Wheels of Heaven, to turn the Mills day and night

Art thou not Newtons Pantocrator weaving the Woof of Locke
To mortals thy Mills seem everything & the Harrow of Shaddai
A scheme of Human conduct invisible and incomprehensible
Get to thy Labours at the Mills & leave me to my wrath.

(Blake 1977: 518)

"Pantocrator" is Newton's epithet for God. Newton writes:

This Being governs all things, not as the soul of the world, but as Lord over all; and on account of his dominion he is wont to be called "Lord God" or "Universal Ruler"; for "God" is a relative word and has a respect to servants; and Deity is the dominion of God, not over his own body, as those imagine who fancy God to be the soul of the world, but over servants.

(Newton, *Principia*, Book III, "General Scholium")

Apparently, Newton used the word "Pantocrator" as a name for a copying machine of his invention.

59. For an amusing recital of the kind of scenario Locke feared, consider the career of John Law as found in J.K. Galbraith, *Money: Whence It Came, Where it Went* (1975: 22–27).

CONCLUSION

1. These dichotomies have their root in the substance/mixed-mode distinction discussed in Chapter 3.
2. For a discussion and survey, cf. Alex Page (1972: 12–21).
3. For a contrasting perspective, consider Aristotle. The first words of the *Metaphysics* are: "All men by nature desire to know. An indication of this is the delight we take in our senses; for even apart from their usefulness they are loved for themselves" (1924: 980a). On reaching the climax of that work, Aristotle asks: what is thought of? He rejects the Buddhist's answer: Nothing. Can it be just of anything? For example, a humiliating scatological scene? Clearly not. Hence, "it must be of itself that the divine thought thinks (since it is the most excellent of things) and its thinking is a thinking of thinking" Aristotle, *Metaphysics* (1924: 1074^b35). Locke was appalled by Aristotle, not surprisingly. Wittgenstein tries to compromise; cf. *Philosophical Investigations*.

466. What does a man think for? What use is it? Why does he make boilers according to calculations and not leave the thickness of their walls to chance?...
467. Does man think, then, because he has found that thinking pays?— Because he thinks it advantageous to think? (Does he bring his children up because he has found it pays?)
467. What would show why he thinks?

470. So we do sometimes think because it has been found to pay.

(Wittgenstein 1953: 134)

Clearly Wittgenstein lived the "crisis of the bourgeois intellectual."

4. In *Some Thoughts Concerning Education*, especially sections 24–27, Locke appears as an innovator in pedagogical theory. He was the first to stress the importance of "toilet training." His views on this matter flow directly from his comments in the *Essay Concerning Human Understanding*. "The great thing to be minded in education is what habits you settle," and the most important of these is "going to stool regularly." Locke's interest in toilet training was not motivated by physiological concerns, but by disciplinary ones. He values toilet training as an exercise in body-control. The purpose of this regimen is to cultivate the body "so that it may be able to obey and execute the orders of the mind." The Pantocrator is everywhere.

5. This arises from the fallacy of composition that is so frequent in "social thought," for example, in Say's law as pointed out by Keynes.

6. Hume was to develop the notion that convention is essential to the "analysis" of property. Cf. Hume, *A Treatise of Human Nature* (2000: Book III, sec. ii).

7. Leibniz, though never writing a "treatise" on the matter, had an expectedly different theory of the origin of society and a different method of explanation. Consider his use of the "anthropological evidence":

> The Iroquois and Hurons, uncivilized neighbors of New France and New England, have upset the two universal political maxims of Aristotle and Hobbes. By their surprising conduct they have shown that entire peoples can live *without magistrates and without quarrels* and as a result that men are neither carried far enough by their natural goodness nor forced by their malice to provide themselves with a government and so renounce their freedom. Yet the roughness of these savages shows that it is not so much necessity as the inclination to advance to a better state and to arrive at happiness through mutual assistance which is the foundation of societies and states.
>
> (Leibniz 1969: 630)

That is, the mental monads, by recognizing the higher good, create relations through it. Inevitably, Leibniz was interested in China, while Locke barely mentions it (except as a source of "commodities"). Undoubtedly China's bureaucratic state, managing an extremely diverse empire, drew him as much as the *I Ching*'s binary calculus and the rationalism of Confucianism. For a discussion of this connection, cf. David E. Mungello, *Leibniz and Confucianism: The Search for an Accord* (1977).

8. Locke is commenting on an important contemporary theme: how to best impose social discipline especially on the working classes: informally or through an organized police? That is, through civil laws or laws of fashion? How this question was answered in Locke's time is described in Peter Burke, *Popular Culture in Early Modern Europe*:

In England in the 1690s, societies were founded for what was called the "reformation of manners." These societies promoted measures against fairs, gambling, masquerades, plays, taverns, whores, and "obscene ballads." The concern of the reformers for the "profanation of the Lord's Day" links them to an earlier generation of puritans, but the movement was essentially concerned with morals rather than theology, with "licence" rather than superstition.

(Burke 1978: 240)

Next consider Thomas A. Critchley's stem professional judgment on the efforts of these early amateurs of order in *A History of Police in England and Wales*.

Towards the end of the seventeenth century a campaign for moral regeneration had achieved astonishing vigour under the leadership of the King and the Archbishop of Canterbury. Royal proclamations called for an end to drunkenness and debauchery, and societies were promoted to lay information against profane cursers and swearers, prostitutes, adulterers, Sabbath-breakers, and many others. Common informers multiplied and zealots of the worst type brought misery to multitudes of the poor; for it was fashionable to view crime as a by product of poverty, debauchery and sexual irregularity; and an influential school of thought insisted on drawing a distinction between the dissolute ways of the wealthy, which harmed no one but themselves and those of the poor, which if persisted in deprived the nation of the produce of their toil.

However, societies for the suppression of vice and promotion of virtue achieved little in the long run, and the reformers, accordingly turned their bewildered attention to the state of criminal law, which, they concluded, was too lax to provide an effective deterrent. The death penalty was extended to, and implemented in an increasing number of cases, but still there was criticism of excessive leniency and voices spoke up in favour of breaking men on the wheel, castration, hanging in chains alive, and other refinements of cruelty.

(Critchley 1979: 22)

Linebaugh in *The London Hanged* gives a detailed account of the network of informers created in this period (2006). The problem for these "moral regeneration societies" was, of course, that they were trying to intervene in a very large-scale law of fashion of the poor.

9. For a wide-ranging survey of "primitive money," as well as theories about it, see Paul Einzig, *Primitive Money* (1966).

10. Ilya Prigogine has studied this irreversibility and its remarkable stability in thermodynamic systems.

11. There is a major lacuna in Locke's theory which requires more attention than it has been given: the turning of the land into a private possession, in contrast to the "fruits" of the land. Lawrence C. Becker discusses this problem in *Property Rights: Philosophic Foundations* (1977).

12. Writes Marx:

> Accumulate! Accumulate! Accumulate, accumulate! That is Moses and
> the prophets! "Industry furnishes the material which saving accumulates."
> Therefore, save, save, i.e., reconvert the greatest possible portion of sur-
> plus-value, or surplus-product into capital! Accumulation for accumulation's
> sake, production for production's sake: by this formula classical economy
> expressed the historical mission of the bourgeoisie, and did not for a single
> instant deceive itself over the birth-throes of wealth. But what avails lamenta-
> tion in the face of historical necessity?
>
> (Marx 1976: 652)

13. Deuteronomy 23 is the chapter that contains the "antiusury" commandment; it
    also contains many other interesting orders from God:

> 13. And thou shalt have a paddle upon thy weapon; and it shall be, when thou
> wilt ease thyself abroad, thou shalt dig therewith, and shalt turn back and
> cover that which cometh from thee...
> 17. There shall be no whore of the daughters of Israel, nor sodomite of the
> sons of Israel...
> 19. Thou shalt not lend upon usury to thy brother; usury of money, usury of
> vituals; usury of anything that is lent upon usury;
> 20. Unto a stranger thou mayest lend upon usury; but unto thy brother thou
> shalt not lend upon usury: that the Lord thy God may bless thee in all that
> thou settest thine hand to in the land whither thou goest to possess it.
> 24. When thou comest into thy neighbor's vineyard, then thou mayest eat
> grapes thy fill at thine own plessure; but thou shalt not put any in thy vessel.
> 25. When thou comest into the standing corn of thy neighbor, then thou
> mayest pluck the ears with thy hand; but thou shalt not move a sickle unto
> thy neighbor's standing corn.
>
> (Deuteronomy 23: 13–25)

14. With Christianity, since all become "brothers" and there are no "strangers,"
    usury becomes taboo; however, the automatic "charity" (which is a sort of
    communal appropriation) decreed in verses 24 and 25 ends as well. Charity
    becomes a form of grace.

15. It is interesting to note that our notion of "interest" comes from "interesse,"
    a term first used by the Bolognese civil lawyer Aso, writing in the first two
    decades of the thirteenth century. Lester K. Little describes Aso's use of the term
    in *Religious Poverty and the Profit Economy in Medieval Europe*:

> Interest was not part of the loan agreement, or a price for the loan, but
> something related only accidentally or extrinsically to the loan. It referred
> to the penalty which was to correspond to the difference between, or the
> amount that came in between (quod interest) the present financial position

of the lender and the position he would have been in if he had not made the loan in the first place.

(Little 1978: 180)

Hence, the original use of interest was in the context of the defaulting of a non-usurous loan. Here indeed we do have the negation of the negation!

16. The real problem for Locke is not to explain why the rich get together by consent and set up laws and magistrates to protect and preserve their property. That was obvious. His problem was to explain how it is that people consented to be poor. Not an easy task, even for a great philosopher.

17. Apparently, Boyle's deathbed schemes included an alchemical process that for a while attracted the interest of Newton and Locke. Cf. Cranston, *John Locke: A Biography* (1957).

18. A work that well describes the dramas connected with the transmission of inheritance in the context of the bourgeois family is Thomas Mann's *Buddenbrooks*.

19. For a recent discussion of Locke's theory of personal identity, cf. David Wiggins (1980: 150ff.).

20. Sol Yurick in *Behold Metatron: The Recording Angel* (1984) discusses the relation between capitalism and inheritance. As inheritance became important so did legitimacy and illegitimacy, as well as the gap between subsistence and full inheritance share. M. Dorothy George in *London Life in the Eighteenth Century* describes how "illegitimate" children were settled at the time:

The law … was that of the parish in which the children were born, irrespective of the parents' settlement, and the general presumption was that an illegitimate child would sooner or later be a burden to his parish, so parish officers kept a watchful eye on all non-residents who were expected to lie in. Even apparently well-to-do and respectable visitors to a place where visitors were as frequent as Bath, did not lightly escape, if we may credit Defoe.

(George 1976 (1925): 214)

If one was caught, a lump sum of £10 freed the parent from any responsibility in terms of "taxes, charges and payments" and from the obligation to "maintain the child." With the money, there would be a party for the infant called "saddling the spit," where much of the maintenance money was eaten and drunk by the parish authorities. After the party, the babe was put into the arms of a "nurse" and in most cases was never heard from again. A Parliamentary report of 1715 writes:

[Children] are inhumanly suffered to die by the barbarity of nurses who are a sort of people void of commiseration or religion, hir'd by the church warden to take off a burden from the parish at the cheapest and easiest rate they can, and those know the manner of doing it effectually.

(George 1976 (1925): 215)

What was £10 in those days? Consider that Locke's funeral cost £60, ceremony to casket, and that was done in typical Lockean minimalist fashion. Cf. Cranston, *John Locke: A Biography* (1957: 480–481).

POSTFACE

1. The three volumes of *Theories of Surplus Value* were to be the repository of Marx's direct critique of the texts of political economy, whereas *Capital*, Vols I–III were to be critiques of the system itself. In *Theories of Surplus Value*, however, there is no systematic review of the bourgeois texts dealing with the origins of the accumulation process.
2. See Chapter 3, "Abused Words."
3. See Conclusion: "Weaving an Origin."

Bibliography

TEXTS BY JOHN LOCKE

Locke, John (1823a) *Essay Concerning Human Understanding. Volume I–III, The Works of John Locke in Ten Volumes* (Reprint Darmstadt: Scientia Verlag Aalen, 1963).

Locke, John (1823b) *Fundamental Constitutions of Carolina. Volume X, The Works of John Locke in Ten Volumes.*(Reprint Darmstadt: Scientia Verlag Aalen, 1963), 175–199.

Locke, John (1823c) *Further Considerations Considering Raising the Value of Money. Volume V, The Works of John Locke in Ten Volumes* (Reprint Darmstadt: Scientia Verlag Aalen, 1963), 139–206.

Locke, John (1823d) *A History of Navigation from its Origin to the Year 1704. Volume X, The Works of John Locke in Ten Volumes* (Reprint Darmstadt: Scientia Verlag Aalen, 1963), 357–512.

Locke, John (1823e) Letters on *Toleration. Volume VI, The Works of John Locke in Ten Volumes* (Reprint Darmstadt: Scientia Verlag Aalen, 1963).

Locke, John (1823f) *Some Considerations of the Consequences of lowering the Interest and raising the Value of Money, Volume V, The Works of John Locke in Ten Volumes* (Reprint Darmstadt: Scientia Verlag Aalen, 1963), 1–116.

Locke, John (1823g) *Two Treatises on Government. Volume V, The Works of John Locke in Ten Volumes* (Reprint Darmstadt: Scientia Verlag Aalen, 1963), 207–485.

Locke, John (1959) *An Essay Concerning Human Understanding.* Collated and annotated by Alexander Campbell Fraser, 2 Vols. New York: Dover.

Locke, John (1963) *Two Treatises of Government.* Edited by Peter Laslett, rev. edn. Cambridge: Cambridge University Press.

Locke, John (1975) *An Essay Concerning Human Understanding.* Edited by Peter Nidditch. Oxford: Oxford University Press.

Locke, John (1991) *Locke on Money.* Edited by Patrick H. Kelly. Oxford: Clarendon Press.

OTHER TEXTS CITED

Aaron, Richard I. (1965) *John Locke,* 2nd edn. Oxford: Oxford University Press.

Alexander, Peter (1980) "Locke on Substance-in-General." *Ratio* 21(1) (December 1980): 91–105.

Alexander, Peter (1981) "Locke on Substance-in-General." *Ratio* 23(1) (June 1981): 1–19.

Allison, Henry E. (1977) "Locke's Theory of Personal Identity: A Re-Examination." In I.C. Tipton (Ed.), *Locke on Human Understanding*. Oxford: Oxford University Press, 105–122.

Alsop, James D. (1979) "Gerrard Winstanley's Later Life." *Past and Present* 82(1) (February): 73–81.

Andrews, Charles M. (1964) *The Colonial Period of American History, Vol. III*. New Haven, CT: Yale University Press.

Anstey, Roger (1975) *The Atlantic Slave Trade and British Abolition 1760–1810*. London: Humanities Press.

Appleby, Joyce O. (1978) *Economic Thought and Ideology in Seventeenth Century England*. Princeton, NJ: Princeton University Press.

Aristotle (1924) *Metaphysics*. Translated by W.D. Ross. Oxford: Clarendon Press.

Aristotle (1998) *Metaphysics*. Translated by Hugh Lawson-Tancred. New York: Penguin Classics.

Arendt, Hannah (1959) *The Human Condition*. New York: Doubleday Anchor Books.

Arneil, Barbara (1996) *John Locke and America: The Defense of English Colonialism*. Oxford: Clarendon Press, 169–187.

Ayers, Michael R. (1981) "Mechanism, Superaddition and the Proof of God's Existence in Locke's *Essay*." *The Philosophical Review* (April): 210–251.

Balibar, Étienne (2006) "My Self and My Own: One and the Same?" In B. Mauer and G. Schwab (Eds.), *Accelerating Possession: Global Futures of Property and Personhood*. New York: Columbia University Press.

Balibar, Étienne (2013) *Identity and Difference: John Locke and the Invention of Consciousness*. London: Verso.

Barker, Anthony J. (1978) *The African Link: British Attitudes to the Negro in the Seventeenth and Eighteenth Centuries*. London: Frank Cass.

Barthes, Roland (1976) *Sade, Fourier, Loyola*. Translated by R. Miller. New York: Farrar, Strauss & Giroux.

Bartley III, William W. (1973) *Wittgenstein*. Philadelphia, PA: J.P. Lippincott.

Becker, Lawrence C. (1977) *Property Rights: Philosophic Foundations*. London: Routledge.

Bennett, Jonathan (1971) *Locke, Berkeley, Hume: Central Themes*. Oxford: Oxford University Press.

Birrell, T.A. (1963) "Roger North and Political Morality in the Later Stuart Period." *Scrutiny: Reissued in 20 Volumes with an Index and Retrospect*. Cambridge: Cambridge Books, 282–298.

Blake, William (1977) *William Blake: The Collected Poems*. Harmondsworth: Penguin.

Borneman, Ernest (1976) *The Psychoanalysis of Money*. New York: Urizen Books.

Boyer, Carl B. (1949) *The History of the Calculus*. New York: Dover Publications.

Burke, Peter (1978) *Popular Culture in Early Modern Europe*. London: Harper Torchbooks.

Caffentzis, C. George (1989) *Clipped Coins, Civil Government and Abused Words: John Locke's Philosophy of Money*. New York: Autonomedia.

Caffentzis, George C. (1995) "On the Scottish Origin of 'Civilization.'" In Silvia Federici (Ed.), *Enduring Western Civilisation: The Construction of the Concept of Western Civilisation and its Others*. Westport, CT: Praeger, 13–36.

Caffentzis, C. George (2000) *Exciting the Industry of Mankind: George Berkeley's Philosophy of Money*. London: Kluwer.

Caffentzis, C. George (2001) "Hume, Money, & Civilization: or, Why Was Hume a Metallist?" *Hume Studies* 27(2) (November): 301–335.

Caffentzis, C. George (2005) "Civilizing the Highlands: Hume, Money and the Annexing Act." *Historical Reflections/Réflections Historiques* 31(1): 169–194.

Caffenztis, George (2010) "Locke, Berkeley and Hume as Philosophers of Money." In Silvia Parigi (Ed.), *George Berkeley: Religion and Science in the Age of Enlightenment*. London: Springer.

Caffenztis, George (2013) *In Letters of Blood and Fire: Work, Machines and the Crisis of Capitalism*. Oakland, CA: PM Press.

Caffenztis, George (2017) *No Blood for Oil: Essays on Energy, Class Struggle and War 1998–2016*. New York: Autonomedia.

Caffenztis, George (2021) *Civilizing Money: Hume, His Monetary Project, and the Scottish Enlightenment*. London: Pluto Press.

Cameron, William J. (1971) (Ed.) *Augustan Satirical Verse, Vol. V: 1688–1697*. New Haven, CT: Yale University Press.

Carey, Daniel (2013) "Locke's Species: Money and Philosophy in the 1690s." *Annals of Science* 70(3): 357–380.

Casson, Douglas (2016): "John Locke, Clipped Coins, and the Unstable Currency of Reason." *Ethica & Politica* 18(2): 153–180.

Chomsky, Noam (1966) *Cartesian Linguistics*. New York: Harper & Row.

Clark, George (1955) *The Later Stuarts 1660–1714*. Oxford: The Clarendon Press.

Cleaver, Harry (1996) "The Subversion of Money-As-Command in the Current Crisis." In Werner Bonefeld and John Holloway (Eds.), *Global Capital, National State and the Politics of Money*. London: Palgrave Macmillan.

Clower, Robert W. (1971) *Monetary Theory: Selected Readings*. London: Penguin.

Colletti, Lucio (1975) "Introduction." *Karl Marx: Early Writings*. Translated by Rodney Livingstone and Gregor Benton. London: Penguin.

Coupland, Reginald (1964) *The British Anti-Slavery Movement*, 2nd edn. London: Frank Cass & Co.

Craig, John (1946) *Newton at the Mint*. Cambridge: Cambridge University Press.

Cranston, Maurice (1957) *John Locke: A Biography*. London: Longman.

Craton, Michael (1974) *Sinews of Empire: A Short History of British Slavery*. London: Anchor Press.

Critchley, Thomas A. (1979) *A History of Police in England and Wales*, rev. edn. London: Constable.

Davidson, Basil (1961) *The African Slave Trade*. Boston, MA: Atlantic Monthly Press.

Davidson, Basil (1964) *The African Past: Chronicles from Antiquity to the Modern Times*. London: Longmans.

Davidson, Donald (1970) "The Individuation of Events." In Carl G. Hempel, Donald Davidson and Rescher (Eds.), *Essays in Honor of Carl Hempel*. Dordrecht: D. Reidel.

Davis, David B. (1966) *The Problem of Slavery in Western Culture*. Ithaca, NY: Cornell University Press.

Defoe, Daniel (1701) *The True-Born Englishman*. London.

Defoe, Daniel (1710) *A Letter to Mr. Bisset Eldest Brother of the Collegiate Church of St. Catherines; in Answer to his Remarks on Dr. Sacheverel's Sermon*. London.

Defoe, Daniel (1724) *A General History of the Pyrates: From their First Rise and Settlement in the Island of Providence to the Present Time*. London.

Defoe, Daniel (1970) *The History and Remarkable Life of the Truly Honourable Col. Jack*. Edited by Samuel H. Monk. London: Oxford University Press.

Dickson, P.G.M. and Sperling, J.G. (1970) "War Finance, 1689–1714." In J.S. Bromley (Ed.), *The Rise of Great Britain and Russia*, Vol. VI of *The New Cambridge Modern History*. Cambridge: Cambridge University Press.

Dryden, John (1913) *The Poems of John Dryden*, edited by John Sargeant. Oxford: Oxford University Press.

Duff, Koshka (2017) "The Criminal is Political: Real Existing Liberalism and the Construction of the Criminal." PhD Dissertation, University of Sussex, December.

Dunn, John (1969) *The Political Thought of John Locke*. Cambridge: Cambridge University Press.

Edwards, Elwin (1964) *Information Transmission: An Introductory Guide to the Application of the Theory of Information to the Human Sciences*. London: Chapman & Hall.

Einzig, Paul (1966) *Primitive Money in its Ethnological, Historical, and Economic Aspects*, 2nd edn. Oxford: Pergamon Press.

Eysenck, Hans Jürgen (1977) *Crime and Personality*. London: Routledge & Kegan Paul.

Ezejiofor, Gaius (1980) "The Law of Property." In Cyprian O. Okonkwo (Ed.), *Introduction to Nigerian Law*. London: Sweet & Maxwell.

Faulkner, Joanne (2011) "Innocents and Oracles: The Child as a Figure of Knowledge and Critique in the Middle-Class Imagination." *Critical Horizons* (12)3: 323–346.

Feavearyear, Albert E. (1963) *The Pound Sterling: A History of English Money*. Oxford: Oxford University Press.

Federici, Silvia (2004) *Caliban and the Witch: Women, the Body and Primitive Accumulation*. New York: Autonomedia.

Feinstein, Charles H. (1964) "National Income and Expenditure, 1870–1963." *London & Cambridge Economic Bulletin* (June).

Fischer Sybille (2015) "Atlantic Ontologies: On Violence and Being Human." *Caribbean Rasamblaj* 1–2, https://hemisphericinstitute.org/en/emisferica-121-

caribbean-rasanblaj/12-1-essays/e-121-essay-fischer-atlantic-ontologies.html (accessed August 7, 2020).

Flew, Antony (1951) "Locke and the Problem of Personal Identity." *Philosophy* 96: 53–68.

Forster, E.M. (1924) *A Passage to India*. London: Harcourt Brace.

Foucault, Michel (1970) *The Order of Things: An Archaeology of the Human Sciences*. New York: Pantheon Books.

Foucault, Michel (2000) "What is an Author?" In J. Faubion (Ed.), *Aesthetics, Method & Epistemology: The Essential Works of Michel Foucault Volume 2*. London: Penguin.

Foucault, Michel (1978) *Discipline and Punish: The Birth of the Prison*. Translated by Alan Sheridan. Harmondsworth: Penguin.

Frege, Gottlob (1960) *The Foundations of Arithmetic*. Translated by J.L. Austin. New York: Harper & Brothers.

Furniss, Edgar S. (1957) *The Position of the Laborer in a System of Nationalism*. New York: Kelley and Millman.

Galbraith, John K. (1975) *Money: Whence It Came, Where it Went*. Harmondsworth: Penguin.

George, M. Dorothy (1976 [1925]) *London Life in the Eighteenth Century*. Harmondsworth: Penguin.

Glymour, Clark N. (1980) *Theory and Evidence*. Princeton, NJ: Princeton University Press.

Goldstein, Jesse (2013) "Terra Economica: Waste and the Production of Nature." *Antipode* 54(2): 357–375.

Goodman, Nelson (1955) *Fact, Fiction and Forecast*. Cambridge, MA: Harvard University Press.

Grant, Douglas (1968) *The Fortunate Slave: An Illustration of African Slavery in the Early Eighteenth Century*. London: Oxford University Press.

Grice, Herbert P. (1969) "Utterer's Meaning and Intentions." *The Philosophical Review* 78: 147–177.

Hacking, Ian (1975a) *The Emergence of Probability*. Cambridge: Cambridge University Press.

Hacking, Ian (1975b) *What Does Language Matter to Philosophy?* Cambridge: Cambridge University Press.

Hacking, Ian (1981) (Ed.) *Scientific Revolutions*. Oxford: Oxford University Press.

Harney, Stefano and Moten, Fred (2013) *The Undercommons: Fugitive Planning and Black Study*. Wivenhoe: Minor Compositions.

Hegel, Georg W.F. (1952) *Philosophy of Right*. Translated by T.M. Knox. Oxford: Clarendon Press.

Hempel, Carl G. (1966) *Philosophy of Natural Science*. Englewood Cliffs, NJ: Prentice-Hall.

Hibbert, Christopher (1977) *London: The Biography of a City*. London: Allen Lane.

Higginbotham, Jr., A. Leon (1978) *In the Matter of Color: Race and the American Legal Process*. New York: Oxford.

Hill, Christopher (1961) *The Century of Revolution 1603–1714*. London: T. Nelson.

Hill, Christopher (1970) *The World Turned Upside Down*. London, Penguin.

Hill, Christopher (1977) *Milton and the English Revolution*. London: Faber & Faber.

Holloway, John and Black, Joan (1975) *Later English Broadside Ballads*. London: Routledge and Keegan Paul.

Horsby, Stephen J. (2005) *British Atlantic, American Frontier: Spaces of Power in Early Modern America*. Hanover, NH: University Press of New England.

Horwitz, Henry (1977) *Parliament, Policy and Politics in the Reign of William III*. Manchester: Manchester University Press.

Hughes, M.W. (1975) "Personal Identity: A Defense of Locke." *Philosophy* 50: 169–187.

Hume, David (2000) *A Treatise of Human Nature*. Edited by David F. Norton and Mary J. Norton. Oxford: Oxford University Press.

Ince, Onur Ulas (2011) "Enclosing in God's Name, Accumulation for Mankind: Money, Morality, and Accumulation in John Locke's Theory of Property." *Review of Politics* 73: 29–54.

Ince, Onur Ulas (2018) *Colonial Capitalism and the Dilemmas of Liberalism*. Oxford: Oxford University Press.

Inglis, Brian (1971) *Poverty and the Industrial Revolution*. London: Panther Books.

Jappe, Anselme (2013) "Sohn-Rethel and the Origin of 'Real Abstraction': A Critique of Production or a Critique of Circulation?" *Historical Materialism* 21(1): 3–14.

Jeffrey, Richard C. (1965) *The Logic of Decision*. New York: McGraw Hill.

Jevons, William S. (1921) *Money and the Mechanism of Exchange*. New York: D. Appleton and Co.

Jevons, William S. (1926) "Barter." *Money and the Mechanism of Exchange*. New York, Keegan Paul, Trench & Co.

Jones, D.W. (1972) "London Merchants and the Crisis of the 1690s." In P. Clark and P. Slack (Eds.), *Crisis and Order in English Towns 1500–1700: Essays in Urban History*. London: Routledge.

Johnson, Samuel (1969) *The Rambler*. Edited by W.J. Bates and Albrecht B. Strauss, Vol. 5 of the *Yale Edition of Samuel Johnson*. New Haven, CT: Yale University Press.

Kelly, Patrick (2009) "'Monkey' Business: Locke's 'College' Correspondence and the Adoption of the Plan for the Great Recoinage of 1696." *Locke Studies* 9: 139–165.

Keynes, John M. (1927) "One of Wells' Worlds." *The New Republic* (February), 2.

Keynes, John M. (1937) "The General Theory of Employment." *Quarterly Journal of Economics* (February): 215–216.

Keynes, John M. (1964) *The General Theory of Employment, Interest, and Money*. New York: St. Martin's Press.

Keynes John M. (1971a) *The Economic Consequences of the Peace, Vol. II, Collected Writings of J.M. Keynes*. London: Macmillan.

Keynes, John M. (1971b) *Indian Currency and Finance, Vol. I, The Collected Writings of J.M. Keynes*. London: Macmillan.

Keynes, John M. (1972a) *Essays in Persuasion*, Vol. 9, *The Collected Writings of J.M. Keynes*. London: Macmillan.

Keynes, John M. (1972b) *Essays in Biography*, Vol. 10, *The Collected Writings of J.M. Keynes*. London: Macmillan.

Keynes, John M. (1973a) *A Treatise on Probability*, Vol. 8, *Collected Writings*. London: Macmillan.

Keynes, John M. (1973b) "The General Theory of Employment." *Quarterly Journal of Economics* (February): 215–216. Republished in *Collected Writings*, Vol. 14. London: Macmillan.

King, Peter (1971) *The Development of the English Economy to 1750*. London: Macdonald & Evans.

King, Peter (1984) *The Life and Letters of John Locke*. New York: Garland Publishing.

Koyré, Alexandre (1957) *From the Closed to the Infinite Universe*. Baltimore, MD: Johns Hopkins University Press.

Kretzmann, Norman (1977) "The Main Thesis of Locke's Semantic Theory." In I.C. Tipton (Ed.), *Locke on Human Understanding: Selected Essays*. Oxford: Oxford University Press, 123–140.

Kripke, Saul A. (1980) *Naming and Necessity*. Cambridge, MA: Harvard University Press.

Kripke, Saul A. (1982) *Wittgenstein: On Rules and Private Language*. Cambridge, MA: Harvard University Press.

Laslett, Peter (1963) "Introduction." In John Locke, *Two Treatises of Government*. Edited by Peter Laslett, rev. edn. Cambridge: Cambridge University Press.

Laudan, Larry (1977) *Progress and its Problems*. Berkeley, CA: University of California Press.

Laureen, Karsten and Pedersen, Jorgen (1964) *The German Inflation 1918–1923*. Amsterdam: North-Holland.

Leibniz, Gottfried W. (1969) *Philosophical Papers and Letters*, 2nd edn. Edited and translated by Leroy E. Loemker. Dordrecht: D. Reidel.

Leijonhufvud, Axel (1967) "Keynes and the Keynesians: A Suggested Interpretation." *American Economic Review* 57(2) (May): 401–410.

Linebaugh, Peter (1982) "All the Atlantic Mountains Shook." *Labour/Le Travailleur* 10: 87–121.

Linebaugh, Peter (2006) *The London Hanged: Crime and Civil Society in the Eighteenth Century*, 2nd edn. London: Verso.

Linsky, Leonard (Ed.) (1971) *Reference and Modality*. Oxford: Oxford University Press.

Little, Lester K. (1978) *Religious Poverty and the Profit Economy in Medieval Europe*. London: Paul Elek.

Lovejoy, Arthur O. (1960) *The Great Chain of Being: The History of an Idea*. New York: Harper Torchbooks.

Lowndes, William (1933) "A Report Containing an Essay for the Amendment of the Silver Coins." In J.R. McCulloch (Ed.), *Old and Scarce Tracts on Money*. London: P.S. King & Son.

McNally, David (2014) "The Blood of the Commonwealth: War, the State, and the Making of World Money." *Historical Materialism* 22(2): 3–32.

Macpherson, Crawford B. (1962) *The Political Theory of Possessive Individualism: Hobbes to Locke*. Oxford: Oxford University Press.

Macpherson, Crawford B. (1980) "Introduction." In John Locke, *Second Treatise of Government*. Indianapolis, IN: Hackett.

Macpherson, Crawford B. (2011) *The Political Theory of Possessive Individualism: Hobbes to Locke*. Oxford: Oxford University Press.

Mann, F.A. (1982) *The Legal Aspect of Money*, 4th edn. Oxford: Oxford University Press.

Marx, Karl (1970) *A Contribution to the Critique of Political Economy*. Moscow: Progress Publishers.

Marx, Karl (1976) *Capital: A Critique of Political Economy, Vol. I*. Translated by Ben Fowkes. Harmondsworth: Penguin.

Marx, Karl (1978) *Capital: A Critique of Political Economy, Vol. II*. Translated by David Fernbach. Harmondsworth: Penguin.

Marx, Karl (1992) "Critique of Hegel's Doctrine of the State." In *Early Writings*. Translated by Rodney Livingstone and George Benton. London: Penguin.

Merton, Robert K. (1970) *Science, Technology, and Society in Seventeenth-Century England*. New York: Howard Fertig.

Miers, Suzanne (1975) *Britain and the Ending of the Slave Trade*. London: Longman.

Moten, Fred (2018) *Stolen Life*. Durham, NC: Duke University Press.

Mungello, David E. (1977) *Leibniz and Confucianism: The Search for Accord*. Honolulu, HI: University of Hawai'i Press.

Neocleous, Mark (2011) "War on Waste: Law, Original Accumulation and the Violence of Capital." *Science and Society* 75(4): 506–528.

Novak, Maximillian E. (1963) *Defoe and the Nature of Man*. Oxford: Oxford University Press.

Novak, Maximillian E. (1977) "Introduction." In Maximillian E. Novak (Ed.), *English Literature in the Age of Disguise*. Berkeley, CA: University of California.

Nozick, Robert (1974) *Anarchy, State and Utopia*. New York: Basic Books.

Page, Alex (1972) "The Origin of Language and Eighteenth-Century English Criticism." *The Journal of English and Germanic Philology* 71(1): 12–21.

Pashukanis, Evgeny (1978) *General Theory of Law and Marxism*. Translated by Dragan Milovanovic. New Brunswick, NJ: Transaction Publishers.

Phelps Brown, Ernest H. (1968) *A Century of Pay*. London: Macmillan.

Plant, Marjorie (1974) *The English Book Trade*, 3rd edn. London: Allen & Unwin.

Pocock, J.G.A (1975) *The Machiavellian Moment: Florentine Political Thought and the Atlantic Republic Tradition*. Princeton, NJ: Princeton University Press.

Pompa, Leon (1975) *Vico: A Study of the New Science.* Cambridge: Cambridge University Press.

Postone, Moishe (2006) *Time, Labour And Social Domination: A Reinterpretation of Marx's Critical Theory.* Cambridge: Cambridge University Press.

Putnam, Hilary (1975) *Mind, Language and Reality: Philosophical Papers,* Vol. 2. Cambridge: Cambridge University Press.

Quine, W.V.O. (1969) *Ontological Relativity and Other Essays.* New York: Columbia University Press.

Radnitzky, Gerard (1973) *Contemporary Schools of Metascience.* Chicago, IL: Regnery.

Rediker, Marcus (1981) "'Under the Banner of King Death': The Social World of Anglo American Pirates: 1716–1726." *The William and Mary Quarterly* 3rd series(38): 203–227.

Rekret, Paul (2019) "Cogito Ergo Habo." In Camille Barbagallo, Nicholas Beuret and David Harvie (Eds.), *Commoning with George Caffentzis and Silvia Federici.* London: Pluto Press.

Rekret, Paul and Choat, Simon (2016) "From Political Topographies to Political Logics: Post-Marxism and Historicity." *Constellations* 23(2) (June): 281–291.

Robinson, Cedric (2000) *Black Marxism: The Making of the Black Radical Tradition.* Chapel Hill, NC: University of North Carolina Press.

Rose, Mark (1994) "The Author as Proprietor: Donaldson v. Beckett and the Genealogy of Modern Authorship." In B. Sherman and A. Strowel (Eds.), *Of Authors and Origins: Essays on Copyright Law.* Oxford: Clarendon Press.

Rousseau, Jean-Jacques (2018) *Rousseau: The Social Contract and Other Later Political Writings,* 2nd edn. Edited by Victor Gourevitch. Cambridge: Cambridge University Press.

Russell, Bertrand (1937) *The Principles of Mathematics.* London: G. Allen & Unwin.

Sanford, Stella (2013) "The Incomplete Locke: Balibar, Locke and the Philosophy of the Subject." In Étienne Balibar, *Identity and Difference: John Locke and the Invention of Consciousness.* London: Verso.

Sartre, Jean-Paul (2004) *Critique of Dialectical Reason.* Translated by Jonathan Rée. London: Verso.

Schumpeter, Joseph A. (1954) *History of Economic Analysis.* Edited from manuscript by Elizabeth Broody Schumpeter. New York: Oxford University Press.

Selin, Ivan (1965) *Detection Theory.* Princeton, NJ: Princeton University Press.

Shackle, G.L.S. (1973) "Keynes and Today's Establishment in Economic Theory: A View." *Journal of Economic Literature* 11(2) (June).

Simmel, Georg (1978) *The Philosophy of Money.* Translated by translated by Tom Bottomore and David Frisby from a first draft by Kaethe Mengelberg. Boston, MA: Routledge and Kegan Paul.

Simmel, Georg (1990) *The Philosophy of Money,* 2nd edn. Translated by Tom Bottomore and David Frisby. London: Routledge.

Skinner, Quentin (1998) *Liberty Before Liberalism*. Cambridge: Cambridge University Press.

Sohn-Rethel, Alfred (1978) *Intellectual and Manual Labour: A Critique of Epistemology*. London: Macmillan Press.

Spinoza, Baruch de (1901) *Ethics, Vol. II, The Chief Works of Benedict of Spinoza*. Edited and translated by R.H.M. Elwes. London: George Bell & Sons.

Spinoza, Baruch de (2018) *Ethics Proved in Geometrical Order*. Edited by Matthew I. Kisner. Translated by Michael Silverthorne and Matthew J. Kisner. Cambridge: Cambridge University Press.

Stam, James H. (1976) *Inquiries into the Origin of Language: The Fate of a Question*. New York: Harper and Row.

Swift, Jonathan (1726) *Gulliver's Travels*. London: Benjamin Motte.

Toscano, Alberto (2008) "The Open Secret of Real Abstraction." *Rethinking Marxism* 20(2): 273–287.

Tully, James (1980) *A Discourse on Property: John Locke and His Adversaries*. Cambridge: Cambridge University Press.

Tully, James (1993) *An Approach to Political Philosophy: Locke in Contexts*. Cambridge: Cambridge University Press.

Ver Steeg, Clarence L. (1965) *The Formative Years, 1607–1763*. London: Macmillan.

Vickers, Douglas. (1959) *Studies in the Theory of Money 1690–1776*. London: Peter Owen.

Vilar, Pierre (1976) *A History of Gold and Money 1450–1920*. London: New Left Books.

Wallerstein, Immanuel (1974) *The Modern World-System I: Capitalist Agriculture and the Origins of the European World-Economy in the Sixteenth Century*. New York: Academic Press.

Weber, Max (1947) *The Theory of Social and Economic Organization*. Translated by A.M. Henderson and T. Parsons. New York: The Free Press.

Wegmark, J.A. (1980) "Money and Locke's Theory of Property." *History of Political Economy* 12(2): 282–290.

Whittaker, Edmund (1940) *History of Economic Ideas*. London: Longmans, Green and Company.

Whorf, Benjamin L. (1956) *Language, Thought and Reality: Selected Writings by Benjamin Lee Whorf*. Edited by J.B. Carroll. Cambridge, MA: Harvard University Press.

Wiggins, David (1980) *Sameness and Substance*. Oxford: Blackwell.

Wilson, Charles (1965) *England's Apprenticeship, 1603–1763*. London: Longmans.

Wittgenstein, Ludwig (1953) *Philosophical Investigations*. Oxford: Blackwell.

Wood, Ellen Meiksins (2002) *The Origins of Capitalism: A Longer View*. London: Verso.

Wood, Ellen Meiksins (2008) *Citizens and Lords: A Social History of Western Political Thought from Antiquity to the Middle Ages*. London: Verso.

Wood, Ellen Meiksins (2012) *Liberty and Property: A Social History of Western Political Thought from the Renaissance to Enlightenment*. London: Verso.

Wood, Neal (1983) *The Politics of John Locke's Philosophy: A Study of An Essay Concerning Human Understanding*. Berkeley, CA: University of California Press.

Woolhouse, Roger S. (1971) *Locke's Philosophy of Science and Knowledge: A Consideration of Some Aspects of An Essay Concerning Human Understanding*. New York: Barnes and Noble.

Yates, Frances (1968) *The Art of Memory*. Harmondsworth: Penguin Books.

Young, John F. (1971) *Information Theory*. London: Butterworth.

Yurick, Sol (1984) *Behold Metatron: The Recording Angel*. New York: Semiotext(e).

Index

The Pluto Press Newsletter

Hello friend of Pluto!

Want to stay on top of the best radical books
we publish?

Then sign up to be the first to hear about our
new books, as well as special events,
podcasts and videos.

You'll also get 50% off your first order with us
when you sign up.

Come and join us!

Go to bit.ly/PlutoNewsletter

Printed and bound by CPI Group (UK) Ltd, Croydon, CR0 4YY

23/04/2025

14661019-0002